Interactive Dashboards and Data Apps with Plotly and Dash

Harness the power of a fully fledged frontend web framework in Python – no JavaScript required

Elias Dabbas

BIRMINGHAM—MUMBAI

Interactive Dashboards and Data Apps with Plotly and Dash

Group Product Manager: Kunal Parikh
Publishing Product Manager: Reshma Raman
Senior Editor: David Sugarman
Content Development Editor: Joseph Sunil
Technical Editor: Devanshi Deepak Ayare
Copy Editor: Safis Editing
Project Coordinator: Aparna Nair
Proofreader: Safis Editing
Indexer: Manju Arasan
Production Designer: Nilesh Mohite

First published: May 2021
Production reference: 2250521

Published by Packt Publishing Ltd.
Livery Place
35 Livery Street
Birmingham
B3 2PB, UK.

ISBN 978-1-80056-891-4

www.packt.com

Contributors

About the author

Elias Dabbas is an online marketing and data science practitioner. Combining both fields, He produces open source software for building dashboards and data apps, as well as software for online marketing. He is the author and maintainer of advertools, a Python library that provides various digital marketing tools, with a focus on SEO, SEM, crawling, and text analysis.

About the reviewer

Leonardo Ferreira is an accountant and self-taught data scientist with the title of Kaggle Grandmaster and also acts as a data platform developer. He started his studies in data science in 2017 and started working in the field a few months after starting his apprenticeship. Since then, he has worked for large companies in Brazil and worldwide, with more than 100 open source projects adding GitHub, Kaggle, and their portfolio of web applications. He is currently a Top Rated Plus freelancer on the Upwork platform, where he has already carried out more than 20 data science and data platform projects. He is also enthusiastic about solutions on the Cardano blockchain.

Table of Contents

3

Working with Plotly's Figure Objects

4

Data Manipulation and Preparation, Paving the Way to Plotly Express

Section 2: Adding Functionality to Your App with Real Data

5

Interactively Comparing Values with Bar Charts and Dropdown Menus

6

Exploring Variables with Scatter Plots and Filtering Subsets with Sliders

7

Exploring Map Plots and Enriching Your Dashboards with Markdown

8

Calculating the Frequency of Your Data with Histograms and Building Interactive Tables

Section 3: Taking Your App to the Next Level

9
Letting Your Data Speak for Itself with Machine Learning

10
Turbo-charge Your Apps with Advanced Callbacks

11
URLs and Multi-Page Apps

12
Deploying Your App

13
Next Steps

Other Books You May Enjoy

Index

Preface

Plotly's Dash framework allows Python programmers to develop complete analytic data apps and interactive dashboards. This book will help you explore the functionalities of Dash for visualizing data in different ways and getting the most out of your data.

You'll start with an overview of the Dash ecosystem, its main packages, and the available third-party packages crucial for structuring and building different parts of your apps. Next, you will learn how to create a basic Dash app and add different features to it. You'll then integrate controls such as dropdowns, checkboxes, sliders, date pickers, and more in the app, and then link them to charts and other outputs. Depending on the data you are visualizing, you will also add several types of charts, including scatter plots, line plots, bar charts, histograms, maps, and more, as well as exploring the options available for customizing them.

By the end of this book, you will have developed the skills you need to create and deploy an interactive dashboard, be able to handle complexity and code refactoring, and understand the process of improving your application.

Who this book is for

This Plotly Dash book is for data professionals and data analysts who want to gain a better understanding of their data with the help of different visualizations and dashboards. Basic to intermediate-level knowledge of the Python programming language is expected to grasp the concepts covered in this book more effectively.

What this book covers

Chapter 1, *Overview of the Dash Ecosystem*, will help you attain a good understanding of the Dash ecosystem, the main packages used, as well as the available third-party packages. By the end of this chapter, you will be able to differentiate between the different elements of an app and what each is responsible for, and you will have built a minimal app.

Chapter 2, Exploring the Structure of a Dash App, demonstrates how to add some interactive functionality to the app we created earlier. We will go through the app callbacks and see how they allow your users to connect visual elements of your app, and how you can let users use some of those elements to control others by creating special callback functions.

Chapter 3, Working with Plotly's Figure Objects, provides an in-depth introduction to the `Figure` object, its components, how it can be manipulated, and how it can be converted to different formats. Later on, we will use this understanding to build specific types of charts as needed in our application.

Chapter 4, Data Manipulation and Preparation - Paving the Way to Plotly Express, introduces an overview of tidy data, as well as the high-level Plotly Express package, and shows how it uses the grammar of graphics to easily produce charts and map data to visual elements.

Chapter 5, Interactively Comparing Values with Bar Charts and Dropdown Menus, goes in some depth into the available options for graphs and explores further possibilities. Then, we will see how to allow users to select which values they want to compare using drop-down menus.

Chapter 6, Exploring Variables with Scatter Plots and Filtering Subsets with Sliders, moves on to one of the most frequently used chart types: scatter plots. Like we did with bar charts, we will see many different ways to customize them. Scatter plots provide even more options that we will explore, such as mapping the size of the points to a certain variable, dealing with overplotting, and handling a large number of points.

Chapter 7, Exploring Map Plots and Enriching Your Dashboards with Markdown, explores a new type of chart that we see in many situations. There are many ways to plot data on maps, and we will explore two of the most frequently used types: scatter maps and choropleth maps.

Chapter 8, Calculating the Frequency of Your Data with Histograms and Building Interactive Tables, explores the different ways of creating histograms and customizing them, as well as splitting the data in different ways and then counting the resulting values.

Chapter 9, Letting Your Data Speak for Itself with Machine Learning, shows us how clustering works, and also uses a test model to evaluate performance. We will also explore a technique to evaluate various clusters and finally, we will design an interactive app using KMeans clustering.

Chapter 10, Turbo-charge Your Apps with Advanced Callbacks, introduces the pattern-matching callback to achieve dynamic app modification based on user interaction and various other conditions.

Chapter 11, *URLs and Multi-Page Apps*, introduces a new architecture that allows us to incorporate multiple pages in one app. The other interesting feature we will explore is using URLs either as inputs or outputs, interacting with different elements in the app.

Chapter 12, *Deploying Your App*, shows you how to deploy your app on a server, where people can access it from anywhere so you can share it with the world. Different options are available, and we will go through two simple options that might be useful.

Chapter 13, *Next Steps*, showcases the different options in taking your app(s) to the next level. This chapter provides some pointers on things you might want to explore.

To get the most out of this book

You will need a system with a stable internet connection.

If you are using the digital version of this book, we advise you to type the code yourself or access the code via the GitHub repository (link available in the next section). Doing so will help you avoid any potential errors related to the copying and pasting of code.

Download the example code files

You can download the example code files for this book from GitHub at `https://github.com/PacktPublishing/Interactive-Dashboards-and-Data-Apps-with-Plotly-and-Dash`. In case there's an update to the code, it will be updated on the existing GitHub repository.

We also have other code bundles from our rich catalog of books and videos available at `https://github.com/PacktPublishing/`. Check them out!

Download the color images

We also provide a PDF file that has color images of the screenshots/diagrams used in this book. You can download it here: `https://static.packt-cdn.com/downloads/9781800568914_ColorImages.pdf`.

Code in Action

Code in Action videos for this book can be viewed at (`https://bit.ly/3vaXYQJ`).

Conventions used

There are a number of text conventions used throughout this book.

`Code in text`: Indicates code words in text, database table names, folder names, filenames, file extensions, pathnames, dummy URLs, user input, and Twitter handles. Here is an example: "Our dataset will consist of the files in the `data` folder in the root of the repository."

A block of code is set as follows:

```
import plotly.express as px
gapminder = px.data.gapminder()
gapminder
```

When we wish to draw your attention to a particular part of a code block, the relevant lines or items are set in bold:

```
import os
import pandas as pd
pd.options.display.max_columns = None
os.listdir(,data')
['PovStatsSeries.csv',
 'PovStatsCountry.csv',
 'PovStatsCountry-Series.csv',
 'PovStatsData.csv',
 'PovStatsFootNote.csv']
```

Bold: Indicates a new term, an important word, or words that you see onscreen. For example, words in menus or dialog boxes appear in the text like this. Here is an example: "Another important column is the **Limitations and exceptions** column."

> **Tips or important notes**
> Appear like this.

Get in touch

Feedback from our readers is always welcome.

General feedback: If you have questions about any aspect of this book, mention the book title in the subject of your message and email us at `customercare@packtpub.com`.

Errata: Although we have taken every care to ensure the accuracy of our content, mistakes do happen. If you have found a mistake in this book, we would be grateful if you would report this to us. Please visit www.packtpub.com/support/errata, selecting your book, clicking on the Errata Submission Form link, and entering the details.

Piracy: If you come across any illegal copies of our works in any form on the Internet, we would be grateful if you would provide us with the location address or website name. Please contact us at copyright@packt.com with a link to the material.

If you are interested in becoming an author: If there is a topic that you have expertise in and you are interested in either writing or contributing to a book, please visit authors.packtpub.com.

Reviews

Please leave a review. Once you have read and used this book, why not leave a review on the site that you purchased it from? Potential readers can then see and use your unbiased opinion to make purchase decisions, we at Packt can understand what you think about our products, and our authors can see your feedback on their book. Thank you!

For more information about Packt, please visit packt.com.

Section 1: Building a Dash App

This section provides a general overview of the Dash ecosystem, and shows how to get started with a minimal functional app.

This section comprises the following chapters:

- *Chapter 1, Overview of the Dash Ecosystem*
- *Chapter 2, Exploring the Structure of a Dash App*
- *Chapter 3, Working with Plotly's Figure Objects*
- *Chapter 4, Data Manipulation and Preparation - Paving the Way to Plotly Express*

1
Overview of the Dash Ecosystem

One of the few constants in our work with data is the amount of change in the volume, sources, and types of data that we deal with. Being able to quickly combine data from different sources and explore them is crucial. **Dash** is not only for exploring data; it can be used for almost all phases of the data analysis process, from exploration to operational production environments.

In this chapter, we will get an overview of Dash's ecosystem and focus on building the layout, or the user-facing part, of the app. By the end of the chapter, you will be able to build a running app with almost any visual component you want, but without interactivity.

The following topics will be covered:

- Setting up your environment
- Exploring Dash and other supporting packages
- Understanding the general structure of a Dash app
- Creating and running the simplest app
- Adding HTML and other components to the app
- Learning how to structure the layout and managing themes

Technical requirements

Every chapter will have slightly different requirements, but there are some that you will need throughout the book.

You should have access to Python 3.6 or higher, which can be easily downloaded from `https://www.python.org`, as well as a text editor or an **integrated development environment** (IDE) so you can edit code.

For this chapter, we will be using **Dash**, **Dash HTML Components**, and **Dash Bootstrap Components**, which can be installed together with all other required packages by following the instructions in the following section. All code and data required for this book can be downloaded from the book's GitHub repository, which can be found at `https://github.com/PacktPublishing/Interactive-Dashboards-and-Data-Apps-with-Plotly-and-Dash`. As I just mentioned, the following section will show in detail how to get started with your setup.

The code files of this chapter can be found on GitHub at `https://github.com/PacktPublishing/Interactive-Dashboards-and-Data-Apps-with-Plotly-and-Dash/tree/master/chapter_01`.

Check out the following video to see the Code in Action at `https://bit.ly/3atXPjc`.

Setting up your environment

With the fast pace of change in all the packages used in the book, you will most likely come across some differences in functionality, so in order to reproduce the exact outcomes described in the book, you can clone the book's repository, install the packages used (in the specified versions), and use the included dataset. From the command line, go to a folder in which you want to build the project and do the following:

1. Create a Python virtual environment in a folder called `dash_project` (or any other name you want). This will also create a new folder with the name you chose:

   ```
   python3 -m venv dash_project
   ```

2. Activate the virtual environment.

   On Unix or macOS, run this:

   ```
   source dash_project/bin/activate
   ```

   On Windows, run this:

   ```
   dash_project\Scripts\activate.bat
   ```

3. Go to the created folder:

```
cd dash_project
```

4. Clone the book's GitHub repository:

```
git clone   https://github.com/PacktPublishing/
Interactive-Dashboards-and-Data-Apps-with-Plotly-and-Dash
```

5. You should now have a file containing the required packages and their versions called requirements.txt. You can install those packages by going to the repository's folder and running the install command as follows:

```
cd Interactive-Dashboards-and-Data-Apps-with-Plotly-and-
Dash/
pip install -r requirements.txt
```

You should find a copy of the dataset in the data folder, which was downloaded from this link: https://datacatalog.worldbank.org/dataset/poverty-and-equity-database. You can get the latest version if you want, but as with packages, if you want to get the same results, it's better to work with the provided dataset.

In order for Plotly figures and apps to be displayed in JupyterLab, you will need to install Node.js, which can be install from https://nodejs.org.

You will also need to install the JupyterLab Plotly extension, which can be done by running the following from the command line in your virtual environment:

```
jupyter labextension install jupyterlab-plotly@4.14.1
```

Note that the version number at the end should correspond to the version of Plotly that you are running. You can replace the preceding version numbers if you want to upgrade (making sure to upgrade the Plotly Python package as well).

Once you have run the preceding code, you should have everything you need to follow along. You will see that each chapter of this book builds on the previous one: we will be building an app that adds more and more functionality and complexity as we go through the chapters.

The main objective is to put you in a practical setting as much as possible. In general, it is straightforward to create any standalone Dash component, but it gets more challenging when you already have a few components in a running app. This becomes clear when you have to decide how to change the layout to accommodate new changes and how to refactor code, focusing on the details without losing sight of the big picture.

Now that the environment has been established, let's get an overview of Dash.

Exploring Dash and other supporting packages

Although not strictly necessary, it's good to know the main components that are used to make Dash and its dependencies, especially for more advanced usage, and in order to know how and where to get more information:

Figure 1.1 – What Dash is made of

> **Note**
>
> One of the main advantages of using Dash is that it allows us to create fully interactive data, analytics, and web apps and interfaces, using pure Python, without having to worry about HTML, CSS, or JavaScript.

As you can see in Figure 1.1, Dash uses **Flask** for the backend. For producing charts, it uses **Plotly**, although it is not strictly required, but it is the best-supported package for data visualization. **React** is used for handling all components, and actually a Dash app is rendered as a single-page React app. The most important things for us are the different packages that we will be using to create our app, which we will be covering next.

> **Tip**
>
> For people who are familiar with or invested in learning Matplotlib, there is a special set of tools to convert Matplotlib figures to Plotly figures. Once you have created your figure in Matplotlib, you can convert it to Plotly with one command: mpl_to_plotly. As of the time of this writing, this is supported for Matplotlib<=3.0.3 only. Here is a full example:

```
%config InlineBackend.figure_format = 'retina'
import matplotlib.pyplot as plt
from plotly.tools import mpl_to_plotly


mpl_fig, ax = plt.subplots()
ax.scatter(x=[1, 2, 3], y=[23, 12, 34])
plotly_fig = mpl_to_plotly(mpl_fig)
plotly_fig
```

The different packages that Dash contains

Dash is not one big package that contains everything. Instead, it consists of several packages, each handling a certain aspect. In addition, as we will see later, there are several third-party packages that are used, and the community is encouraged to develop their own functionality by creating special Dash packages.

The following are the main packages that we will mostly be using in this chapter, and we will explore others in later chapters:

- **Dash**: This is the main package, which provides the backbone of any app, through the `dash.Dash` object. It also provides a few other tools for managing interactivity and exceptions, which we will get into later as we build our app.

- **Dash Core Components**: A package that provides a set of interactive components that can be manipulated by users. Dropdowns, date pickers, sliders, and many more components are included in this package. We will learn how to use them to manage reactivity in *Chapter 2, Exploring the Structure of a Dash App*, and will be focusing on how to use them in detail in *Part 2* of the book.

- **Dash HTML Components**: This package provides all the available HTML tags as Python classes. It simply converts Python to HTML. For example, you can write `dash_html_components.H1('Hello, World')` in Python, and it will be converted to `<h1>Hello, World</h1>` and rendered as such in the browser.

- **Dash Bootstrap Components**: This is a third-party package that adds Bootstrap functionality to Dash. This package and its components take care of a lot of options related to layouts and visual signals. Laying out elements side by side or on top of one another, specifying their sizes based on the browser's screen size, and providing a set of encoded colors for better communicating with users are some of the benefits of using it.

> **Tip**
> The recommended way to install the main packages of Dash is to simply install Dash, and it will automatically handle installing the other packages, ensuring that they get installed with the correct versions. Simply run `pip install dash` from the command line. For upgrades, that would be `pip install dash --upgrade`.

We will now take a brief look at the general structure of a typical Dash app, after which we will start coding.

Understanding the general structure of a Dash app

The following diagram shows what generally goes into creating a Dash app. We typically have a file called app.py, although you can name it whatever you want. The file is shown as the column on the right, with the different parts split by lines, just to visually distinguish between them, while on the left is the name of each part:

App parts	app.py

imports (boilerplate)	`import dash`
	`import dash_html_components as html`
	`import dash_core_components as dcc`

app instantiation	`app = dash.Dash(__name__)`

app layout: a list of HTML and/or interactive components	`app.layout = html.Div([`
	    `dcc.Dropdown()`
	    `dcc.Graph()`
	    `...`
	`])`

callback functions	`@app.callback()`
	`...`
	`@app.callback()`
	`...`

running the app	`if __name__ == '__main__':` `app.run_server()`

Figure 1.2 – The structure of a Dash app

Let's look at each app part in detail:

- **Imports (boilerplate):** Like any Python module, we begin by importing the required packages, using their usual aliases.

- **App instantiation**: A straightforward way to create the app, by creating the app variable in this case. The __name__ value for the name parameter is used to make it easy for Dash to locate static assets to be used in the app.

- **App layout**: The subject of this chapter, which we will focus on in detail. This is where we set the user-facing elements, or the frontend. We usually define a container element, html.Div in the figure, that takes a list of components for its children parameter. These components will be displayed in order when the app renders, each placed below the previous element. In the following section, we will create a simple app with a minimal layout.

- **Callback functions**: This is the subject of Chapter 2, *Exploring the Structure of a Dash App*, where we will go through how interactivity works in detail; this won't be covered in this chapter. For now, it's enough to know that this is where we define as many functions as needed to link the visible elements of the app to each other, defining the functionality that we want. Typically, functions are independent, they don't need to be defined within a container, and their order does not matter in the module.

- **Running the app**: Using the Python idiom for running modules as scripts, we run the app.

As I promised, we are now ready to start coding.

Creating and running the simplest app

Using the structure that we just discussed, and excluding callback functions, let's now build our first simple app!

Create a file and name it app.py, and write the following code:

1. Import the required packages using their usual aliases:

```
import dash
import dash_html_components as html
```

2. Create (instantiate) the app:

```
app = dash.Dash(__name__)
```

3. Create the app's layout:

```
app.layout = html.Div([
    html.H1('Hello, World!')
])
```

4. Run the app:

```
if __name__ == '__main__':
    app.run_server(debug=True)
```

A few points before running the app. First, I strongly suggest that you don't copy and paste code. It's important to make sure you remember what you coded. It's also useful to explore the possibilities provided by each component, class, or function. Most IDEs provide hints on what is possible.

This app's layout contains one element, which is the list passed to html.Div, corresponding to its children parameter. This will produce an H1 element on the page. Finally, note that I set debug=True in the app.run_server method. This activates several developer tools that are really useful while developing and debugging.

You are now ready to run your first app. From the command line, in the same folder where you saved your app file, run this:

```
python app.py
```

You might need to run the preceding command using python3 if your system is not configured to use version three by default:

```
python3 app.py
```

You should now see an output like that shown in Figure 1.3, indicating that the app is running:

```
> python app.py
Dash is running on http://127.0.0.1:8050/

 * Serving Flask app "app" (lazy loading)
 * Environment: production
   WARNING: This is a development server. Do not use it in a production deployment.
   Use a production WSGI server instead.
 * Debug mode: on
```

Figure 1.3 – Command-line output while running the app

Congratulations on running your very first Dash app! Now, if you point your browser to the URL shown in the output, http://127.0.0.1:8050, you should see the "Hello, World!" message in H1 on the page. As you can see, it shows that it is serving a Flask app called "app," with a warning that this server is not designed for production use. We will cover deployment in a later chapter, but this server is good enough for developing and testing your apps. You can also see that we are in debug mode:

Hello, World!

Figure 1.4 – App rendered in the browser

As specified, we see the text in H1, and we can also see the blue button as well. Clicking on this button will open some options in the browser, and it will be more useful once there are callback functions and/or errors while running the app. We wouldn't have gotten the blue button if we had run the app with debug=False, which is the default.

Now that we have established a good-enough understanding of the main elements that go into creating a Dash app, and we have run a minimal one, we are ready to explore two packages that are used for adding and managing visible elements: first, Dash HTML Components, and after that, we will explore how to use Dash Bootstrap Components.

Adding HTML and other components to the app

From now until the end of this chapter, we will mainly be focusing on the app.layout attribute of our app and making changes to it. It's straightforward to do so; we simply add elements to the top-level html.Div element's list (the children parameter):

```
html.Div(children=[component_1, component_2, component_3, …])
```

Adding HTML components to a Dash app

Since the available components in the package correspond to actual HTML tags, it is the most stable package. Let's quickly explore the parameters that are common to all its components.

At the time of this writing, Dash HTML Components has 131 components, and there are 20 parameters that are common to all of them.

Let's go over some of the most important ones that we will frequently be using:

- children: This is typically the main (and first) container of the content of the component. It can take a list of items, or a single item.

- className: This is the same as the class attribute, only renamed as such.

- id: While we won't be covering this parameter in this chapter, it is the crucial one in making interactivity work, and we will be using it extensively while building the app. For now, it's enough to know that you can set arbitrary IDs to your components so you can identify them and later use them for managing interactivity.

- `style`: This is similar to the HTML attribute of the same name, but with a few differences. First, its attributes are set using camelCase. So, say you wanted to set the following attributes in Dash HTML Components:

```
<h1 style="color:blue; font-size: 40px; margin-left:
20%">A Blue Heading</h1>
```

You would specify them this way:

```
import dash_html_components as html
html.H1(children='A Blue Heading',
          style={'color': 'blue',
                 'fontSize': '40px',
                 'marginLeft': '20%'})
```

As you have most likely noticed, the `style` attribute is set using a Python dictionary.

The other parameters have different uses and rules, depending on the respective component that they belong to. Let's now practice adding a few HTML elements to our app. Going back to the same `app.py` file, let's experiment with adding a few more HTML elements and run the app one more time, as we just did. I kept the top and bottom parts the same, and I mainly edited `app.layout`:

```
...
app = dash.Dash(__name__)
app.layout = html.Div([
    html.H1('Poverty And Equity Database',
            style={'color': 'blue',
                   'fontSize': '40px'}),
    html.H2('The World Bank'),
    html.P('Key Facts:'),
    html.Ul([
        html.Li('Number of Economies: 170'),
        html.Li('Temporal Coverage: 1974 - 2019'),
        html.Li('Update Frequency: Quarterly'),
        html.Li('Last Updated: March 18, 2020'),
        html.Li([
            'Source: ',
            html.A('https://datacatalog.worldbank.org/dataset/
poverty-and-equity-database',            href='https://
datacatalog.worldbank.org/dataset/poverty-and-equity-database')
```

```
        ])
    ])
])
...
```

```
python app.py
```

That should produce the following screen:

Poverty And Equity Database

The World Bank

Key Facts:

- Number of Economies: 170
- Temporal Coverage: 1974 - 2019
- Update Frequency: Quarterly
- Last Updated: March 18, 2020
- Source: https://datacatalog.worldbank.org/dataset/poverty-and-equity-database

Figure 1.5 – Updated app rendered in the browser

> **Tip**
> If you are familiar with HTML, this should look straightforward. If not, please check out a basic tutorial online. A great source to start would be W3Schools: `https://www.w3schools.com/html/`.

In the updated part, we just added a `<p>` element and an unordered list, `<ul>`, within which we added a few list items, `<li>` (using a Python list), the last of which contained a link using the `<a>` element.

Note that since these components are implemented as Python classes, they follow Python's conventions of capitalizing class names: `html.P`, `html.Ul`, `html.Li`, `html.A`, and so on.

Feel free to experiment with other options: adding new HTML components, changing the order, trying to set other attributes, and so on.

Learning how to structure the layout and managing themes

So far, we have discussed the basic structure of a Dash app and gone through a brief overview of its main elements: the imports, app instantiation, app layout, callbacks (which we will cover in the next chapter), and running the app. We created a bare-bones app, and then we learned how to add a few HTML elements to it. We are now ready to take our app to the next level—from a layout perspective. We will keep working with the app.layout attribute and control it in a more powerful and flexible way using the Dash Bootstrap Components package.

Bootstrap is basically a set of tools that abstract away many details for handling the layout of web pages. Here are some of the most important benefits of using it:

- **Themes**: As we will see in a moment, changing the app's theme is as simple as providing an additional argument while instantiating the app. Dash Bootstrap Components ships with a set of themes that you can select from and/or edit.
- **Grid system**: Bootstrap provides a powerful grid system, so we can think about our pages more from a user perspective (rows and columns) and not have to focus on the screen attributes (pixels and percentages), although we still have access to those low-level details whenever we need to.
- **Responsiveness**: Having a large number of possible screen sizes makes it almost impossible to properly design page layouts. This is handled for us, and we can also fine-tune the behavior of page elements to control how their sizes change as the screen size changes.
- **Prebuilt components**: A set of prebuilt components is also provided, which we will be using. Alerts, buttons, drop-down menus, and tabs are some of the components that Bootstrap provides.
- **Encoded colors**: We also get a set of colors for easy communication with users, in case we have a warning, an error, simple information, and so on.

Let's explore these features one by one.

Themes

First, let's see how easy it is to change the theme of an app. In the same app.py file, add the following import and the new argument to the app creation call:

```
import dash_bootstrap_components as dbc

...

app = dash.Dash(__name__, external_stylesheets=[dbc.themes.
BOOTSTRAP])

...
```

Running the app again, you should see that the theme has changed. As shown in Figure 1.6, you can also see other sample themes, and I also added their names and how to set them at the bottom of each page:

Figure 1.6 – Theme samples and how to set them

You can see how easy it is to completely change the look and feel of the app, simply by changing one argument. Note also that the color and font size of the <h1> element were overridden in the style argument. We specifically set the color to "blue" and the size to "40px". Usually, this is not advisable; for example, in the two dark themes in the figure it is very difficult to read the blue text. So, be careful when you make such changes.

Grid system and responsiveness

Another powerful benefit that we get from Bootstrap is its grid system. When adding Dash HTML Components, we saw that we can do so by appending items to the children parameter of the main html.Div element. In this case, every added item occupies the full width of the screen and takes as much screen height as it needs to display its contents. The order of the elements in the list determines their order of display on the screen as well.

Displaying elements side by side in columns

While it's possible to do this by editing the `style` parameter of any HTML element, it is a bit tedious and can be brittle. You have to worry about too many details, and it might break in unexpected ways. With Bootstrap, you simply define a column, and that in turn behaves as an independent screen, displaying its elements on top of one another, with each element occupying the full width of this mini screen. Columns' widths can also be specified in powerful and flexible ways. The grid system divides the screen into 12 columns, and the width of a column can be specified by using a number from 1 to 12 inclusive. Figure 1.7 shows how the columns can be defined, and how they would change for screens of different size:

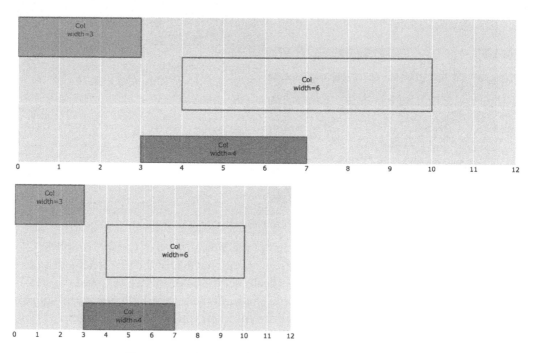

Figure 1.7 – The same column layout on two screen sizes

As you can see, the two screens are identical, and the resizing happens automatically, while maintaining the proportions.

In many cases, this might not be exactly what you want. When the screen width becomes smaller, it might make more sense to expand the columns to be more easily readable by the users. For this, we have the option of specifying the width of columns for each of five possible screen widths: `xs` (extra-small), `sm` (small), `md` (medium), `lg` (large), and `xl` (extra-large). These are also the names of the parameters that you can set:

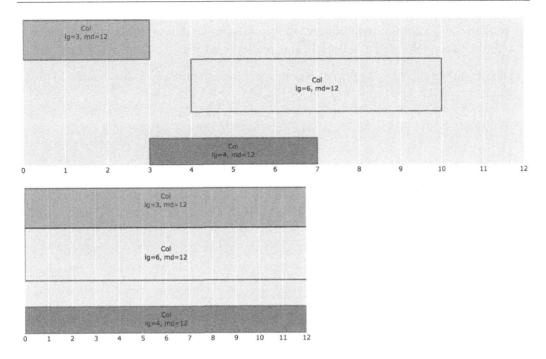

Figure 1.8 – Granular control of column width based on screen size

Figure 1.8 shows how this is achieved by setting two arguments for the column. The way to set these values is simple, as indicated in the figure. The full code would be something like this:

```
import dash_boostrap_components as dbc
dbc.Col(children=[child1, child2, ...], lg=6, md=12)
```

The lg=6, md=12 arguments simply mean that we want this column to have a width of six when the screen is large (lg), which means 6 ÷ 12, or half the screen's width. On screens of medium size (md), set the column width to 12, which means the full width of the screen (12 ÷ 12).

You might be wondering how we can have the columns in the middle of the page, and not starting from the left, as is the case in Figures 1.7 and 1.8. The width and the different size parameters can also take a dictionary, one of the keys of which can be offset, and this is how you set its horizontal location on the screen:

```
dbc.Col(children=[child1, child2, ...], lg={'size': 6, 'offset':
4}, md=12)
```

As you can see, `lg` became a dictionary where we indicated that we want that column to skip the first four columns from the left, and be displayed after that, in the specified size.

Finally, if you want to place multiple columns next to each other, you simply have to place them in a row (with `Row`), and they will be placed next to each other:

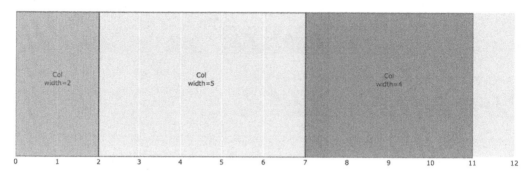

Figure 1.9 – Columns side by side in a row

In order to produce the layout in Figure 1.9, we can simply place the three columns in a list and pass it as the `children` parameter to a row element:

```
dbc.Row([
    dbc.Col('Column 1', width=2),
    dbc.Col('Column 2', width=5),
    dbc.Col('Column 3', width=4),
])
```

Prebuilt components

While we won't cover them all, we will be using several of those components, and they are generally straightforward to create. Please check the documentation for ideas and details of each component: `https://dash-bootstrap-components.opensource.faculty.ai/`. We will shortly modify the app to include some prebuilt components.

Encoded colors

Although you can set any color you want for text, background colors, and many other elements using its hexadecimal representation, Bootstrap provides a set of named colors based on the type of information you are trying to convey. This can be set as the `color` parameter in several components, and it would have a visual meaning to users. For example, setting `color="danger"` would cause the component to appear in red, and `color="warning"` as yellow. The available color names are *primary, secondary, success, warning, danger, info, light,* and *dark.*

Adding Dash Bootstrap components to our app

We will now add two new related components to the app: Tabs and Tab. As you might have guessed, Tabs is simply a container of Tab components. The result we are aiming for is adding a little more information to the page, and organizing it under new tabs, as you can see in Figure 1.10:

Figure 1.10 – Adding tabs to the app

> **Tip**
>
> One of the most important skills to develop while learning Dash is code refactoring. While the latest version of the app is still very simple, it is a very good idea to make sure you know how to manually refactor the code from the previous version to the new one. The more components you have in your app, the more attention you will need to give to the refactoring details. I suggest you always do this manually and do not simply copy and paste the latest version of the app.

In order to create the tabs, and get the new content in the form you see in Figure 1.10, you will need to make the following changes:

```
html.H2('The World Bank'),
dbc.Tabs([
    dbc.Tab([
        html.Ul([
            # same code to define the unordered list
        ]),

    ], label='Key Facts'),
    dbc.Tab([
        html.Ul([
            html.Br(),
```

```
            html.Li('Book title: Interactive Dashboards and
    Data Apps with Plotly and Dash'),
            html.Li(['GitHub repo: ',
                html.A('https://github.com/
    PacktPublishing/Interactive-Dashboards-and-Data-Apps-with-
    Plotly-and-Dash',
                    href='https://github.com/
    PacktPublishing/Interactive-Dashboards-and-Data-Apps-with-
    Plotly-and-Dash')])
        ])


    ], label='Project Info')
```

As you can see, we have added one Tabs element, within which we added two Tab elements. In the first one, we simply used the same code that went into defining our ordered list. In the second, we added a similar unordered list with new content. OK, you can copy this part if you want! You can also see how to specify the labels of the tabs, by setting a value for the label parameter.

Now you can run your updated app again, and make sure that the new content went to the right place, and that the tabs work as expected.

We are now ready to add some interactivity to our app.

Summary

We have learned how to create a minimal app and saw indeed how simple the process is. We then explored the main Dash packages used to create visual elements on a web page. With what we covered in this chapter, you have enough information to create almost any layout, with any elements you want on a page. The discussion and examples were not comprehensive, however. We will be using and discussing those components and many others, so you can master their use.

In the next chapter, we will turn our attention to the mechanism of adding interactivity to our app. We will set up the app such that the user will be able to explore different options by selecting what exactly they would like to analyze from our dataset.

2
Exploring the Structure of a Dash App

We are now ready to tackle the mechanism through which Dash creates interactivity – the heart of Dash, if you will. Once you are comfortable with creating **callback functions** that link different elements of the layout, combined with what you learned in *Chapter 1, Overview of the Dash Ecosystem*, you should be well equipped to be able to convert datasets into interactive apps in a very short period of time. The remainder of this book will go into much more detail and offer many more options of how to do this. However, these two chapters should be sufficient for creating visual layouts, as well as connecting them and making them interactive. We will mainly explore callback functions in this chapter; the following topics will be covered:

- Using Jupyter Notebooks to run Dash apps
- Creating a standalone pure Python function
- Understanding the ID parameter of Dash components
- Using Dash inputs and outputs
- Incorporating the function into the app – creating your first reactive program
- Running your first interactive app

Technical requirements

In addition to the packages that we used in *Chapter 1, Overview of the Dash Ecosystem* (for example, Dash, Dash HTML Components, and Dash Bootstrap Components), we will be, most importantly, working with **Dash Core Components**. We will also look at how to run Dash apps within a Jupyter Notebook environment, and for that, we will be using the `jupyter_dash` package along with **JupyterLab**. Later in the chapter, when we incorporate new functionality into the app, we will use `pandas` for data manipulation.

The code files of this chapter can be found on GitHub at `https://github.com/PacktPublishing/Interactive-Dashboards-and-Data-Apps-with-Plotly-and-Dash/tree/master/chapter_02`.

Check out the following video to see the Code in Action at `https://bit.ly/3tCOZsW`.

Using Jupyter Notebooks to run Dash apps

With a change to imports and a minor change to app instantiation, we can easily start to run our apps within Jupyter Notebook environments. The package that makes this possible is `jupyter_dash`. Essentially, the difference is that we import the **JupyterDash** object (instead of importing Dash), and app instantiation occurs by calling this object, as follows:

```
from jupyter_dash import JupyterDash
app = JupyterDash(__name__)
```

One of the advantages of running apps in a notebook environment is that it is less tedious to make small changes, iterate them, and see results. Working with an IDE, the command line, and the browser, you need to constantly shift between them, while in a notebook environment, everything is in one place. This makes introducing simple changes and testing them easier. It can make your notebooks far more powerful and interesting as well.

The `jupyter_dash` package also provides an additional option while running the app, where you can determine whether you want to run the app in one of three modes:

- `external`: In a separate browser window, exactly as we have done so far
- `inline`: In the code output area of the notebook, right underneath the code cell
- `jupyterlab`: In a separate tab while/if running in JupyterLab

You can also set your desired width and height if you wish to. Running the app takes additional optional parameters, as follows:

```
app.run_server(mode='inline', height=600, width='80%')
```

As you can see, setting the height and width can be done either by specifying an integer, that is, the number of pixels, or, for `width`, a percentage of the screen size as a string.

Still, there is another important benefit of running apps in a Jupyter Notebook environment, other than keeping the code and narrative in one place.

Isolating functionality for better management and debugging

When running and developing apps, you inevitably come across bugs and issues. In order to handle them, you need to isolate the cause and create the simplest reproducible example that causes the bug to happen. Only then can you properly troubleshoot the problem. And only then can you ask others for help. We won't wait for bugs to happen to isolate issues and figure them out. We will preemptively isolate all new features before incorporating them, so we can better handle and manage them.

From now on, introducing new features will be done by, first, creating them in an isolated environment, where we create a minimal app containing only this functionality. Once we are comfortable that we understand how it works, and that it functions as expected, we will keep a copy for reference, and see how to incorporate it into the existing app. This will also help us if we want to make changes to that specific functionality in the future, in which case we go through the same process again.

Let's start with our first example, which will be a drop-down menu with three values. The user selects one, and right underneath it, they see a message showing the value they chose. *Figure 2.1* shows an example of what this might look like in its simplest form:

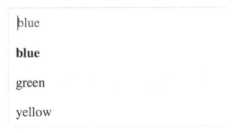

You selected <color>

Figure 2.1 – The user's selection is displayed based on the value selected

The following code will create this, except for the function that shows the user's selection:

1. Import the required packages with their aliases:

    ```
    from jupyter_dash import JupyterDash
    import dash_core_components as dcc
    import dash_html_components as html
    ```

2. Instantiate the app:

    ```
    app = JupyterDash(__name__)
    ```

3. Create the layout of the app. We will now introduce a new component, the Dash Core Components **Dropdown**. This will be covered in much more detail later. However, for now, we will primarily use its `options` attribute to set the options that the user can select from. This parameter is set by using a list of dictionaries, one for each option, where `label` is what the user will see, and `value` is the actual value that we will be dealing with:

    ```
    app.layout = html.Div([
        dcc.Dropdown(options=[{'label': color, 'value':
    color}
                            for color in ['blue', 'green',
    'yellow']]),
        html.Div()
    ])
    ```

4. Run the app as usual, with the minor change of running this in the `inline` mode for easier interactive work in JupyterLab:

    ```
    if __name__ == '__main__':
        app.run_server(mode='inline')
    ```

Figure 2.2 shows an example of what this would look like in a notebook environment:

```
1   from jupyter_dash import JupyterDash
2   import dash_core_components as dcc
3   import dash_html_components as html
4
5   app = JupyterDash(__name__)
6
7 ▼ app.layout = html.Div([
8 ▼     dcc.Dropdown(options=[{'label': color, 'value': color}
9                              for color in ['blue', 'green', 'yellow']]),
10        html.Div()
11
12  ])
13 ▼ if __name__ == '__main__':
14        app.run_server(mode='inline')
```

green	× ▲
blue	
green	
yellow	

Figure 2.2 – The Dash app running in JupyterLab

I'm sure you have noticed the empty html.Div component that was added right underneath the drop-down list. Let's examine how that fits into the structure of the app and how to implement the remaining functionality. We will now look at how to create the function that will link the dropdown to the empty div tag.

Creating a standalone pure Python function

This function is what we will be using to take the selected value from the dropdown, process it somehow, and use its return value to do something that is visible to the user.

The function is so simple that it doesn't require much explanation:

```
def display_selected_color(color):
    if color is None:
        color = 'nothing'
    return 'You selected ' + color
```

If the user doesn't input anything (or deselects the current option), then the color variable is set to 'nothing', and the function returns 'You selected ' + <color>, with whatever value color takes. Later in the chapter, we will create a more involved function to get some information on countries.

A function is essentially a procedure. It takes in one or more arguments (inputs), does something to them, and returns one or more outputs. So, for this function, what will Input be, and what happens to its Output? You decide by selecting from the available components from the layout.

For this function, the dropdown will provide Input. Then, after processing it, the return value of the function, that is, its Output, will influence what to display in the currently empty html.Div right underneath the dropdown. Building on the diagram in *Figure 2.1*, *Figure 2.3* shows what we are trying to achieve. We will build a way to connect the dropdown (Input) to the div that shows the text (Output) by using the function we just defined as an intermediary:

blue

blue

green

yellow

```
def display_selected_color(color):
    if color is None:
        color = 'nothing'
    return 'You selected ' + color
```

You selected <color>

Figure 2.3 – Input, Output, and a standalone function

In order for it to work in the context of this app, the function needs to know what its inputs and outputs are.

Let's now look at how to identify components by setting their id values. After that, we will learn how to declare a component as Input or Output.

The id parameter of Dash components

As briefly mentioned in *Chapter 1*, *Overview of the Dash Ecosystem*, every Dash component has an id parameter that you can easily set in order to uniquely identify it. There is actually nothing more to this parameter than making sure that your components have unique and descriptive names.

> **Note**
> There are more advanced ways of using the **id** parameter, and they will be tackled in a later, more advanced chapter. However, for now, we will just focus on it being a unique identifier.

Using descriptive and explicit names for the id parameter becomes more important as the app grows in complexity. This parameter is optional when there is no interactivity, but it becomes mandatory when there is. The following example snippet shows how easy it is to set the id parameter for a basic use case:

```
html.Div([
    html.Div(id='empty_space'),
    html.H2(id='h2_text'),
    dcc.Slider(id='slider'),
])
```

Applying this to our current isolated app, we set a descriptive name to each id parameter:

```
app.layout = html.Div([
    dcc.Dropdown(id='color_dropdown',
                 options=[{'label': color, 'value': color}
                          for color in ['blue', 'green',
'yellow']]),
    html.Div(id='color_output')
])
```

Our app is now complete from a layout perspective, exactly as we did in *Chapter 1, Overview of the Dash Ecosystem*. The difference here is that we set values for the id parameter, and we are running it in a Jupyter Notebook environment. Once we can identify components using their id parameter, we can determine which become Input and which become Output. By updating our conceptual diagram with the ID values that we set, we can view the labels, as shown in *Figure 2.4*:

Figure 2.4 – Visible app elements are given names (IDs)

Having given our components descriptive names, we are now ready to use them beyond simply displaying them.

Dash inputs and outputs

The next step is to determine which component is going to become an input (to our pure Python function) and which component will get the return value of the function (as an output) to be displayed to the user.

Determining your inputs and outputs

The `dash.dependencies` module has several classes, two of which we will be using here: `Output` and `Input`.

These classes can be imported by adding the following line to the `imports` section of our app:

```
from dash.dependencies import Output, Input
```

Let's quickly recap what we did earlier before adding the final element that will make this functionality work:

1. We instantiated an app in the Jupyter Notebook environment.

2. We created a dropdown containing three colors.

3. We created a regular function that returns a string, together with the value provided to it: `'Your selected'` `+ <color>`.

4. The components were identified with descriptive names through their `id` parameters.

5. `Input` and `Output` were imported from `dash.dependencies`.

    We will now define our callback function.

Callback functions are decorators, and in the most basic use case, they require three things:

1. **Output**: The page element that will be changed as a result of running the function. Dash gives us the flexibility to also determine which **property** of the component we want to modify. In our case, we want to modify the `children` property of the empty div. In this case, it can be specified like this:

    ```
    Output(component_id='color_output',
    component_property='children')
    ```

2. **Input**: Using the same logic, we need to specify which property of which component will serve as our input to the callback function. In our case, this would be the `value` property:

```
Input(component_id='color_dropdown',
component_property='value')
```

3. **A normal Python function**: Any function can be used, but obviously, it needs to make sense in the context of the `Input` and `Output` that we have chosen.

Figure 2.5 shows an updated view of how things are coming together:

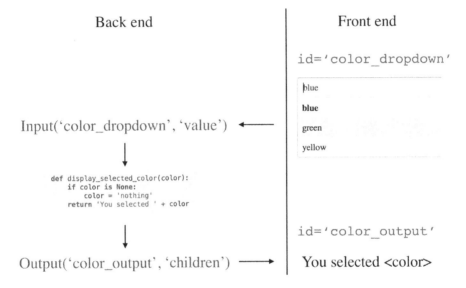

Figure 2.5 – Visible app elements connected through certain properties

> **Tip**
> The distinction between the frontend and the backend in Dash is massively simplified for us. They both exist in the same module, and we don't need to worry about many of the conventional details. For now, anything in `app.layout` can be considered the frontend, and any callback functions that we define outside it can be collectively thought of as the backend.

Specifying your callback function

The general format to specify a callback function is to define it as an attribute of the app variable, using the Python classes' dot notation, and then set the output and input, as shown here:

```
@app.callback(Output(component_id, component_property)
              Input(component_id, component_property))
```

Now that we have created a callback as an attribute of our app and determined which components' IDs and properties we want to influence each other, we bring our Python function and simply place it underneath the callback:

```
@app.callback(Output(component_id, component_property)
              Input(component_id, component_property)
def regular_function(input):
    output = do_something_with(input)
    return output
```

Now our callback is complete and ready to be incorporated into our app.

Implementing the callback

Let's take this abstract structure and implement it using the details of our standalone app:

```
@app.callback(Output('color_output', 'children'),
              Input('color_dropdown', 'value')
def display_selected_color(color):
    if color is None:
        color = 'nothing'
    return 'You selected ' + color
```

Please keep in mind that the order is important. Output has to be provided before Input.

Now we have a complete callback function that belongs to our app. It knows which property of which Output it will modify, as well as which property of which Input it will be using for this. It then uses the display_selected_color function for processing, taking the output value and sending it to the component where id='color_output'. This will, in turn, modify the specified property (children).

For running it in JupyterLab, you can see the full code in *Figure 2.6*, as well as several possible outputs based on the selected value:

```
1    from jupyter_dash import JupyterDash
2    import dash_core_components as dcc
3    import dash_html_components as html
4    from dash.dependencies import Output, Input
5
6    app = JupyterDash(__name__)
7
8 ▾ app.layout = html.Div([
9 ▾     dcc.Dropdown(id='color_dropdown',
10 ▾                  options=[{'label': color, 'value': color}
11                             for color in ['blue', 'green', 'yellow']]),
12         html.Br(),
13         html.Div(id='color_output')
14    ])
15
16 ▾ @app.callback(Output('color_output', 'children'),
17              Input('color_dropdown', 'value'))
18 ▾ def display_selected_color(color):
19 ▾     if color is None:
20             color = 'nothing'
21         return 'You selected ' + color
22
23 ▾ if __name__ == '__main__':
24         app.run_server(mode='inline')
```

Select...   ▾

You selected nothing

blue   ✕ ▾

You selected blue

green   ✕ ▾

You selected green

Figure 2.6 – An interactive Dash app in a Jupyter Notebook

I also introduced a simple new component, html.Br, which simply provides a regular HTML <br> element, for better readability of the output.

With this, we have completed our first isolated and interactive app. We ran it in JupyterLab, and we did so step by step, analyzing every tiny detail. The app that we have just built uses a toy dataset and implements extremely simple functionality. We did this so that we could focus on the mechanism that creates interactivity. There's not much practical value in telling the user what color they know they just selected.

With this knowledge, we will now add functionality to answer a real question for the user – a question that might be tedious to answer if they were to skim through the whole dataset.

We will also incorporate this new feature into our app and examine how it fits with the other content and functionality that we created already.

Incorporating the function into the app

Here is the plan for the functionality that we are going to introduce:

1. Create a drop-down list using the countries and regions available in our dataset.

2. Create a callback function that takes the selected country, filters the dataset, and finds the population of that country in the year 2010.

3. Return a small report about the found data. *Figure 2.7* shows the desired end result:

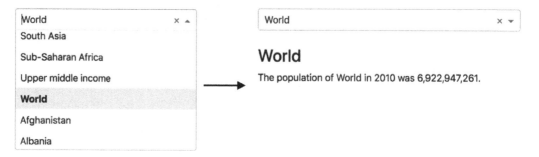

Figure 2.7 – A drop-down list used to display the selected country's population

> **Important note**
>
> Now that we are beginning to use our dataset, we will start opening files from the data folder. This assumes that the app you are running is in the same folder. The code for each chapter in the GitHub repository is placed in its own folder for easy access; however, the code only works if the data folder and app.py are both in the same folder.

Figure 2.8 shows what this folder structure might look like:

Figure 2.8 – The assumed folder structure for the app

As agreed, we will run a minimal app in JupyterLab, make sure it is running properly, keep a copy, and then add it to the app.

We first need to take a look at the dataset, explore it a little bit, and learn how to implement the new functionality.

To view what files we have in the dataset, we can run the following code:

```
import os
os.listdir('data')


['PovStatsSeries.csv',
 'PovStatsCountry.csv',
 'PovStatsCountry-Series.csv',
 'PovStatsData.csv',
 'PovStatsFootNote.csv']
```

Feel free to check out the files and their contents if you wish to. For now, we will be working with the PovStatsData.csv file. For a quick overview of its structure, we can run the following:

```
import pandas as pd
poverty_data = pd.read_csv('data/PovStatsData.csv')
poverty_data.head(3)
```

Running this code snippet in JupyterLab displays the first three rows of the dataset, as follows:

	Country Name	Country Code	Indicator Name	Indicator Code	1974	1975	1976	1977	1978	1979	1980	1981	1982	1983
0	East Asia & Pacific	EAS	Annualized growth in per capita real survey me...	SI.SPR.PC40.ZG	NaN	NaN	NaN	NaN	NaN	NaN	NaN	NaN	NaN	NaN
1	East Asia & Pacific	EAS	Annualized growth in per capita real survey me...	SI.SPR.PT10.ZG	NaN	NaN	NaN	NaN	NaN	NaN	NaN	NaN	NaN	NaN
2	East Asia & Pacific	EAS	Annualized growth in per capita real survey me...	SI.SPR.PT60.ZG	NaN	NaN	NaN	NaN	NaN	NaN	NaN	NaN	NaN	NaN

Figure 2.9 – The first few rows and columns of the poverty dataset

It seems that we have two fixed variable columns (**Country Name** and **Indicator Name**). Measured variables in the form of numeric data (or missing NaN) values are available under their respective year column. Here, the years span from 1974 to 2019 (note that not all of the years are shown for better readability). The countries and indicators also have codes, which can be useful later when we want to merge different DataFrames.

> **Tip**
>
> Fixed variables refers to variables that are known in advance and don't change; in this case, they are the countries and the indicators. The measured variables are the values that we are interested in knowing, for example, the population of country A in year B. Fixed variables are also known as "dimensions." Technically, they are all columns in the dataset, and this is a conceptual distinction that is useful for analysis.

In *Chapter 4, Data Manipulation and Preparation - Paving the Way to Plotly Express*, we will explore data formats and how they might affect our analysis and visualization. The current structure can be improved by having a column for "year," and another column for "values," which makes it standardized and more intuitive for analysis. For now, since we are focusing on callback functions, we will keep the data format as it is so that we don't get distracted.

Let's now implement the plan with code:

1. First, let's create a drop-down list. Here, we use the pandas `Series.unique` method to deduplicate countries and regions. Right underneath that, we create an empty div with `id='report'`:

```
dcc.Dropdown(id='country',
            options=[{'label': country, 'value':
country}
                    for country in
                    poverty_data['Country Name'].
unique()])
html.Div(id='report')
```

2. Next, we create a callback function that takes the selected country, filters the dataset, and finds the population of that country in the year 2010. The filtering will take two steps.

Check whether no country has been provided to the function, which happens when the user first accesses the page or when the user deselects values from the dropdown. Here, we simply return the empty string:

```
if country is None:
    return ''
```

Now, let's focus on the filtering part. First, we take the selected country and filter the `poverty_data` DataFrame to get the population value. We then define the `filtered_df` variable. This takes the selected country and gives the rows where the **Country Name** column is equal to the selected country, and the **Indicator Name** column is equal to **Population, total**. After that, we create the `population` variable. We do this by using the pandas `loc` method, where we take all of the : rows and the column name **2010**. We then extract the `values` attribute and get the number at index zero:

```
filtered_df = countrydata[(countrydata['Country
Name']==country) & (countrydata['Indicator
Name']=='Population, total')]
population = filtered_df.loc[:, '2010'].values[0]
```

3. Finally, let's return a small report about the data that has been found. Now that we have the population number that we are interested in, we return a list that contains two elements. The first is an <h3> element, showing the `country` variable using a large font. The second is a sentence that takes two dynamic values, which are inserted where they belong, as you can see in the following code snippet:

```
return [
    html.H3(country),
    f'The population of {country} in 2010 was
{population:,.0f}.'
]
```

Note that since we already have a div element in the layout, and we have indicated that we are modifying its `children` property (which takes a single value or a list), the return value of the function can simply be a list (or a single value).

I have formatted the `population` value in the report to make it easier to read. The colon indicates that the following string is how we want to format it. The comma indicates that we want thousands to be separated by a comma. The dot indicates how to format decimal places. A zero after the dot indicates the number of decimal places, and the `f` indicates that we are dealing with floats.

Now, we are ready to refactor our code to include the new visual elements, as well as the new functionality.

Picking up where we left off in the last version of our app in *Chapter 1, Overview of the Dash Ecosystem*, the dropdown and report div should go between the `H2` and `Tabs` components:

```
...
html.H2('The World Bank'),
dcc.Dropdown(id='country',
             options=[{'label': country, 'value': country}
                      for country in poverty_data['Country
Name'].unique()]),
html.Br(),
html.Div(id='report'),

dbc.Tabs([
    dbc.Tab([
...
```

The callback function should come after the closing parentheses of the top-level `html.Div` of the app. Here is the full code of the function:

```
@app.callback(Output('report', 'children'),
              Input('country', 'value'))
def display_country_report(country):
    if country is None:
        return ''
    filtered_df = poverty_data[(poverty_data['Country
Name']==country) &
                              (poverty_data['Indicator
Name']=='Population, total')]
    population = filtered_df.loc[:, '2010'].values[0]
```

```
return [html.H3(country),
        f'The population of {country} in 2010 was
{population:,.0f}.']
```

By running the app again, you should get this updated view:

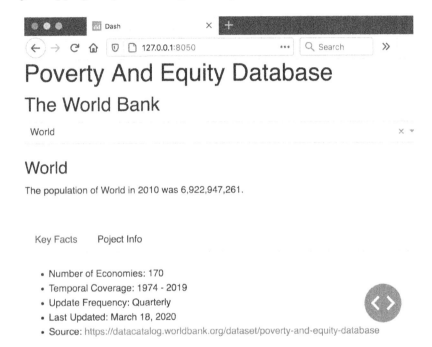

Figure 2.10 – The updated app with the dropdown and simple population report

---

Tip

The `app.run_server` method takes an optional `port` argument, which defaults to **8050**, as you can see in the URL in *Figure 2.10*. While developing apps, you might want to run two or more apps side by side. The way to do that is to simply run the second app on a different port, for example, `app.run_server(port=1234)`. This also applies to `jupyter_dash`.

Now that we have our callbacks enabled and working, we can finally start using that blue button in the bottom-right corner! Clicking on it and then selecting **Callbacks** shows an interactive diagram displaying the components exactly as we specified them. The **country** and its **value**, and the **report** and its **children**. *Figure 2.11* shows this:

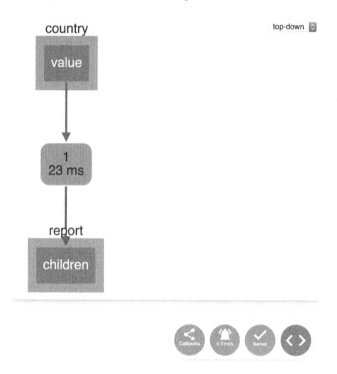

Figure 2.11 – The Dash visual debugger in action

The **Server** button is green, which means it's running fine. We also see that we have "0 Errors." When you have this debugger opened in a running app, and while modifying the components, you can also see the path of the callbacks and what is triggering what. The components that are involved in triggering a callback light up, so you can "see" what is going on. This becomes much more useful in complex situations. The nodes of the graph are also interactive, and you can move them around by increasing/decreasing the size of the overall graph so that you can zoom in and out wherever you want. And yes, this graph is a Dash app, using another one of Dash's packages.

The green rectangle in the middle shows two interesting numbers. The one on top, showing **1**, tells us how many times this callback has been fired so far. The one at the bottom shows how long it took to run this callback function. This is very helpful in tracking and analyzing performance.

So far, we have used a single-value input (not a list, for example) to modify an output. But what if we wanted to get multiple values and do something with them? What if we wanted to process values from multiple sources, for example, drop-down values and a date? All this and more is possible with Dash's callback functions. Did I mention that they were the heart of Dash?

I believe we've done enough coding in this chapter, and I think it's a good idea to have an overview of what lies ahead in terms of the power of callback functions, what they can do, and some of their interesting attributes. These are just things to keep in mind and know for now; we will be exploring how each feature works as we progress through the later chapters.

Properties of Dash's callback functions

Let's recap the properties of Dash's callback function and introduce a few others that will be explored in more detail later on:

- **Multiple inputs**: As I just mentioned, we can give callbacks to more than one input, and create more complex functionality. Using our dataset as an example, we can easily imagine a dropdown to select countries, another to select dates, and yet another to specify the economic indicator that you want to analyze. Those inputs could be used to filter a subset of the DataFrame and return the values that you want, based on multiple criteria.

- **Inputs can be lists** (effectively multiple values from a single `Input`): The country selector can be made to accept multiple values, so we can loop over them and visualize the same trend for the same indicator for multiple countries in one chart (or a chart per country).

- **Multiple outputs**: As with multiple inputs, multiple outputs can be modified using one callback function. In our example, we might imagine producing two outputs – one that is a chart visualizing the filtered data and another that is a table – providing the user with the raw data if they want to export and further analyze this particular subset.

- **They can do other things before returning**: We have mainly focused on callbacks being simple processors of data, but they can really do anything before returning. For example, you can imagine a function sending an email under certain conditions. Logging is another interesting thing to explore. All you have to do is simply log the arguments given to each function. This can give you insights into what people are interested in, which functionality is being used, and more. You can even parse those logs and develop your own separate analytics app based on that!

- **Order matters**: Outputs have to come before inputs. Additionally, the order of inputs corresponds to the parameters and their order of the callback function. For example, take a look at the following:

```
@app.callback(Output('div_1', 'children'),
              Input('dropdown', 'value'),
              Input('date', 'value)
def my_function(dropdown, date):
    output = process(dropdown, date)
    return output
```

Here, the first given `Input` in the decorator should correspond to the first parameter of `my_function`. I used the same names in the preceding snippet to make it explicit and clear (`dropdown` and `date`). The same applies to outputs.

- **State**: Another optional parameter for callbacks is `State`. In the examples we have discussed so far, the callbacks immediately fire when the values change. Sometimes, you don't want that. For example, if you have multiple inputs, it might be annoying for the user to have the outputs change while they are configuring their options. Imagine having a textbox that modifies another element on the page. Every letter the user enters would modify it, which is not the best user experience. The typical scenario for using `State` is to have buttons. The user selects or enters values, and once they are ready, they can click on a button, which only then triggers the callback function.

Figure 2.12 presents a conceptual diagram of a more complex callback function and what it might look like:

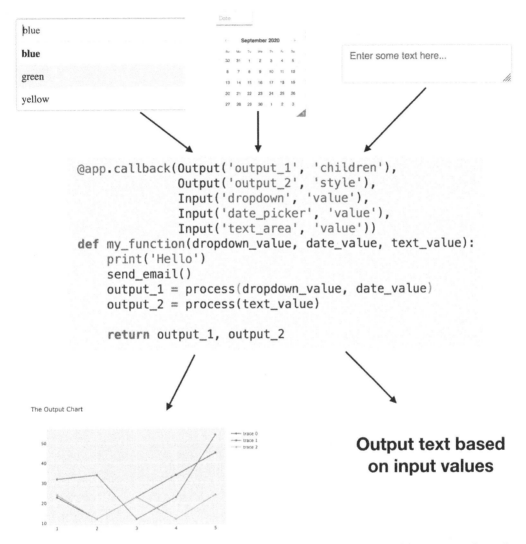

Figure 2.12 – A callback function handling multiple inputs and outputs, as well as running other tasks

We have now created and run two callback functions in two different contexts. We also incorporated one of them and built on the work we did in *Chapter 1, Overview of the Dash Ecosystem*. With a few more examples, you will have mastered callback functions. The next skills you need to conquer are managing complexity and being comfortable with refactoring code while keeping things organized and under control.

Let's quickly recap what we learned in this chapter.

Summary

First, we introduced a new way to run Dash apps, which is by running them in a Jupyter Notebook environment. We saw how familiar the process is, and we created our first interactive app in a notebook. We went through every detail in the process from creating layout components, giving them IDs, and selecting which of their properties will be used, to connecting all of this with the callback function. We ran another example and familiarized ourselves with our dataset. Most importantly, we learned how to incorporate the new work into the app, and we ran an updated version that produced simple population reports. Congratulations!

In the next chapter, we will take a deep dive into Plotly's data visualization capabilities. We will mainly focus on the **Figure** object, its components, how to query them, and how to modify them. This will give us fine-grained control over the visualizations that we will make.

3
Working with Plotly's Figure Objects

Imagine that you have published an article that contains a chart. Assume that your readers will, on average, spend 1 minute looking at the chart. If your chart is easy to understand, then they will probably spend 10 seconds understanding it and 50 seconds thinking, analyzing, and pondering its implications. On the other hand, if the chart is difficult to understand, they will spend 50 seconds "reading" it, and very little time thinking about its implications.

This chapter aims to equip you with tools that will help you to minimize the time an audience spends understanding your charts, and to maximize their analysis and thinking time. The two previous chapters were about structuring apps and making them interactive. In this chapter, we will discuss how to create and control the very charts around which your apps are built. Plotly's **Figure** object is what we will primarily explore. In this chapter, we will cover the following main topics:

- Understanding the Figure object
- Getting to know the data attribute
- Getting to know the layout attribute

- Learning about figure traces and how to add them

- Exploring the different ways of converting figures

Technical requirements

We will focus on using the `Figure` object from the `graph_objects` module of the `plotly` package. Later in the chapter, we will utilize the other packages that we have been using to improve our app and add an interactive chart to it. As a reminder, the packages that we will use are Dash, Dash HTML Components, Dash Core Components, Dash Bootstrap Components, JupyterLab, Jupyter Dash, and pandas.

The packages can be individually installed by running `pip install <package-name>`, but it would be better to install the exact same versions that we use here, to reproduce the same results. You can install them all by running one command, `pip install -r requirements.txt`, from the root folder of the repository. The latest version of the poverty dataset can be downloaded from this link: `https://datacatalog. worldbank.org/dataset/poverty-and-equity-database`. However, as with the packages, if you want to reproduce the same results, you can access the dataset from the `data` folder in the root of the Git repository, along with the rest of the code for this chapter can be found on GitHub at `https://github.com/PacktPublishing/ Interactive-Dashboards-and-Data-Apps-with-Plotly-and-Dash/tree/ master/chapter_03`.

Check out the following video to see the Code in Action at `https://bit.ly/3x9VhAA`.

Understanding the Figure object

Plotly is a fully fledged data visualization system, which ships with more than 50 types of charts out of the box (for example, bar charts, scatter plots, and histograms). It supports 2D and 3D visualizations, ternary plots, maps, and more. The available options for customizing almost any aspect of your charts are very detailed and can be overwhelming. This, as they say, is a good problem to have!

We use charts to uncover certain characteristics of our data or the relationships between different datasets. However, pure data visualization would be meaningless if we didn't know what is being visualized. Imagine a rectangle that has a bunch of dots on it with clear patterns. It would still be meaningless if you didn't know what the x axis represented, for example. If you have different shapes and colors in a plot, then they would mean nothing without a legend. Usually, titles and annotations are also needed to give us context around the data we are trying to understand.

Those two groups, `data` and other supporting elements, which are collectively called `layout`, are two top-level attributes of Plotly's `Figure` object. Each attribute has several subattributes, at multiple levels, forming a tree-like structure. There is also the `frames` attribute, which is mainly used with animations, and it is not as common as the other two that are always present in every chart. We will not cover it in this chapter.

Let's now explore these attributes and start plotting to get a better understanding of how they fit together within the `Figure` object:

- `data`: The different attributes of data, and the relationships between them, are expressed using graphical/geometrical shapes, for example, circles, rectangles, lines, and more. The graphical attributes of those shapes are used to express various attributes of the data. The relative size, length, and distance between those shapes are how we understand this. Due to their visual and, therefore, intuitive nature, those attributes are easy to understand and don't require much explanation. The `data` attribute corresponds to the essence of what we are trying to understand. The values you need to provide for the `data` attribute depend on the chart type. For a scatter plot, for example, you need to provide `x` and `y` values. For maps, you need to have `lat` and `lon`. You can overlay several sets of data on top of each other on the same chart; each one is referred to as a **trace**. Each chart type can take many other optional values, and many of them will be covered in more detail later on in the book.

- `layout`: Everything else around the data belongs to this attribute. Elements of the `layout` attribute are more abstract in nature. They typically use text to inform the user what they are looking at. Many of them are also styling elements, which might not add as much information, but they make the charts easier to understand or conform to certain branding guidelines. There are many attributes that we will explore, but the most prominent ones are the title, axis titles, ticks, and legend. These, in turn, have subattributes, such as the font size, location, and more.

It's much easier to learn by doing, and we can now start by creating our first figure. The graph_objects module is usually imported as go, and we instantiate a figure by calling go.Figure! *Figure 3.1* shows an empty Figure object and how it is created and displayed:

```
1  import plotly.graph_objects as go
2
3  go.Figure()
```

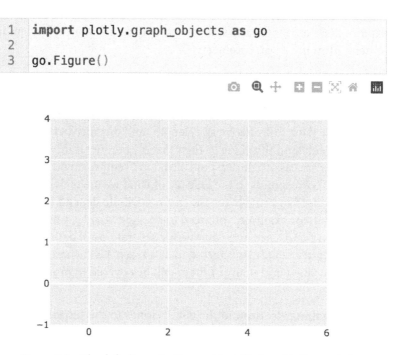

Figure 3.1 – The default empty Figure object displayed in JupyterLab

Of course, we don't get anything from this empty figure, but it is the first step before adding the elements we want to it. Although we can create and display Figure objects by defining everything in the go.Figure call, we will use a slightly easier and more convenient approach. We will assign the created object to a variable, and then iteratively add and/or modify the elements that we want. An important benefit of this approach is that we can make changes to our charts after creating them.

> **Important note**
> Once you assign a Figure object to a variable, this variable becomes available in the global scope. Since it is mutable, you can make changes to it in other places in your code. Displaying the figure after making such changes will show it with the changes you have made. We will be utilizing this important feature in order to manage our charts.

Having created the basic object, we are now ready to start adding our first data traces to our first chart.

Getting to know the data attribute

First, we start by adding a scatter plot using a very small and simple dataset. Later in the chapter, we will use our poverty dataset to create other plots. Once you have created your `Figure` object and assigned it to a variable, you have access to a large number of convenient methods for manipulating that object. The methods related to adding data traces all start with `add_`, followed by the type of chart we are adding, for example, `add_scatter` or `add_bar`.

Let's go through the full process of creating a scatter plot:

1. Import the `graph_objects` module:

   ```
   import plotly.graph_objects as go
   ```

2. Create an instance of a `Figure` object and assign it to a variable:

   ```
   fig = go.Figure()
   ```

3. Add a scatter trace. The minimum parameters required for this type of chart are two arrays for the x and y values. These can be provided as lists, tuples, NumPy arrays, or pandas `Series`:

   ```
   fig.add_scatter(x=[1, 2, 3], y=[4, 2, 3])
   ```

4. Display the resulting figure. You can simply have the variable on the last line in your code cell, and it will also be displayed in JupyterLab once you run it. You can also explicitly call the `show` method, which gives you a few more options to customize the display of the figure:

   ```
   fig.show()
   ```

You can see the full code, as well as the final output, in *Figure 3.2*:

```
1  import plotly.graph_objects as go
2
3  fig = go.Figure()
4  fig.add_scatter(x=[1, 2, 3], y=[4, 2, 3])
5  fig.show()
```

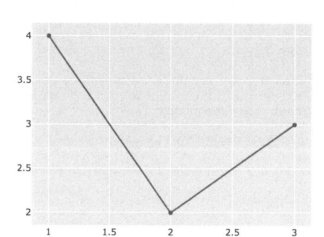

Figure 3.2 – A scatter plot displayed in JupyterLab

We will now add another similar scatter plot, overlaid on top of this one. We simply repeat *step 3*, but with different values:

```
fig.add_scatter(x=[1, 2, 3, 4], y=[4, 5, 2, 3])
```

This will add the new scatter plot to the same figure. If we call `fig.show()` after running this code, we will be able to see the updated figure. Note that this trace has four data points, whereas the previous trace had three. We don't need to worry about this, as this is handled for us using certain default values. We also have the option to modify those default values if we need to.

If we want to modify any aspect of our `data` trace, we can do it through the `add_<chart_type>` method. The call to those methods provides a lot of options through many parameters, and they are specific to the type of chart you are producing. Part 2 of this book will go deeper into several chart types and the different options that they provide. On the other hand, if we want to modify anything related to the `layout` attribute, we can do so by accessing and then assigning the attributes and/or subattributes that we want in a simple, declarative way. This is generally done using Python's dot notation, for example, `figure.attribute.sub_attribute = value`. This guideline is not entirely correct, as there are a few exceptions, and in some cases, there is an overlap where an attribute belongs to the `data` attribute but is managed by the `layout` attribute, for example. In most cases, this is a helpful distinction to keep in mind.

Let's now take a look at some of the things that we can change in our figure's layout.

Getting to know the layout attribute

For the current figure that we are working on, let's add a title (for the whole figure), along with axis titles, to see how it works:

```
fig.layout.title = 'The Figure Title'
fig.layout.xaxis.title = 'The X-axis title'
fig.layout.yaxis.title = 'The Y-axis title'
```

As you can see, we are exploring the tree-like structure of our figure. There is a `title` attribute that falls directly under `fig.layout`, and there are also titles for `fig.layout.xaxis` and `fig.layout.yaxis`. To give you a sense of how detailed the available options are, *Figure 3.3* shows some of the `xaxis` attributes that start with `tick` only:

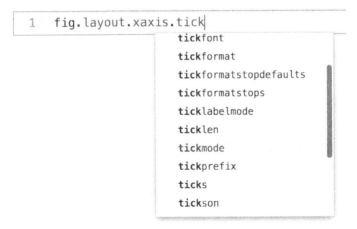

Figure 3.3 – Some of the Figure object's layout.xaxis options

Let's now look at the effect of the four lines of code we just added:

```
1    fig.show()
```

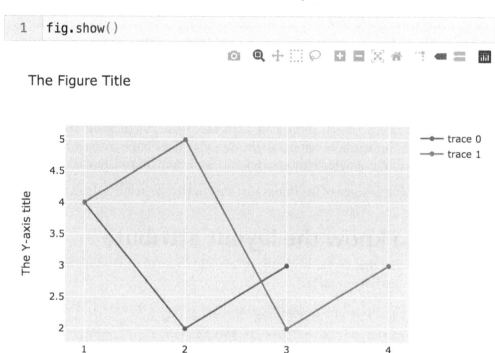

Figure 3.4 – The updated figure containing two traces, a legend, and titles

The three titles we have added are self-explanatory. New traces take on new default colors to differentiate them. Another interesting thing is the legend, which was added automatically. When you just have one trace, there is usually no need for a legend, but it becomes important when you have more than one. Descriptive names are crucial, of course, and **trace 0** doesn't mean much, but I'm keeping it as a memory aid to remember the names of the figure elements.

The figure we just created and displayed is what your users will see. Let's now take an interactive peek at the components of this figure.

Interactively exploring the Figure object

As I mentioned earlier, the `show` method provides a few handy options for customizing what and how your figures are displayed. A particularly helpful one is setting the `renderer` parameter to JSON. *Figure 3.5* shows how this can be useful:

Figure 3.5 – Interactively exploring the Figure object in JupyterLab

In the top-left corner, you can see the default view. The **root** represents the `Figure` object, and the two top-level attributes can be seen right under it. We also get a hint that our **data** attribute contains two items (these are the two traces we added). The triangles and their directions indicate whether the respective attribute has been expanded or collapsed.

In the bottom-left corner, you can see the search functionality in action. This is useful for when you want to access or modify a certain attribute but are not entirely sure what its exact name is, or to what attribute it belongs. On the right-hand side, I have expanded a few of the items, and you can see that they correspond to the figure we created.

> **Important note**
>
> This chapter, and the whole book really, is about how to create the charts and dashboards that you want. It's not about data visualization's best practices or statistical inference. In other words, it's about how to create the things you *want* to create, and not about what you *should* create. I'll still try to share good practices, and hopefully, make reasonable choices for the charts and their details, but it's important to keep this distinction in mind.

I'm sure you have noticed the "mode bar" containing interactive buttons and controls in the top-right corner of the figures we created. There are several ways to control which buttons to show or hide and a few other options. This is available through the `config` parameter of the `show` method.

Configuration options for the Figure object

The `config` parameter takes a dictionary and controls several interesting options. The keys control which aspect to modify. Additionally, the values can be given as strings or lists, depending on which one you are modifying. For example, consider the following code snippet:

```
fig.show(config={'displaylogo': False,
                 'modeBarButtonsToAdd': ['drawrect',
                                         'drawcircle',
                                         'eraseshape']})
```

Here are some of the most important ones:

- `displayModeBar`: This defaults to `True`. It controls whether or not to display the whole mode bar.

- `responsive`: This defaults to `True`. It controls whether or not to change the dimensions of the figure based on the browser window's size. Sometimes, you might want to keep the figure dimensions fixed.

- `toImageButtonOptions`: The camera icon in the mode bar allows users to download the figure as an image. This option controls the default formats of downloading those images. It takes a dictionary in which you can set the default format (that is, SVG, PNG, JPG, or WebP). You can also set default values for the height, width, filename, and scale.

- `modeBarButtonsToRemove`: This is a list of buttons you don't want in the mode bar.

Now that we have learned how to create, examine, and configure basic charts, let's explore what else we can do with them. How can we convert them into other formats? And what other formats are available?

Exploring the different ways of converting figures

The methods that control converting figures start with either `to_` or `write_`. Let's explore some of the most interesting ones.

Converting figures into HTML

Plotly figures are actually HTML objects, together with the JavaScript that makes them interactive. We can easily capture that HTML file if we want to share it with others via email, for example. You might consider having this as a feature in your dashboards. Your users can create the chart or report they want, convert it into HTML, download it, and share it with their colleagues.

All you have to do is provide a file path of where you want it to be saved. The method also takes several optional parameters for further customization. Let's convert our figure into HTML and add a `config` option to make it download the figure image in SVG format. The effect of this will be reflected in the HTML file when clicking on the camera icon. The code for this is straightforward:

```
fig.write_html('html_plot.html',
              config={'toImageButtonOptions':
                     {'format': 'svg'}})
```

We can now open the file in a browser as a separate HTML file, filling the whole browser screen, as shown in *Figure 3.6*:

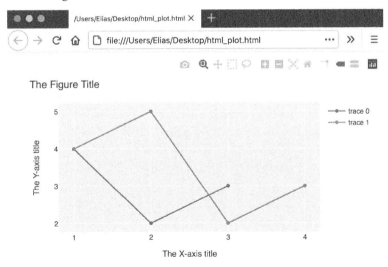

Figure 3.6 – The Figure object is rendered as a separate HTML file in a browser window

Converting figures into images

We have examined the option that allows users to manually download an image of the `Figure` object. There is another way of doing so programmatically, which can also be interesting. Just like the `write_html` method, we also have a `write_image` method. The format of the image can be explicitly provided or inferred from the file extension you provide. You can also set the `height` and `width` values.

This might be interesting for mass image creation. For example, you might want to create many plots, one for each country, and save each in a file for a separate report on each country. It would be very tedious to do this manually. You might also include this in one of your callbacks for your users. You could allow your users to assemble certain reports, and click on a button that converts them into images and then downloads them, for example. This can be run just like the HTML converter:

```
fig.write_image('path/to/image_file.svg',
                height=600, width=850)
```

With this information, we can now get practical and find out more about our dataset.

Plotting using a real dataset

In *Chapter 2*, *Exploring the Structure of a Dash App*, we created a simple report that showed the user the population of the selected country in the year 2010. This type of report is used when the user knows what they want. That is, they have a specific question about a specific country, metric, and period of time in mind, and our functionality provides an answer to their question.

We can think of dashboard functionality falling under two broad categories. The first, as we have done already, are visualizations or reports that answer a specific question. The second, which we will do now, guide the user in a more exploratory approach. In this case, users don't know much about a certain topic and they are looking for an overview.

Your users can go back and forth between those types of charts. For example, first, they explore poverty in the last decade. A certain region stands out. They then ask a specific question about that region. When they realize that that region had an unusually high rate of another metric, they can go on to another exploratory chart in that metric to learn more about it.

Now, we will let the user select a year, and the app will display the top 20 countries by population for the selected year.

As a quick reminder, our poverty dataset contains columns for the countries and their codes, the indicators and their codes, and a column for each year from 1974 to 2019.

As agreed, let's first do this in an isolated environment in JupyterLab:

1. Import `pandas`, use it to open the poverty dataset, and assign it to the `poverty_data` variable:

```
import pandas as pd
poverty_data =
pd.read_csv('data/PovStats_csv/PovStatsData.csv')
```

2. Although the column of interest is called **Country Name**, it actually contains regions as well, which can be really useful, but not in this case. We can extract all the regions so that we can exclude them from the dataset. I manually copied the regions and created the `regions` list:

```
regions = ['East Asia & Pacific', 'Europe & Central
Asia',              'Fragile and conflict affected
situations', 'High income',
'IDA countries classified as fragile situations', 'IDA
total', 'Latin America & Caribbean', 'Low & middle
income', 'Low income', 'Lower middle income', 'Middle
East & North Africa', 'Middle income', 'South Asia',
'Sub-Saharan Africa', 'Upper middle income', 'World']
```

3. Create `population_df`, the subset DataFrame where the **Country Name** column is not in `regions`, and the **Indicator Name** column is equal to **Population, total**. The `isin` method for pandas `Series` checks whether values in the `Series` are in a certain list, and the ~ (tilde) is the logical negation operator:

```
population_df = poverty_data[~poverty_data['Country
Name'].isin(regions) & (poverty_data['Indicator
Name'] == 'Population, total')]
```

4. The first few rows of the resulting DataFrame can be displayed as follows:

```
population_df.head()
```

It looks similar to the following screenshot:

	Country Name	Country Code	Indicator Name	Indicator Code	1974	1975	1976	1977	1978
1051	Afghanistan	AFG	Population, total	SP.POP.TOTL	12412950.0	12689160.0	12943093.0	13171306.0	13341198.0
1115	Albania	ALB	Population, total	SP.POP.TOTL	2350124.0	2404831.0	2458526.0	2513546.0	2566266.0
1179	Algeria	DZA	Population, total	SP.POP.TOTL	16149025.0	16607707.0	17085801.0	17582904.0	18102266.0
1243	Angola	AGO	Population, total	SP.POP.TOTL	6761380.0	7024000.0	7279509.0	7533735.0	7790707.0
1307	Argentina	ARG	Population, total	SP.POP.TOTL	25462302.0	25865776.0	26264681.0	26661398.0	27061047.0

Figure 3.7 – The first few rows of population_df

5. Create a dynamic `year` variable, and create a `year_df` variable containing the countries column along with the selected year's column. Then, sort those values in descending order and extract the first 20:

```
year = '2010'
year_df = population_df[['Country Name',
year]].sort_values(year, ascending=False)[:20]
```

6. With a `year_df` variable containing two sorted columns, we can very easily create a bar chart just as we did with the scatter plots earlier. We can also add a dynamic title, containing the year, as a variable:

```
fig = go.Figure()
fig.add_bar(x=year_df['Country Name'],
y=year_df[year])
fig.layout.title = f'Top twenty countries by
population - {year}'
fig.show()
```

This results in the following output:

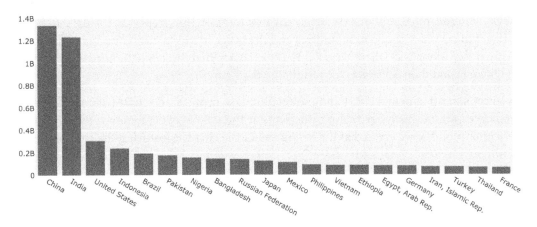

Top twenty countries by population - 2010

Top twenty countries by population - 2010

Figure 3.8 – A bar chart showing the top 20 countries by population in 2010

As you can see, once we have a proper subset with the relevant columns sorted, we can produce the chart we want with a few lines of code. Additionally, note that the numbers on the *y* axis were formatted, by default, as billions (or fractions of billions) to make them easy to read.

We didn't set axis titles. Here, the figure title implicitly tells us about both axes: "countries" and "population." With a numeric *y* axis and the country names listed on the *x* axis, it should be clear to users.

2010 is an arbitrary year, and we actually want users to be able to select the year they want from the ones that are available in the dataset.

The code that produced the figure only requires a def statement and some indentation to become a function:

```
def plot_countries_by_population(year):
    year_df = …
    fig = go.Figure()
    …
    fig.show()
```

This function produces a similar chart to the one that we just produced, but for the given year argument. You might think that it's as easy to convert this function into a callback function, just by adding a line of code. This is exactly what we will be doing, but first, I'd like to highlight an observation about data manipulation and preparation, and how it relates to data visualization because this example illustrates it very well.

Data manipulation as an essential part of the data visualization process

The previous example contains six steps. The first five were for preparing the data and getting it in two arrays: one for countries and the other for population numbers. The sixth and final step alone was where we produced the chart. There was much more code for data preparation than there was for producing the figure.

If you consider the mental effort and time required to produce the chart (that is, the final step only), you can easily see that it is the same as the mental effort required to produce the scatter plot that we created at the beginning of the chapter, featuring the toy dataset. We simply ran `add_scatter(x=[1, 2, 3], y=[4, 2, 3])`, and then we did the same for the bar chart, only with different values.

However, if you consider the mental effort and time spent on preparing the data for the bar chart, you can clearly see that there is a huge difference, compared to the data preparation for the scatter plot. We needed to know that the **Country Name** column did not really refer to *all* countries. We had to explore and manually check that first to know this. We also had to extract the regions and exclude them. How did we know that "South Asia" was a region, while "South Africa" was a country? We had to know this beforehand, or we had to know how to get a list of countries to check against. Additionally, we had to know that the year columns were strings and not integers. I discovered that when I got `KeyError` after trying to access the data for a certain year. We typically spend more time and effort on these things, and once the data is in a suitable format, we can easily visualize it.

In *Chapter 4, Data Manipulation and Preparation - Paving the Way to Plotly Express*, we will spend more time on this topic, and introduce some important techniques that might be useful in a variety of situations. However, keep in mind that your skills in manipulating data, reshaping it, merging datasets, regular expressions, and all the tedious parts of data preparation form a big part of where your contribution lies. It's where most opportunities are, and a lot of it is based on your judgment. Domain knowledge is also essential; for instance, knowing the difference between regions and countries. Once you have data in a certain format, there are numerous advanced techniques and algorithms that you can use to visualize, analyze, and run various machine learning pipelines that require comparatively little code.

Now, let's use our newly created function and learn how to make it interactive with a `Dropdown` component and a callback function.

Making the chart interactive with a callback function

First, we will do this as a completely isolated app in JupyterLab, after which we will add it to our app. In the isolated environment, our `app.layout` attribute will contain two components:

`Dropdown`: This will display all the available years so that the user can select the one they want.

`Graph`: This is a new component that we haven't covered yet, and we will be working extensively with it. Adding a `Graph` component to the layout displays an empty chart. If you remember our discussion about callback functions, when modifying a component in a callback function, we need to provide its `component_id` and `component_property`. The property that we will be modifying, in this scenario, is the `figure` property, and it only belongs to the `Graph` component.

You are now familiar with the imports and app instantiation, so I will mainly focus on the `app.layout` attribute of the app:

```
app.layout = html.Div([
    dcc.Dropdown(id='year_dropdown',
                 value='2010',
                 options=[{'label': year, 'value':
str(year)}
                          for year in range(1974, 2019)]),
    dcc.Graph(id='population_chart'),
])
```

For now, there is nothing special about the `Graph` component. We simply create one underneath the `Dropdown` component and give it a descriptive `id` argument.

I'm sure you have also noticed that this time, we have slightly different values for the `label` and `value` keys in the list of `options` in the `Dropdown` component. The difference is that the `value` key is set to `str(year)`. Since `options` is a list of dictionaries generated by a list comprehension, it will produce a list of integers. The selected number will be used to select the column with that value. In this dataset, the columns are all strings, so using `population_df[2010]` will not work, because there is really no such column (as an integer). The actual column name is **2010**, as a string. So, we are specifying the label as an integer, but the actual value that will be used by the callback function is the string representation of that integer (the year).

We have also added a new parameter that we haven't discussed yet. The `value` parameter of the `Dropdown` component serves as a default that will be shown to users the first time they see the app. This is better than showing an empty chart.

In some cases, you might want to do the opposite of what we did in this example. You might want to keep `value` as it is but modify `label` somehow. For example, if your data was all in lowercase, you might want to display the options as capitalized. In our colors example, in the previous chapter, we could have done something like this:

```
dcc.Dropdown(options=[{'label': color.title(), 'value':
color} for color in ['blue', 'green', 'yellow']])
```

From the callback function's perspective, the colors are still the same, because it mainly deals with the `value` attribute. But for the user, this would display the colors as capitalized: "Blue," "Green," and "Yellow."

Running the app with the two components defined so far produces the app, as shown in *Figure 3.9*:

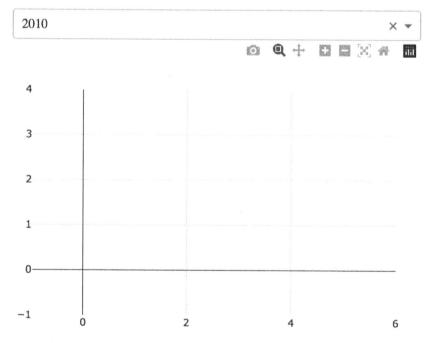

Figure 3.9 – An app with a Dropdown component showing a default value and an empty graph

We have already created a normal function that takes the data as a year and returns a bar chart showing the top 20 countries by population for that year. Converting it into a callback function requires one line of code:

```
@app.callback(Output('population_chart', 'figure'),
              Input('year_dropdown', 'value'))
def plot_countries_by_population(year):
    year_df = …
    fig = go.Figure()
    …
    return fig
```

In the previous function definition, the last line was `fig.show()`, and in the callback function, we return the figure instead. The reason is that, in the first case, we were running it interactively and there was no app or callback context. In this case, we have a component with the `population_chart` ID, and, most importantly, we want to change its `figure` property. Returning the figure will hand it to the `Graph` component and modify its `figure` attribute.

Running this app will produce dynamic charts based on the user selection, as you can see in *Figure 3.10*:

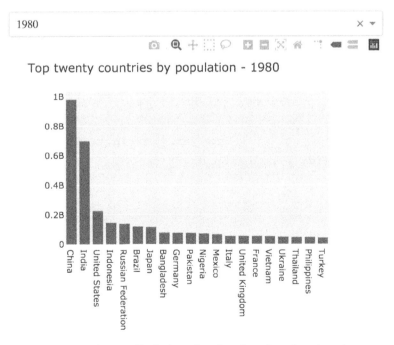

Figure 3.10 – An app displaying a bar chart based on the selected year

If you compare this to *Figure 3.8*, you will notice that the country names are displayed vertically here, while, previously, they were displayed at a certain angle. This is simply because the chart was displayed in a wider browser window. This is another convenient default that Plotly handles for us without us having to do anything. This means that our figures are responsive, which gives them great flexibility. This is the same with the apps and their components that we style with Dash Bootstrap Components.

Now that we have created an isolated app that works independently, let's look at how to add this to our app.

Adding the new functionality to our app

So far, the latest version of the app contains a `Dropdown` component, and underneath that, the `Div` for the population report of 2010. Underneath that, we have the `Tabs` component. Let's now insert the new `Dropdown` and `Graph` components right underneath the report area, and above the `Tabs` component. Let's also add the new callback function:

1. Copy the two new components to where they belong in the `app.layout` attribute:

```
...
html.Br(),
html.Div(id='report'),
html.Br(),
dcc.Dropdown(id='year_dropdown',
             value='2010',
             options=[{'label': year, 'value':
str(year)}
                      for year in range(1974, 2019)]),
dcc.Graph(id='population_chart'),

dbc.Tabs([
...
```

2. Copy the callback function definition and place it anywhere after the closing tag of the top-level `Div` of `app.layout`. You can place it under the previous callback function that we created for better organization, but it doesn't matter where you place it in terms of functionality:

```
@app.callback(Output('population_chart', 'figure'),
              Input('year_dropdown', 'value'))
def plot_countries_by_population(year):
    fig = go.Figure()
    year_df = population_df[['Country Name',
year]].sort_values(year, ascending=False)[:20]
    fig.add_bar(x=year_df['Country Name'],
                y=year_df[year])
    fig.layout.title = f'Top twenty countries by
population - {year}'
    return fig
```

3. Add the definition of the `regions` list and then `population_df` after the definition of `poverty_data`. The order is important because `population_df` depends on `regions` to be defined before it, and since it is a subset of `poverty_data`, it also needs to be defined after it. This is the order in which these variables need to be defined:

```
poverty_data = …
regions = …
population_df = …
```

Now, if we run the app, you can see what it looks like in *Figure 3.11*:

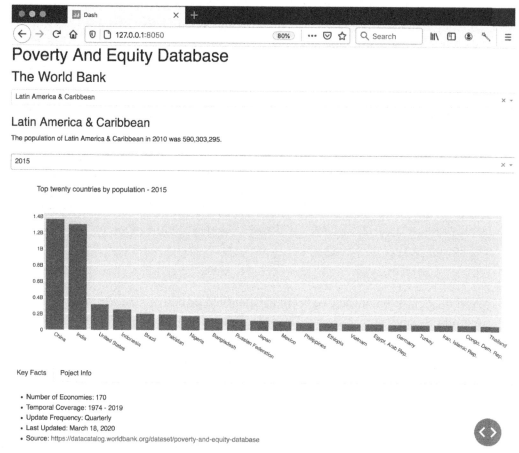

Figure 3.11 – The app with the new components added (Dropdown and Graph).

If you open the debugger and click on the **Callbacks** button, you can also see an updated view of the available callbacks, along with the names of the components that they link to (the component IDs and the component properties). *Figure 3.12* shows this:

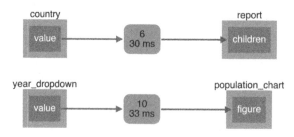

Figure 3.12 – The app callbacks in the visual debugger

Our app now displays more information. It allows users to get information interactively from the dataset. We defined two callback functions and have a layout that contains several components of different types. We also have about 90 lines of code in total. Simply adding new components by inserting them somewhere works fine until you have a large enough number of them in the app. Then, we will need to learn how to better organize the code and refactor it.

Let's close this chapter with a fun, easy-to-use aspect of the Plotly `Figure` object, which does not require much coding, and then recap the topics covered.

Theming your figures

Theming your figures (as opposed to your apps) can be interesting and saves a lot of time if you need to change themes. This can be accessed and modified through the `template` attribute under `layout`:

```
fig.layout.template = template_name
```

Figure 3.13 shows four different templates and their names:

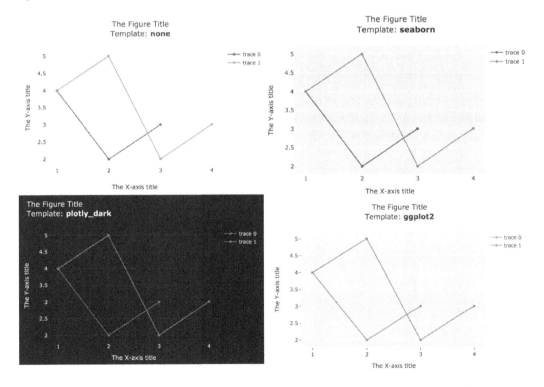

Figure 3.13 – Four different Figure templates

The full list of templates is available in `plotly.io.templates`.

This is helpful when you want your figures to have a template that is compatible with the app's theme. It is also a good starting point to enable you to select one of the templates and then modify a few of its elements as you see fit.

Let's now recap the topics that we have covered in this chapter.

Summary

We started by introducing the `Figure` object, its components, and subcomponents. We looked at how to create figures step by step, and how to modify various aspects of them. We also took an extensive look at the two main attributes of figures, the `data` and `layout` attributes. A few ways of converting figures were also explored, and we then created a chart based on our dataset and incorporated it into our app.

With the chapters you have read so far, you now know how to create and structure apps, how to make them interactive by creating callbacks that link various page components together, and how to build charts that fit into the whole system.

You now know how to build fully interactive apps, and with the understanding developed in this chapter, you also know how to manage the various aspects of your figures and make sure that they are easy to read, so your users can spend more time on analysis and less time on understanding the charts themselves.

We briefly observed the importance of data preparation and manipulation, and we are now ready to take a more extensive look at it. In the next chapter, we will introduce **Plotly Express**, a powerful and higher-level interface that is used to create charts concisely.

4
Data Manipulation and Preparation, Paving the Way to Plotly Express

We saw that preparing data can take much more mental effort and code than the process of creating charts. Or, to put it differently, if we invest a good amount of time in preparing our data and making certain decisions about how and what we intend to do with it, the process of visualization can be made much easier. So far, we have used a small part of our dataset and didn't make any changes to its shape or format. And when making our charts, we followed the approach of building them from scratch by creating a figure and then adding different layers and options for traces, titles, and so on.

In this chapter, we will go through a thorough familiarization with the dataset and reshape it to an intuitive and easy-to-use format. This will help us in using a new approach for creating visualizations, using **Plotly Express**. Instead of starting with an empty rectangle and building layers on top of it, we will start with the features (columns) of our dataset, and create visualizations based on them. In other words, instead of being screen- or chart-oriented, we will work with more of a data-oriented approach. We will also compare the two approaches and discuss when to use them.

We will mainly cover the following topics:

- Understanding long format (tidy) data
- Understanding the role of data manipulation skills
- Learning Plotly Express

Technical requirements

Technically, no new packages will be used in this chapter, but as a major module of Plotly, we can consider Plotly Express to be a new one. We will also be extensively using `pandas` for data preparation, reshaping, and general manipulation. This will mainly be done in JupyterLab. Our dataset will consist of the files in the `data` folder in the root of the repository.

The code files of this chapter can be found on GitHub at `https://github.com/PacktPublishing/Interactive-Dashboards-and-Data-Apps-with-Plotly-and-Dash/tree/master/chapter_04`.

Check out the following video to see the Code in Action at `https://bit.ly/3suvKi4`.

Let's start by exploring the different formats in which we can have data, and what we can do about it.

Understanding long format (tidy) data

We have a moderately complex dataset that we will be working with. It consists of four CSV files, containing information on almost all the countries and regions in the world. We have more than 60 metrics spanning more than 40 years, which means that there are quite a lot of options and combinations to choose from.

But before going through the process of preparing our dataset, I'd like to demonstrate our end goal with a simple example, so you have an idea of where we are heading. It will also hopefully show why we are investing time in making those changes.

Plotly Express example chart

Plotly Express ships with a few datasets for practicing and testing certain features whenever you want to do so. They fall under the `data` module of `plotly.express`, and calling them as functions returns the respective dataset. Let's take a look at the famous Gapminder dataset:

```
import plotly.express as px
gapminder = px.data.gapminder()
gapminder
```

Running this code displays sample rows of the `gapminder` DataFrame as you can see in *Figure 4.1*:

	country	continent	year	lifeExp	pop	gdpPercap	iso_alpha	iso_num
0	Afghanistan	Asia	1952	28.801	8425333	779.445314	AFG	4
1	Afghanistan	Asia	1957	30.332	9240934	820.853030	AFG	4
2	Afghanistan	Asia	1962	31.997	10267083	853.100710	AFG	4
3	Afghanistan	Asia	1967	34.020	11537966	836.197138	AFG	4
4	Afghanistan	Asia	1972	36.088	13079460	739.981106	AFG	4
...	...	...	...	...	...	...	...	...
1699	Zimbabwe	Africa	1987	62.351	9216418	706.157306	ZWE	716
1700	Zimbabwe	Africa	1992	60.377	10704340	693.420786	ZWE	716
1701	Zimbabwe	Africa	1997	46.809	11404948	792.449960	ZWE	716
1702	Zimbabwe	Africa	2002	39.989	11926563	672.038623	ZWE	716
1703	Zimbabwe	Africa	2007	43.487	12311143	469.709298	ZWE	716

1704 rows × 8 columns

Figure 4.1 – The Gapminder dataset included in Plotly Express

The dataset structure seems straightforward. For each unique combination of **country**, **continent**, and **year**, we have three metrics: **lifeExp**, **pop**, and **gdpPercap**. The **iso_alpha** and **iso_num** columns seem to be encoded values for the countries.

Let's see how we might summarize the `gapminder data_frame` with a `scatter` plot.

On the x axis, we can have the **gdpPercap** values, and as a function of that, on the y axis, it would be good to see the **lifeExp** values and check whether/how they vary from each other. It would also be good to have the `size` of the markers reflect the population of the respective countries.

We might also split the chart horizontally (`facet_col`), into sub-plots, one for each continent, on one row, and make the sub-plot titles reflect that as well. We can also assign a separate `color` to each continent's markers. For more clarity, we can set the `title` of the figure to `'Life Expectancy and GDP per capita. 1952 - 2007'`.

To make them clearer, we can change the `labels` of the X and Y axes' titles from `'gdpPercap'` to `'GDP per Capita'`, and from `'lifeExp'` to `'Life Expectancy'` respectively.

We would expect the GDP per capita to have outliers and not to be normally distributed, so we can set the type of the X-axis scale to logarithmic (`log_x`). The range of the Y-axis (`range_y`) should be the interval [20, 100], so we can see how life expectancy varies on a fixed vertical range.

Hovering over the markers should show the full information for that particular country, and the title of the hover label (`hover_name`) should take the name of the country. Having the same chart overlaid on top of itself for all years would be really cluttered and almost impossible to read. So let's have a separate `animation_frame` for each of the years.

It would be great if we could have a play button that would move the markers across years when clicked, one frame per year, like a video, with the option to stop it at a certain year.

The `height` of the figure should be 600 pixels:

```
px.scatter(data_frame=gapminder,
           x='gdpPercap',
           y='lifeExp',
           size='pop',
           facet_col='continent',
           color='continent',
           title='Life Expectancy and GDP per capita. 1952 -
2007',
```

```
labels={'gdpPercap': 'GDP per Capita',
        'lifeExp': 'Life Expectancy'},
log_x=True,
range_y=[20, 100],
hover_name='country',
animation_frame='year',
height=600,
size_max=90)
```

Running the preceding code would produce the visualization in *Figure 4.2*:

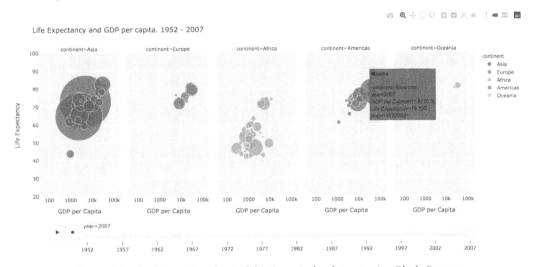

Figure 4.2 – An interactive chart of the Gapminder dataset using Plotly Express

My first observation for this process is that it took us much more text than code to describe the chart. Actually, it was a single line of code that produced it.

Clicking the play button would animate the chart, and you would see a new frame for each year. You could also pause or move to a certain year if you want. This way you can see how the relationship between the two variables progressed through the years, like watching a short movie.

You can also see that hovering over a certain marker representing a country would show all relevant data that was used to specify the location, size, color, and whatever other attributes we might have set. The hover_name argument was set to 'country' and this is why you see it in bold as the title of the label.

In most cases, we have markers overlapping, which makes it difficult to understand the chart. Because Plotly figures are interactive by default, we can easily use the modebar buttons to zoom in/out, or we can manually select a certain rectangle to zoom into.

Zooming into Africa by selecting the rectangle that contains only its markers, *Figure 4.3* shows how the chart changes, and now it is much easier to read the African sub-plot:

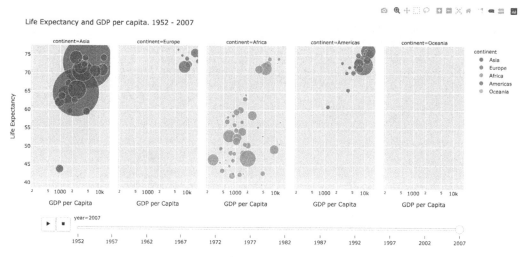

Figure 4.3 – Zooming into specific regions in charts

Note that all other continent charts were also zoomed in to the same zoom level of Africa. Feel free to explore more of the interactive features, but I hope this shows how powerful and intuitive this approach is.

> **Tip**
>
> There are many colored charts in this chapter. I did my best to make sure you can easily distinguish between colored markers as much as possible. It's still better to refer to the color version of the book, which is available online, if you are reading the print version.

There are two main reasons that allowed us to create such a rich chart with one line of code. First, Plotly Express has powerful features and is specially designed to produce such charts with minimal code. This will be covered in more detail later. Second, the structure of the dataset plays an important role in the process. Once we have our data in a consistent format, it becomes easy to model, visualize, or run any kind of analysis.

Let's take a look at the main aspects of this data format.

Main attributes of long format (tidy) data

One of the key features of this structure is that it allows each marker on the chart to be independently represented by a row. Each value in those rows belongs to a distinct column. In turn, those columns each represent a separate variable and have their own data types. This makes it easy to map color, size, or whatever visual attributes we want, simply by declaring which column values we want to express with which visual attribute.

Notice that what I just said is close to the definition of a DataFrame:

- A set of columns, where each has exactly one type of data.
- Columns in a DataFrame can be of different types.
- All columns have the same length, even though they might contain missing values.

From a conceptual point of view, the main difference between a long form DataFrame and a regular one is having one observation per row (country, person, brand, or a combination of them), and one variable per column (population, size, length, height, revenue, and so on). For example, the **country** column contains countries and only countries. Additionally, countries are only present in this column. So, there is no ambiguity about where or how to access them.

This format is not required and is not any more "correct" than other formats. It is simply intuitive, consistent, and easy to use. The actual requirement for producing the visualization we just did is to have a set of values for the X axis and another set of values of the same length for the Y axis. For other features such as color and size, we also need sets of numbers or names of the same length, so we can properly map them together. The DataFrame is a natural fit for such a requirement.

In the chart we just produced, you can easily see that we can have all markers the same size, simply by removing the `size` argument. Changing `facet_col` to `facet_row` would immediately have the sub-plots vertically stacked on top of one another as opposed to side by side. Minimal tweaks allow us to introduce big changes to our visualizations. This is as simple as flipping switches on a dashboard, pun intended!

I hope the end goal is now clear. We want to check the four files of our dataset and see how to generate long format (tidy) DataFrames. As a result, every column would contain data about one variable (year, population, Gini index, and so on), and every row would describe an observation (a combination of country, year, metric, and other values). Once that is done, we should be able to look at the data, specify what we want, and express that with a concise Plotly Express function call.

The process will be much clearer once we start the preparation, so let's start right away.

Understanding the role of data manipulation skills

In practical situations, we rarely have our data in the format that we want; we usually have different datasets that we want to merge, and often, we need to normalize and clean up the data. For these reasons, data manipulation and preparation will always play a big part in any data visualization process. So, we will be focusing on this in this chapter and throughout the book.

The plan for preparing our dataset is roughly the following:

1. Explore the different files one by one.

2. Check the available data and data types and explore how each can help us categorize and analyze the data.

3. Reshape the data where required.

4. Combine different DataFrames to add more ways to describe our data.

Let's go through these steps right away.

Exploring the data files

We start by reading in the files in the `data` folder:

```
import os
import pandas as pd
pd.options.display.max_columns = None
```

```
os.listdir('data')
['PovStatsSeries.csv',
 'PovStatsCountry.csv',
 'PovStatsCountry-Series.csv',
 'PovStatsData.csv',
 'PovStatsFootNote.csv']
```

To make things clear, I'll use the distinct part of each filename as the variable name for each DataFrame: 'PovStats<name>.csv'.

The series file

We start by exploring the series file, using the following code:

```
series = pd.DataFrame('data/'PovStatsSeries.csv')
print(series.shape)
series.head()
```

This will display the shape attribute of the DataFrame, as well as the first five rows, as you can see in *Figure 4.4*:

```
(64, 21)
```

	Series Code	Topic	Indicator Name	Short definition	Long definition	Unit of measure	Periodicity	Base Period	Other notes	Aggregation method	Limitations and exceptions	Notes from original source	General comments
0	SI.DST.02ND.20	Poverty: Income distribution	Income share held by second 20%	NaN	Percentage share of income or consumption is t...	%	Annual	NaN	NaN	NaN	Despite progress in the last decade, the chall...	NaN	The World Bank's internationally comparable po...
1	SI.DST.03RD.20	Poverty: Income distribution	Income share held by third 20%	NaN	Percentage share of income or consumption is t...	%	Annual	NaN	NaN	NaN	Despite progress in the last decade, the chall...	NaN	The World Bank's internationally comparable po...
2	SI.DST.04TH.20	Poverty: Income distribution	Income share held by fourth 20%	NaN	Percentage share of income or consumption is t...	%	Annual	NaN	NaN	NaN	Despite progress in the last decade, the chall...	NaN	The World Bank's internationally comparable po...
3	SI.DST.05TH.20	Poverty: Income distribution	Income share held by highest 20%	NaN	Percentage share of income or consumption is t...	%	Annual	NaN	NaN	NaN	Despite progress in the last decade, the chall...	NaN	The World Bank's internationally comparable po...
4	SI.DST.10TH.10	Poverty: Income distribution	Income share held by highest 10%	NaN	Percentage share of income or consumption is t...	%	Annual	NaN	NaN	NaN	Despite progress in the last decade, the chall...	NaN	The World Bank's internationally comparable po...

Figure 4.4 – The first few rows and columns of the PovStatsSeries file

It seems we have 64 different indicators, and for each one of them, we have 21 attributes, explanations, and notes. This is already in long format – columns contain data about one attribute, and rows are complete representations of an indicator, so there is nothing to change. We just need to explore what data is available and get familiar with this table.

Using this information, you can easily imagine creating a special dashboard for each indicator and placing it on a separate page. Each row seems to have enough information to produce an independent page with a title, description, details, and so on. The main content area of the page could be a visualization of that indicator, for all countries and across all years. This is just one idea.

Let's take a closer look at some interesting columns:

```
series['Topic'].value_counts()
Poverty: Poverty rates         45
Poverty: Shared prosperity     10
Poverty: Income distribution    8
Health: Population: Structure   1
Name: Topic, dtype: int64
```

We can see that the indicators are spread across four topics, the counts of which can be seen above.

There is a column for Unit of measure, which might be interesting to explore:

```
series['Unit of measure'].value_counts(dropna=False)
%            39
NaN          22
2011 PPP $    3
Name: Unit of measure, dtype: int64
```

It seems we have indicators whose units of measure are either percentages (rates) or not available (NaN). This might help us later in grouping certain types of charts together.

Another important column is the **Limitations and exceptions** column. Usually, this kind of metadata is extremely important, because it tells us about where the biases might be, or what we should keep in mind while exploring our data. You can read those limitations, and it might be interesting to count them and see whether they fall under certain groups, or whether they are duplicated. The following code groups the `series` DataFrame by the **Topic** column, and then summarizes the **Limitations and Exceptions** column values by their count and number of unique values:

```
(series
 .groupby('Topic')
 ['Limitations and exceptions']
 .agg(['count', pd.Series.nunique])
 .style.set_caption('Limitations and Exceptions'))
```

The output can be seen in *Figure 4.5*:

Limitations and Exceptions

Topic	count	nunique
Health: Population: Structure	1	1
Poverty: Income distribution	8	2
Poverty: Poverty rates	25	3
Poverty: Shared prosperity	4	2

Figure 4.5 – Counts and unique values of Limitations and Exceptions

It looks like this is going to be a good reference point for us to learn more about the different indicators that we have. It would also be very helpful for the users so they can also get a better understanding of what they are analyzing.

The country file

Let's now take a look at the next file, `'PovStatsCountry.csv'`:

```
country =\
pd.read_csv('data/PovStatsCountry.csv',na_values='',
                   keep_default_na=False)
print(country.shape)
country.head()
```

This will display the shape of the DataFrame as well as a sample of rows and columns, as in *Figure 4.6*:

(184, 31)

	Country Code	Short Name	Table Name	Long Name	2-alpha code	Currency Unit	Special Notes	Region	Income Group	WB-2 code	National accounts base year	National accounts reference year	SNA price valuation	Lending category	Other groups	System of National Accounts	Alternative conversion factor
0	AFG	Afghanistan	Afghanistan	Islamic State of Afghanistan	AF	Afghan afghani	NaN	South Asia	Low income	AF	2002/03	NaN	Value added at basic prices (VAB)	IDA	HIPC	Country uses the 1993 System of National Accou...	NaN
1	AGO	Angola	Angola	People's Republic of Angola	AO	Angolan kwanza	NaN	Sub-Saharan Africa	Lower middle income	AO	2002	NaN	Value added at basic prices (VAB)	IBRD	NaN	Country uses the 1993 System of National Accou...	1991–96
2	ALB	Albania	Albania	Republic of Albania	AL	Albanian lek	NaN	Europe & Central Asia	Upper middle income	AL	Original chained constant price data are resca...	2010	Value added at basic prices (VAB)	IBRD	NaN	Country uses the 2008 System of National Accou...	NaN
3	ARG	Argentina	Argentina	Argentine Republic	AR	Argentine peso	NaN	Latin America & Caribbean	Upper middle income	AR	2004	NaN	Value added at basic prices (VAB)	IBRD	NaN	Country uses the 2008 System of National Accou...	1971–84; 2012-15
4	ARM	Armenia	Armenia	Republic of Armenia	AM	Armenian dram	NaN	Europe & Central Asia	Upper middle income	AM	Original chained constant price data are resca...	2012	Value added at basic prices (VAB)	IBRD	NaN	Country uses the 2008 System of National Accou...	1990–95

Figure 4.6 – Sample rows and columns from the country file

In the call to `read_csv`, we have specified `keep_default_na=False` and `na_values=''`. The reason is that `pandas` interprets strings such as NA and NaN as indicators of missing values. One of the countries, Namibia, has a **2-alpha code** value of NA, so it was missing from the DataFrame. That's why we had to make this change. That's a very good example of how things might go wrong in unexpected ways.

This is very interesting metadata about the countries and regions in our dataset. It is a very small dataset but can be very useful in enriching our understanding, as well as giving us more options to filter and group our countries. It is also in long (tidy) format. Let's take a look at some of its interesting columns.

The **Region** column seems straightforward. We can check to see what regions are available, as well as the counts of countries in each region:

```
country['Region'].value_counts(dropna=False).to_frame().style.
background_gradient('cividis')
```

The result can be seen in *Figure 4.7*:

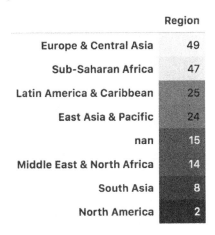

	Region
Europe & Central Asia	49
Sub-Saharan Africa	47
Latin America & Caribbean	25
East Asia & Pacific	24
nan	15
Middle East & North Africa	14
South Asia	8
North America	2

Figure 4.7 – Counts of countries per region

Another column that might be helpful is **Income Group**. Once we have this properly mapped to the right values, we might consider splitting our sub-plots by income group, as we previously did with continents in the first example of this chapter:

```
country['Income Group'].value_counts(dropna=False)
Upper middle income     52
Lower middle income     47
High income             41
Low income              29
NaN                     15
Name: Income Group, dtype: int64
```

Having fifteen NaN values is consistent with the number of regions and classifications combined, which we will see shortly. The income level of countries is independent of their geographic locations.

If you look at the **Short Name** column, you will notice that not all entries are countries. There are geographic regions such as **Middle East & North Africa**, as well as classifications, for example, **Lower middle income**. I think it's important to distinguish between them, and we can easily create a special column for that, so we can differentiate between countries and non-countries.

The **Region** column shows which region the entity in **Short Name** falls under. In the cases where it is a region, the value is missing. We can use this to make our distinction, and create an `is_country` Boolean column:

```
country['is_country'] = country['Region'].notna()
```

Figure 4.8 shows a sample of rows containing countries and regions, as well as classifications:

	Short Name	Region	is_country
170	Upper middle income	NaN	False
42	East Asia & Pacific	NaN	False
155	Syrian Arab Republic	Middle East & North Africa	True
84	Kyrgyz Republic	Europe & Central Asia	True
40	Dominican Republic	Latin America & Caribbean	True
21	Central African Republic	Sub-Saharan Africa	True
105	Middle East & North Africa	NaN	False
150	Slovak Republic	Europe & Central Asia	True
95	Lower middle income	NaN	False
28	Dem. Rep. Congo	Sub-Saharan Africa	True

Figure 4.8 – A sample of countries and regions with the is_country column

The full listing of those categories can be found by getting a subset of the `country` DataFrame where the **Region** column contains missing values and then getting the **Short Name** column:

```
country[country['Region'].isna()]['Short Name']
37      IDA countries classified as fragile situations
42                                 East Asia & Pacific
43                               Europe & Central Asia
50               Fragile and conflict affected situations
70                                           IDA total
92                           Latin America & Caribbean
93                                          Low income
95                                 Lower middle income
```

96	Low & middle income
105	Middle East & North Africa
107	Middle income
139	South Asia
147	Sub-Saharan Africa
170	Upper middle income
177	World

Name: Short Name, dtype: object

Going through this process is very important in helping you plan your dashboards and apps. For example, knowing that we have four classifications for income levels means that it makes sense to create sub-plots for them side by side. But if we had 20 classifications, it might not be a good idea to do so.

Let's create one more column and then move on to the next file.

Since we are dealing with countries, we can use flags as visual and easy-to-spot identifiers. Since flags are emojis, and they are basically Unicode characters, they can be rendered as text on our charts, just like other regular text. We can later consider using other emojis as symbols that make it easy for the reader to spot growth and decline, for example (using the relevant arrow symbols and colors). This can also be useful when you don't have much space and you still need to communicate something to the users, especially on smaller screens. An emoji is worth a thousand words!

The interesting thing about country flag emojis is that they are a concatenation of two special letters whose name is "REGIONAL INDICATOR SYMBOL LETTER <letter>". For example, these are the regional indicator symbols for the letters A and B: **AB**. You simply have to get the two-letter code of a certain country, and look up the name from the unicodedata Python Standard Library module. The lookup function takes the name of a character and returns the character itself:

```
from unicodedata import lookup
lookup('LATIN CAPITAL LETTER E')
'E'
lookup("REGIONAL INDICATOR SYMBOL LETTER A")
'A'
```

Once we have two letters representing a country, we can look them up, and concatenate them to produce the respective country's flag. We can create a simple function that does that. We just need to handle the situation where the provided letters are either NaN or not part of the country code list.

We can create a `country_codes` variable and check against it. If the provided letters are not in the list, we return the empty character, otherwise we create an emoji flag:

```
country_codes = country[country['is_country']]['2-alpha code'].
dropna().str.lower().tolist()
```

We can now easily define the `flag` function:

```
def flag(letters):
    if pd.isna(letters) or (letters.lower() not in country_
codes):
        return ''
    L0 = lookup(f'REGIONAL INDICATOR SYMBOL LETTER
{letters[0]}')
    L1 = lookup(f'REGIONAL INDICATOR SYMBOL LETTER
{letters[1]}')
    return L0 + L1
```

Using this function, we can create our `flag` column:

```
country['flag'] =\
[flag(code) for code in country['2-alpha code']]
```

Figure 4.9 shows a random sample of countries, their flags, and the **is_country** column:

	Short Name	flag	is_country
173	Uzbekistan	🇺🇿	True
83	Kenya	🇰🇪	True
130	Palau	🇵🇼	True
182	Zambia	🇿🇲	True
31	Comoros	🇰🇲	True
102	Moldova	🇲🇩	True
180	Yemen	🇾🇪	True
170	Upper middle income		False
134	Paraguay	🇵🇾	True
155	Syrian Arab Republic	🇸🇾	True

Figure 4.9 – Sample of rows showing countries and their flags

In the case where **Short Name** is not a country, we get an empty string. We used the empty string and didn't use NaN because in many cases we might want to concatenate the country name with its flag, for titles or labels for instance, and an empty string would not cause any issues. Note that if you save the DataFrame to a file and reopen it, pandas will interpret empty strings as NaN, and you will have to either convert them or prevent them from being interpreted as such.

The country-series file

Our next file "PovStatsCountry-Series.csv" simply contains a list of the country codes and shows the sources of their population data. We'll see if/when we might use this as metadata in a relevant chart.

The footnotes file

Next, we'll take a quick look at the footnotes file PovStatsFootNote.csv:

There is an empty column **Unnamed: 4**, which we need to drop, and then convert the years to integers. They are represented as YR2015 and that's why we extract the characters starting from index 2. We renamed the columns to make them consistent with the series DataFrame, to make it easy to merge them when needed:

```
footnote = pd.read_csv('data/PovStatsFootNote.csv')
footnote = footnote.drop('Unnamed: 4', axis=1)
footnote['Year'] = footnote['Year'].str[2:].astype(int)
footnote.columns = ['Country Code', Series Code', 'year',
'footnote']
footnote
```

Figure 4.10 shows a few rows from the `footnote` DataFrame:

	Country Code	Series Code	year	footnote
0	AFG	SI.POV.NAHC	2007	Source: National Statictis and Information Aut...
1	AFG	SI.POV.NAHC	2011	Source: National Statictis and Information Aut...
2	AFG	SI.POV.NAHC	2016	Source: National Statictis and Information Aut...
3	AFG	SI.POV.NAHC.NC	2007	Source: National Statictis and Information Aut...
4	AFG	SI.POV.NAHC.NC	2011	Source: National Statictis and Information Aut...
...	...	...	...	...
33472	ZWE	SI.POV.NAHC.NC	2011	Source: PICES 2011/12, Poverty and Poverty Dat...
33473	ZWE	SI.POV.NOP1	2011	Estimated from grouped consumption data.
33474	ZWE	SI.POV.UMIC	2011	Estimated from grouped consumption data.
33475	ZWE	SI.POV.UMIC.GP	2011	Estimated from grouped consumption data.
33476	ZWE	SI.POV.UMIC.NO	2011	Estimated from grouped consumption data.

33477 rows × 4 columns

Figure 4.10 – Sample of rows from the footnote file

That looks like a large number of notes about the data. We should make sure to include them somehow, to make sure the readers get the full picture. Those footnotes seem to be based on combinations of country, indicator, and year. Since the three are encoded in a consistent way with other tables, it should be straightforward to incorporate and map them to the relevant values elsewhere.

The data file

Next is the main data file, which we have already worked with in previous chapters, but we want to now reshape and merge with other DataFrames, for a more intuitive and powerful view into our dataset.

Let's now explore this file:

```
data = pd.read_csv('data/PovStatsData.csv')
data = data.drop('Unnamed: 50', axis=1)
print(data.shape)
data.sample(3)
```

The preceding code removes the column named **Unnamed: 50**, prints the shape of the data DataFrame, and displays a random sample of rows, as you can see in *Figure 4.11*:

```
(11840, 50)
```

	Country Name	Country Code	Indicator Name	Indicator Code	1974	1975	1976	1977	1978	1979	1980
11657	Yemen, Rep.	YEM	Income share held by fourth 20%	SI.DST.04TH.20	NaN	NaN	NaN	NaN	NaN	NaN	NaN
2970	Colombia	COL	Number of poor at $5.50 a day (2011 PPP) (mill...	SI.POV.UMIC.NO	NaN	NaN	NaN	NaN	NaN	NaN	NaN
1223	Angola	AGO	Growth component of change in poverty at $3.20...	SI.POV.LMIC.GR	NaN	NaN	NaN	NaN	NaN	NaN	NaN

Figure 4.11 – Sample of rows and columns from the data file

It's always interesting to know how many missing values we have, and what percentage they form of all values. The interesting parts are the columns starting from **1974** till the end of the DataFrame. The `isna` method returns a `Series` of Booleans for each column. Taking the mean of that gets the percentage of missing values per column, as a `Series`. Running `mean` again gives the overall percentage of missing values:

```
data.loc[:, '1974':].isna().mean().mean()
0.9184470475910692
```

91.8% of our cells are empty. This has important implications for the results because most of the time we won't have enough data, or we won't have it for certain countries. Many countries didn't exist in their current form before the early nineties, for example, so this is one of the reasons. You can check out the `series` DataFrame and all the information about the indicators and the data collection issues where applicable.

Let's now explore how we can reshape DataFrames to and from long format, and more importantly, why we would want to do so.

Melting DataFrames

One of the first things you probably noticed is that years are spread across columns, with the values corresponding to them, each in its respective cell under the respective year. The issue is that `1980` is not really a variable. A more useful way is to have a `year` variable, and in that column, the values would vary from 1974 to 2019. If you remember the way we created the first chart in this chapter, you can see how this makes our life much easier. Let me illustrate what I mean, using a small dataset so things are clear, and then we can implement the same approach with the `data` DataFrame.

Figure 4.12 shows how we can have the same data structured differently while containing the same information:

Wide format

	country	indicator	2015	2020
0	country_A	indicator 1	100	120
1	country_B	indicator 1	10	15

Long (tidy) format

	country	indicator	year	value
0	country_A	indicator 1	2015	100
1	country_B	indicator 1	2015	10
2	country_A	indicator 1	2020	120
3	country_B	indicator 1	2020	15

Figure 4.12 – Two datasets containing the same information in two different formats

Our current DataFrame is structured like the Wide format table, and it would be easier to have it in a format like Long (tidy) format table.

The difficulty with the wide format is that the variables are presented in different ways. In some cases, they are displayed vertically in a column (**country** and **indicator**), while in others, they are displayed horizontally across the columns **2015** and **2020**. Accessing the same data in the long format DataFrame is straightforward: we simply specify the columns that we want. In addition to that, we get automatic mapping of values. For example, taking the columns **year** and **value** from the long DataFrame would automatically map 2015 to 100, 2015 to 10, and so on. At the same time, each row is a complete and independent representation of the case we are dealing with.

The good news is that this is doable with one call to the `melt` method:

```
wide_df.melt(id_vars=['country', 'indicator'],
             value_vars=['2015', '2020'],
             var_name='year')
```

Here is an overview of what the preceding code and parameters do:

- `id_vars`: Keep these as rows and duplicate them as needed to keep the mapping in place.

- `value_vars`: Take these columns and make them values, melt them into a new column, and make sure the mapping with other values remains consistent with the previous structure. If we don't specify `value_vars`, then this operation will be used for all unspecified columns (all columns except `id_vars`).

- `var_name`: Optional. What you want this newly created column to be named – "`year`" in this case.

Let's do this operation on our `data` DataFrame:

```
id_vars =['Country Name', 'Country Code', 'Indicator Name',
'Indicator Code']
data_melt = data.melt(id_vars=id_vars,
                      var_name='year').dropna(subset=['value'])
data_melt['year'] = data_melt['year'].astype(int)
print(data_melt.shape)
data_melt.sample(10)
```

The code is almost identical to the previous example. We first created a list of `id_vars` and used it for the argument of the same name. Right after that, we removed the missing values under the `value` column. We could have changed the name of this column by using the `value_name` parameter, but "`value`" seems appropriate. We then converted the years to integers. Running this code displays the shape and a sample of the new `data_melt` DataFrame, shown in *Figure 4.13*:

```
(44417, 6)
```

	Country Name	Country Code	Indicator Name	Indicator Code	year	value
487193	Belgium	BEL	Number of poor at $3.20 a day (2011 PPP) (mill...	SI.POV.LMIC.NO	2015	0.0
218139	Guyana	GUY	Population, total	SP.POP.TOTL	1992	748602.0
431387	Honduras	HND	Population, total	SP.POP.TOTL	2010	8317470.0
246046	Senegal	SEN	Poverty gap at $5.50 a day (2011 PPP) (% of po...	SI.POV.UMIC.GP	1994	62.1
251850	Costa Rica	CRI	Income share held by highest 10%	SI.DST.10TH.10	1995	33.8
430878	Germany	DEU	Poverty gap at $5.50 a day (2011 PPP) (% of po...	SI.POV.UMIC.GP	2010	0.1
518299	Sao Tome and Principe	STP	Population, total	SP.POP.TOTL	2017	207089.0
252830	Ethiopia	ETH	Poverty gap at $5.50 a day (2011 PPP) (% of po...	SI.POV.UMIC.GP	1995	68.9
446409	Pakistan	PAK	Income share held by fourth 20%	SI.DST.04TH.20	2011	21.0
480718	Malta	MLT	Income share held by second 20%	SI.DST.02ND.20	2014	13.5

Figure 4.13 – The data DataFrame after being "melted"

The first four columns are the same as they were, with each unique combination intact. We now have all the year columns and their values, condensed into two columns, **year** and **value**.

Now let's see how we can improve the structure further by doing the reverse operation on other columns.

Pivoting DataFrames

The **Indicator Name** column might be improved by doing the reverse of the operation that we just did to the years columns. Ideally, we should have a column for population, another one for poverty rates, and so on. Let's first do this using our long (melted) example DataFrame so it's clear.

Assume we wanted to convert the unique values in the **country** column and make them column names. We use the `pivot` method for that. This can give us a "round trip" back where we came from, using the `melt` method. Here, I'm using it on different columns:

```
melted.pivot(index=['year', 'indicator'],
             columns='country',
             values='value').reset_index()
```

Running this code would convert the melted DataFrame to a wide format (pivoted) DataFrame as you can see in *Figure 4.14*:

Long (tidy) format

	country	indicator	year	value
0	country_A	indicator 1	2015	100
1	country_B	indicator 1	2015	10
2	country_A	indicator 1	2020	120
3	country_B	indicator 1	2020	15

Pivoted (wide) format

country	year	indicator	country_A	country_B
0	2015	indicator 1	100	10
1	2020	indicator 1	120	15

Figure 4.14 – The conversion from long to wide format

The **Indicator Name** column in `data_melt` contains names that can be better used as column names, so each indicator can be represented independently in its own column, to be consistent with our data representation:

```
data_pivot =\
data_melt.pivot(index=['Country Name', 'Country Code', 'year'],
                       columns='Indicator Name',
                       values='value').reset_index()
print(data_pivot.shape)
data_pivot.sample(5)
```

This will produce our `data_pivot` DataFrame, a sample of which you can see in *Figure 4.15*:

```
(8287, 57)
```

Indicator Name	Country Name	Country Code	year	Annualized growth in per capita real survey mean consumption or income, bottom 40% (%)	Annualized growth in per capita real survey mean consumption or income, top 10% (%)	Annualized growth in per capita real survey mean consumption or income, top 60% (%)	Annualized growth in per capita real survey mean consumption or income, total population (%)	Annualized growth in per capita real survey median income or consumption expenditure (%)	GINI index (World Bank estimate)
5872	Paraguay	PRY	2002	NaN	NaN	NaN	NaN	NaN	57.3
853	Brazil	BRA	2017	NaN	NaN	NaN	NaN	NaN	53.3
2665	Germany	DEU	1989	NaN	NaN	NaN	NaN	NaN	NaN
3333	Indonesia	IDN	1983	NaN	NaN	NaN	NaN	NaN	NaN
2747	Greece	GRC	1981	NaN	NaN	NaN	NaN	NaN	NaN

Figure 4.15 – The long form (tidy) poverty DataFrame

If our work is correct, we should now have a unique combination of country and year in each row. That was the whole point of the exercise actually. Let's test that our work is correct:

```
data_pivot[['Country Code', 'year']].duplicated().any()
False
```

Rows now contain country names, codes, and years, as well as all the values for the different indicators. The country information can be enriched by including the metadata that we have in the `country` DataFrame. Let's take a look at the `merge` function, and after that, we'll start using Plotly Express.

Merging DataFrames

First, let's look at a simple example of how merging works, and then we can merge the data_pivot and country DataFrames. *Figure 4.16* shows how two DataFrames can be merged:

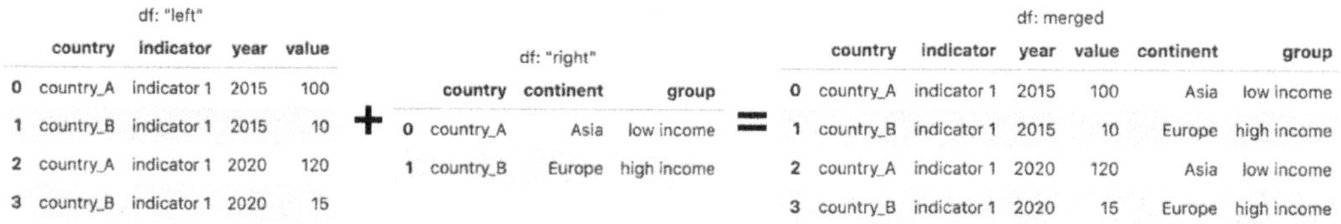

df: "left"						df: "right"				df: merged					
	country	indicator	year	value			country	continent	group		country	indicator	year	value	continent	group
0	country_A	indicator 1	2015	100		0	country_A	Asia	low income	0	country_A	indicator 1	2015	100	Asia	low income
1	country_B	indicator 1	2015	10		1	country_B	Europe	high income	1	country_B	indicator 1	2015	10	Europe	high income
2	country_A	indicator 1	2020	120						2	country_A	indicator 1	2020	120	Asia	low income
3	country_B	indicator 1	2020	15						3	country_B	indicator 1	2020	15	Europe	high income

Figure 4.16 How DataFrames are merged

The merge operation can be done with the merge function:

```
pd.merge(left=left, right=right,
        left_on='country',
        right_on='country',
        how='left')
```

Here are the details of the preceding call to pd.merge:

- left_on: The name of the column(s) from the left DataFrame to merge on.
- right_on: The name of the column(s) from the right DataFrame to merge on.
- how: The merge method. In this case, "left" means to take all the rows in left and only match them with rows in right that have the same values in the **country** columns. Matching rows will be duplicated if needed in the resulting DataFrame, as in this case. Rows in right that don't have matches in the country column will be discarded. The merged DataFrame should end up with the same number of rows as the left DataFrame.

There are several other options for this function, and it's quite powerful. Make sure to check out the other merge methods: inner, outer, and right. For our case, we will be using the options shown in the previous example, so let's do it now. We will merge data_pivot with country the same way:

```
poverty = pd.merge(data_pivot, country,
                left_on='Country Code',
                right_on='Country Code',
                how='left')
```

```
print(poverty.shape)
poverty
```

This merge operation produces the `poverty` DataFrame, which you can see in *Figure 4.17*:

(8287, 89)

	Country Name	Country Code	year	Annualized growth in per capita real survey mean consumption or income, bottom 40% (%)	Survey mean consumption or income per capita, top 60% (2011 PPP $ per day)	Survey mean consumption or income per capita, total population (2011 PPP $ per day)	Short Name	Table Name	Long Name	2-alpha code	Currency Unit	Special Notes	Region	Income Group
6251	Sao Tome and Principe	STP	1976	NaN	NaN	NaN	São Tomé and Principe	São Tomé and Principe	Democratic Republic of São Tomé and Principe	ST	São Tomé and Principe dobra	National account data were adjusted to reflect ..	Sub-Saharan Africa	Lower middle income
153	Angola	AGO	1992	NaN	NaN	NaN	Angola	Angola	People's Republic of Angola	AO	Angolan kwanza	NaN	Sub-Saharan Africa	Lower middle income
5823	Papua New Guinea	PNG	1998	NaN	NaN	NaN	Papua New Guinea	Papua New Guinea	The Independent State of Papua New Guinea	PG	Papua New Guinea kina	NaN	East Asia & Pacific	Lower middle income
2785	Guatemala	GTM	1974	NaN	NaN	NaN	Guatemala	Guatemala	Republic of Guatemala	GT	Guatemalan quetzal	NaN	Latin America & Caribbean	Upper middle income
175	Angola	AGO	2014	NaN	NaN	NaN	Angola	Angola	People's Republic of Angola	AO	Angolan kwanza	NaN	Sub-Saharan Africa	Lower middle income
4494	Madagascar	MDG	1974	NaN	NaN	NaN	Madagascar	Madagascar	Republic of Madagascar	MG	Malagasy ariary	NaN	Sub-Saharan Africa	Low income

Figure 4.17 – Merging data_pivot and country

A quick check to make sure our work is correct:

```
poverty[['Country Code', 'year']].duplicated().any()
False
```

The eight additional columns in the rectangle on the right are some of the additional columns that were added to our `poverty` DataFrame. Now it's very easy to take a certain region or income group, filter by its countries, color by its values, or group it however we want. This is now looking like the Gapminder dataset, only with many more indicators and years, and more metadata about countries.

We now have a DataFrame that has a consistent structure.

Every column contains data about one and only one variable. All values in columns are of the same data type (or missing). Each row can independently represent a complete observation, because it contains the full information available, like all other rows.

> **Important note**
>
> The main drawback of the long format is that it is inefficient for storage. From that perspective, we are unnecessarily repeating a lot of values, which takes a lot of space. We will tackle this later, but keep in mind that this format is extremely efficient in terms of your time as a developer. As we saw in several examples, once the mapping is consistent, creating and changing your visualizations becomes much easier.

I highly recommend reading Hadley Wickham's *Tidy Data* paper, for a deeper discussion on several ways in which data might be formatted and different solutions for that. The examples shown here are inspired by those principles: `https://www.jstatsoft.org/article/view/v059i10`.

We are now ready to explore how to use Plotly Express, first with a toy dataset, and then with the dataset that we prepared.

Learning Plotly Express

Plotly Express is a higher-level plotting system, built on top of Plotly. Not only does it handle certain defaults for us, such as labeling axes and legends, it enables us to utilize our data to express many of its attributes using visual aesthetics (size, color, location, and so on). This can be done simply by declaring what attribute we want to express with which column of our data, given a few assumptions about the data structure. So, it mainly provides us with the flexibility to approach the problem from the data point of view, as mentioned at the beginning of the chapter.

Let's first create a simple DataFrame:

```
df = pd.DataFrame({
    'numbers': [1, 2, 3, 4, 5, 6, 7, 8],
    'colors': ['blue', 'green', 'orange', 'yellow', 'black',
'gray', 'pink', 'white'],
    'floats': [1.1, 1.2, 1.3, 2.4, 2.1, 5.6, 6.2, 5.3],
    'shapes': ['rectangle', 'circle', 'triangle', 'rectangle',
'circle', 'triangle', 'rectangle', 'circle'],
    'letters': list('AAABBCCC')
})
df
```

This will produce the DataFrame in *Figure 4.18*:

	numbers	colors	floats	shapes	letters
0	1	blue	1.1	rectangle	A
1	2	green	1.2	circle	A
2	3	orange	1.3	triangle	A
3	4	yellow	2.4	rectangle	B
4	5	black	2.1	circle	B
5	6	gray	5.6	triangle	C
6	7	pink	6.2	rectangle	C
7	8	white	5.3	circle	C

Figure 4.18 – A simple example DataFrame

We typically create charts with Plotly Express by calling the type of the chart as a function, `px.line`, `px.histogram`, and so on. Each function has its own set of parameters, based on its type.

There are several ways of passing arguments to those functions, and we will focus on two main approaches:

- A DataFrame with column names: In most cases, the first parameter is `data_frame`. You set the DataFrame that you want to visualize, and then you specify the columns you want to use for the parameters that you want. For our example DataFrame, if we want to create a scatter plot with **numbers** on the X axis and **floats** on the Y axis, we call it like this: `px.scatter(data_frame=df, x='numbers', y='floats')`.

- Arrays as arguments: Another way of specifying parameters is by simply passing lists, tuples, or any array-like data structure, without a `data_frame` argument. We can create the same scatter plot by running: `px.scatter(x=df['numbers'], y=df['floats'])`. This is a straightforward and very fast approach, whenever you have lists that you want to explore.

We can also mix the approaches. We can set a `data_frame` argument with a few column names as arguments, and we can pass separate lists for other arguments when needed. A few examples should illustrate these points easily. The following code shows how easy it is to create a scatter plot:

```
px.scatter(df, x='numbers', y='floats')
```

Figure 4.19 shows the resulting figure in JupyterLab:

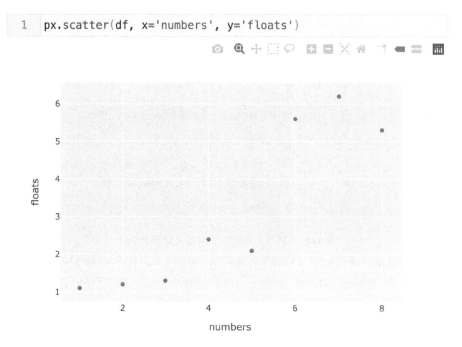

Figure 4.19 – Creating a scatter plot with Plotly Express

I'm sure you noticed that we got the X- and Y-axis titles set for us by default. It takes the names of the arguments we gave (the DataFrame columns in this example) and uses them for that.

We have several other variables in the DataFrame, and we might be interested in checking whether there are any relations between them. For example, let's check whether there is a relationship between **floats** and **shapes**.

We can rerun the same code and add two parameters that allow us to distinguish which markers belong to which shape. We can use the `color` parameter for that, and it will assign a different color to each marker based on the **shapes** that it corresponds to (in the same row). If you are reading this book from the printed grayscale edition, the same argument to the `symbol` parameter was added, to make it easy to distinguish them. This also makes it easier for readers on a colored screen as well, by giving two signals to distinguish the markers:

```
Px.scatter(df,
        x='numbers',
        y='floats',
```

```
        color='shapes',
        symbol='shapes')
```

Figure 4.20 shows the code and resulting figure in JupyterLab:

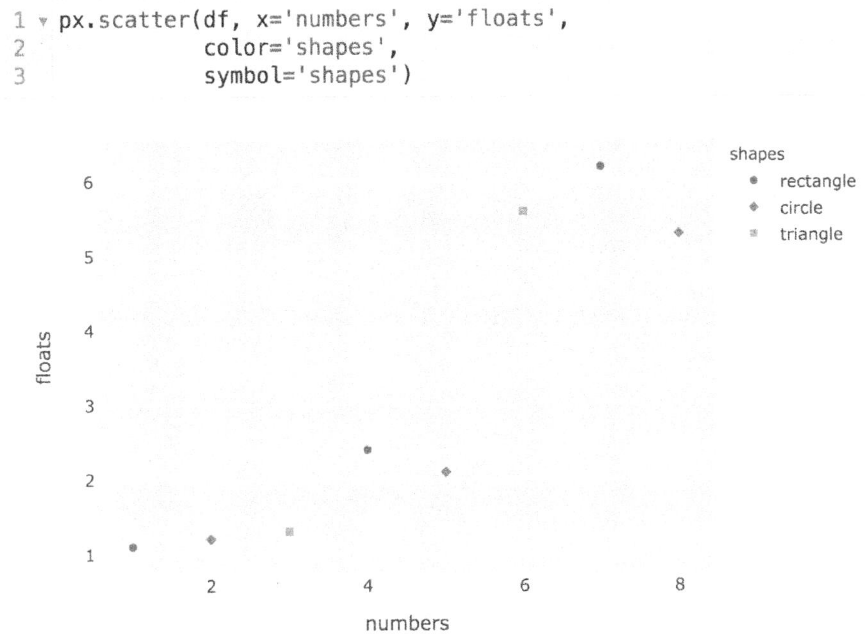

```
1 ▼ px.scatter(df, x='numbers', y='floats',
2              color='shapes',
3              symbol='shapes')
```

Figure 4.20 – Assigning colors and symbols to markers

Note that we have a legend helping us to distinguish the markers by telling us which color and symbol belong to which shape. It also has its own title, all generated by default.

There seems to be no relationship between floats and shapes. So, let's try coloring and setting symbols based on the **letters** column, which can be done with the following code:

```
px.scatter(df,
          x='numbers',
          y='floats',
          color='letters',
          symbol='letters',
          size=[35] * 8)
```

Figure 4.21 demonstrates this:

```
1 ▾ px.scatter(df, x='numbers', y='floats',
2              color='letters',
3              symbol='letters',
4              size=[35] * 8)
```

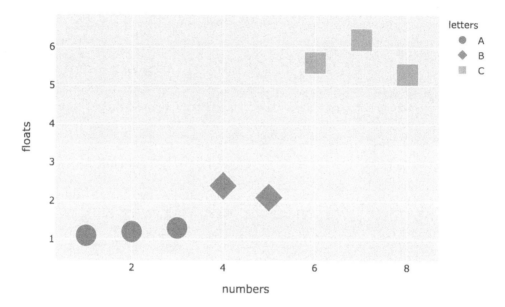

Figure 4.21 – Setting marker sizes using an independent list

We can see a clear difference based on the letters now. This shows how easy it is to explore your datasets by quickly trying out different options. Note that we also mixed the approaches this time by setting a size for the markers. Size wasn't mapped to a value; it was set to make the symbols bigger and easier to see. So, we simply passed a list with the marker size that we wanted. The list had to have the same length as the other variables that we are visualizing.

Let's explore bar charts with the same approach and using the same dataset. We can adjust how the bars are displayed using the barmode parameter like this:

```
px.bar(df, x='letters', y='floats', color='shapes',
barmode='group')
```

Figure 4.22 shows two different ways of displaying the bars – the default, on top of each other, and "group," as you can see:

```
1   px.bar(df, x='letters', y='floats', color='shapes')
```

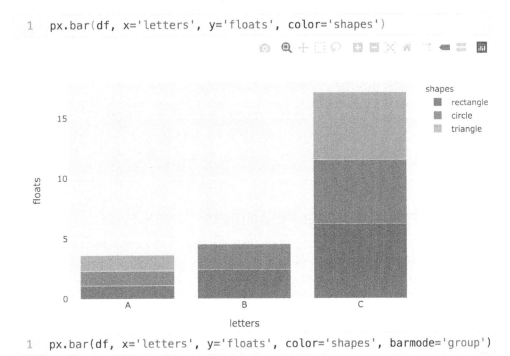

```
1   px.bar(df, x='letters', y='floats', color='shapes', barmode='group')
```

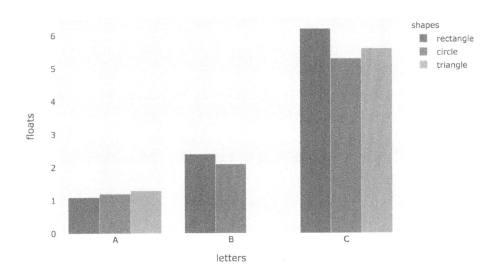

Figure 4.22 – Creating bar charts using different display modes (barmode)

The discussion about long (tidy) format data should should make it very easy to understand how to use Plotly Express. You just need a basic understanding of the chart type, and how it works, and then you can easily set the arguments that you want.

> **Important note**
>
> Plotly Express does not require data to be in long format. It is very flexible and can handle wide, long, as well as mixed format data. Also, pandas and numpy are extremely flexible in data manipulation. I just believe it is better to use a consistent approach for your own productivity.

Now let's see how Plotly Express relates to the `Figure` object and when to use which approach.

Plotly Express and Figure objects

It's helpful to know that all calls to the Plotly Express chart functions return a `Figure` object, the same one we discussed in *Chapter 3, Working with Plotly's Figure Objects*. This is very important for customizing our charts after creating them, in case you want to change the defaults. Let's say you created a scatter plot, and after that, you wanted to add an annotation to it to explain something. You could do it just like we did in the previous chapter:

```
import plotly express as px
fig = px.scatter(x=[1, 2, 3], y=[23, 12, 34])
fig.add_annotation(x=1, y=23, text='This is the first value')
```

Everything you know about the `Figure` object and how it is structured can be used with Plotly Express, so this builds on that knowledge.

This naturally raises the question of when to use Plotly Express and when to use Plotly's `graph_objects` module for creating charts from a lower level.

This question can be tackled by asking the more general question: Given two interfaces that do the same thing at different levels of abstraction, how do we choose between them?

Consider three different approaches to having a pizza:

- **The ordering approach**: You call a restaurant and order your pizza. It arrives at your doorstep in half an hour, and you start eating.

- **The supermarket approach**: You go to a supermarket, buy dough, cheese, vegetables, and all other ingredients. You then make the pizza yourself.

- **The farm approach**: You grow tomatoes in your backyard. You raise cows, milk them, and convert the milk to cheese, and so on.

As we go up to higher-level interfaces, towards the ordering approach, the amount of knowledge required decreases a lot. Someone else holds responsibility, and quality is checked by the market forces of reputation and competition.

The price we pay for this is the diminished freedom and options. Each restaurant has a set of options to choose from, and you have to choose from those options.

Going down to lower levels, the amount of knowledge required increases, we have to handle more complexity, we hold more responsibility for the outcomes, and it takes much more time. What we gain here is much more freedom and power to customize our outcomes the way we want. Cost is a major benefit as well, but only on a large enough scale. If you only want to have a pizza today, it's probably cheaper to order it. But if you plan on having one every day, then you can expect major cost-savings if you do it yourself.

This is the trade-off you have in choosing between the higher-level Plotly Express, and the lower-level Plotly `graph_objects`.

Since Plotly Express returns `Figure` objects, then it's generally not a difficult decision, because you can retroactively modify them. In general, it's good to use the `graph_objects` module in the following cases:

- **Non-standard visualizations**: Many diagrams created in this book were done with Plotly. To create such diagrams with Plotly Express would be quite difficult because they are not standard graphs.

- **When you have a lot of customizations**: If you want to make a lot of changes to most aspects of your charts, you might end up writing the same amount of code and putting in the same amount of effort, so you might consider doing it directly using the `graph_objects` module.

- **Sub-plots**: Sometimes you want to have multiple charts side by side, or in a grid. If these are different charts and not facets as we saw at the beginning of the chapter, then it's better to do them with `graph_objects`.

In general, Plotly Express is usually a better starting point for creating your charts, as we saw how powerful and convenient it is.

You are now ready to use the `poverty` dataset to specify the visualization that you want with Plotly Express, starting from the data.

Creating a Plotly Express chart using the dataset

Let's see how we might summarize the `poverty data_frame` with a scatter plot:

1. Create variables for `year`, `indicator`, and a grouping (`grouper`) metric to use in the visualization. The grouping metric will be used to distinguish between the markers (using color and symbol), and could take any categorical value from the dataset, such as region, income group, and so on:

```
year = 2010
indicator = 'Population, total'
grouper = 'Region'
```

2. Based on these variables, create a DataFrame, where the `year` column is equal to `year`, sort the values by `indicator`, and remove any missing values from the columns of `indicator` and `grouper`:

```
df = (poverty[poverty['year'].eq(year)]
      .sort_values(indicator)
      .dropna(subset=[indicator, grouper]))
```

3. Set the x axis values to `indicator` and set the y axis values to the column "Country Name". The `color` and `symbol` of the markers should be set using `grouper`. The X-axis values are expected to have outliers, and not to be normally distributed, so set `log_x` to `True`. The `hover_name` of each hover label should take the country name together with its flag. Set the `title` of the figure by concatenating `indicator`, "by", `grouper`, and `year`. Give markers a constant `size`, and set the `height` to 700 pixels:

```
px.scatter(data_frame=df,
           x=indicator,
```

```
        y='Country Name',
        color=grouper,
        symbol=grouper,
        log_x=True,
        hover_name=df['Short Name'] + ' ' +
df['flag'],
        size=[1]* len(df),
        title= ' '.join([indicator, 'by', grouper,
str(year)]),
        height=700)
```

This creates the chart in *Figure 4.23*:

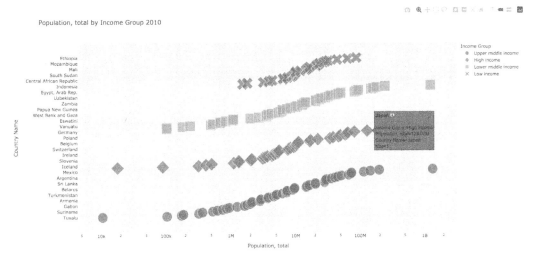

Figure 4.23 – The Plotly Express figure using the poverty dataset

By simply playing with the different combinations of `year`, `grouper`, and `indicator`, you can generate hundreds of charts. *Figure 4.24* shows some samples:

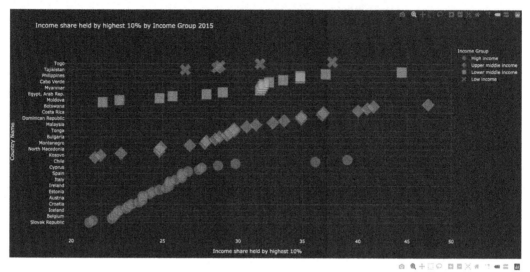

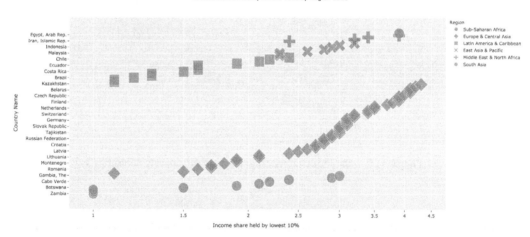

Figure 4.24 – Other figures using the same dataset

With these powerful features, and with data formatted as observations by variables, we can easily visualize six or seven attributes of our data using several visual attributes: X axis, Y axis, marker size, marker symbol, marker color, facets (columns or rows), and animations. We can also add more context and information using hover labels, as well as annotations. Any combination of those attributes can be explored simply by selecting which column to map to which attribute.

Let's now explore how easy it is to enrich our dataset with external resources.

Adding new data and columns to our dataset

There are many ways to add more data, but I would like to highlight two very easy and effective ones:

- **Adding columns or features**: We added our flag column by creating the respective emoji for each country using its two-letter code. You might be interested in segmenting or grouping countries according to other attributes. Maybe you suspect there might be something distinctive about countries using the euro, countries where Spanish or Arabic is spoken, or maybe signatories of a certain trade agreement. Wikipedia contains numerous such lists. Using the pandas read_html function, which downloads all tables on a web page, you can very easily download any such list. Assuming it has the country codes, you can merge it with the main DataFrame and start analyzing accordingly. This can also be a filtering mechanism, where you simply want a subset of all countries.

- **Adding new data**: The World Bank has thousands of other similar datasets. For example, the population figures we have here are for the total population. There are many detailed and segmented population datasets that break the numbers down by gender, age, and other factors. Using the World Bank's API, you can easily obtain other data, merge it, and immediately enrich your analysis.

Let's now review what we have done in this chapter and in *Part 1* of the book.

Summary

You now have enough information and have seen enough examples to create dashboards quickly. In *Chapter 1, Overview of the Dash Ecosystem*, we learned how apps are structured and learned how to build fully running apps, but without interactivity. In *Chapter 2, Exploring the Structure of a Dash App*, we explored how interactivity works, through callback functions, and we added interactive features to our app. *Chapter 3, Working with Plotly's Figure Objects*, introduced how Plotly's charts are created, their components, and how to manipulate them to achieve the results you want. Finally, in this chapter, we introduced Plotly Express, a high-level interface to Plotly that is easy to use but more importantly, follows an intuitive approach that is data-oriented, as opposed to being chart-oriented.

One of the most important and biggest parts of creating visualizations is the process of preparing data in certain formats, after which it becomes relatively straightforward to create those visualizations. Investing in understanding how your dataset is structured, as well as investing time and effort in reshaping your data, pays well in the end, as we saw in the extensive example in this chapter.

Armed with this knowledge and examples, as well as our familiarity with our dataset, and straightforward mechanisms to enrich it, we are now ready to explore in more detail different Dash components, as well as different types of charts.

Part 2 will go deep into different chart types, how to use them, and the different ways we can combine them with the interactivity features that Dash provides.

Section 2: Adding Functionality to Your App with Real Data

This section shows you how to start building with real data and exploring how to utilize the full options of interactivity with Dash.

This section comprises the following chapters:

- *Chapter 5, Interactively Comparing Values with Bar Charts and Drop-down Menus*
- *Chapter 6, Exploring Variables with Scatter Plots and Filtering Subsets with Sliders*
- *Chapter 7, Exploring Map Plots and Enriching Your Dashboards with Markdown*
- *Chapter 8, Calculating the Frequency of Your Data with Histograms and Building Interactive Tables*

5
Interactively Comparing Values with Bar Charts and Dropdown Menus

You now have all the basics you need to easily construct interactive features linking page elements and to produce interactive dashboards. The main concepts have been covered with the help of several examples, and we will now be focusing on specific types of charts and the different options that they provide. More importantly, we will go into additional details for customizing our charts and making them suitable for several purposes, firstly, in order to be good enough to publish and share with a wider audience, as opposed to just for your interactive use, and secondly, to ensure that they properly fit on a page that potentially contains other components, and making sure we utilize the available space in an optimal way. Another important aspect to cover is the dynamic nature of the charts that our users can generate. Based on the user's choice of option in an interactive component, the resulting dataset might contain 7 or maybe 70 elements to plot. In some cases, it might not contain any data. This dramatically affects the resulting charts and their usability, and can even make them difficult to read in certain cases. We will explore a few solutions to cater for these situations.

In other words, we are trying to move from working with a prototype that simply does what it's supposed to do to working with a product that can be shared or published to a wide audience.

The chapters in *Part 2* of this book will each focus on a chart type and an interactive component to explore their options. In this chapter, we will explore **bar charts** and how they can be used with **drop-down** components, from **Dash Core Component**. There is nothing in the nature of these components that links a certain component to a certain chart type. They are just used together for organization purposes. A dropdown can be used with any type of chart, and any type of interactive component can be used to manipulate a bar chart.

We will be focusing on the following topics:

- Plotting bar charts vertically and horizontally

- Linking bar charts and dropdowns

- Exploring different ways of displaying multiple bar charts (stacked, grouped, overlaid, and relative)

- Using facets to split charts into multiple sub-charts – horizontally, vertically, or wrapped

- Exploring additional features of dropdowns (allowing multiple selections, adding placeholder text, and more)

Technical requirements

We will continue to use the packages that we are now familiar with – `JupyterDash` and `Dash`, for prototyping and then integrating into our app, respectively. For data manipulation, we will be using `pandas`, and `JupyterLab` will be our starting point for building and testing various options. Then, we will use Dash Core Component, Dash HTML Components, and Dash Bootstrap Components to update our app.

The dataset that we will be using is the same dataset, specifically the `poverty` DataFrame, that we created in the previous chapter. The code files of this chapter can be found on GitHub at `https://github.com/PacktPublishing/Interactive-Dashboards-and-Data-Apps-with-Plotly-and-Dash/tree/master/chapter_05`.

Check out the following video to see the Code in Action at `https://bit.ly/3ebv8sk`.

Let's start by exploring the two main ways in which we can display bar charts – vertically and horizontally.

Plotting bar charts vertically and horizontally

The default display of bar charts is vertical. This is intuitive and easy to understand. Each category or item takes a separate position on the *x* axis, and the heights of the bars represent a certain quantity on the *y* axis. The same applies when the bars are displayed horizontally, only in this case, the width of the bars is what represents the quantity. Usually, with relatively fewer values, the vertical orientation is good. However, horizontal orientation can be more effective in two cases:

- **When we have many categories**: In this case, the bars might not fit on the screen, and we might need to either make them much thinner than the default width, or we might need to force horizontal scrolling, which is not as natural as vertical scrolling.

- **When the names of the categories are relatively long**: This is not really a big problem, and the solution is easy. Plotly already handles this for us, by automatically changing the angle at which the names (tick labels) are displayed. If needed, the names can be displayed vertically for maximum space utilization. Reading text displayed horizontally is the most natural though, and it is the most suitable way for these situations.

Let's see this in action using our `poverty` DataFrame, so we can see the effects of these options, and also to get to know our dataset a little better. We will take a look at one of the most widely used measures of income/wealth inequality, the Gini index. It is also referred to as the Gini ratio, or coefficient. To learn a bit about it, we can use the `series` DataFrame, which contains information about the indicators that we will be working with:

1. Import `pandas` and create the `series` variable. The name of the variable was chosen based on the filename, as we did in the previous chapter. Please don't confuse this with the `pandas.Series` object:

   ```
   import pandas as pd
   series = pd.read_csv('data/PovStatsSeries.csv')
   ```

2. Create a variable, `gini`, as a string, as an easier alternative to using the long name of the indicator:

   ```
   gini = 'GINI index (World Bank estimate)'
   ```

3. Extract the long definition of the indicator by using the column of the same name:

   ```
   series[series['Indicator Name']==gini]['Long
   definition'].values[0]
   ```

```
Gini index measures the extent to which the distribution
of income (or, in some cases, consumption expenditure)
among individuals or households within an economy
deviates from a perfectly equal distribution. A Lorenz
curve plots the cumulative percentages of total income
received against the cumulative number of recipients,
starting with the poorest individual or household. The
Gini index measures the area between the Lorenz curve
and a hypothetical line of absolute equality, expressed
as a percentage of the maximum area under the line. Thus
a Gini index of 0 represents perfect equality, while an
index of 100 implies perfect inequality.
```

4.   Knowing that the values vary between 0 and 100, let's check what the most extreme values are for all years and countries:

```
poverty[gini].min(), poverty[gini].max()
(20.2, 65.8)
```

5.   We can also learn a little more about this column by using the describe method from pandas:

```
Poverty[gini].describe()
count      1674.000000
mean         38.557766
std           9.384352
min          20.200000
25%          31.300000
50%          36.400000
75%          45.275000
max          65.800000
Name: GINI index (World Bank estimate), dtype: float64
```

We will learn much more about this indicator and interactively explore and compare different countries across different years, but this statement from the Limitations and exceptions column stood out to me: *"Because the underlying household surveys differ in methods and types of welfare measures collected, data is not strictly comparable across countries or even across years within a country."*

So, we will have to be careful not to take those values precisely, as mentioned, and keep this limitation in mind.

Now that we are a bit more familiar with the indicator, we are ready to explore various options for visualizing it with a bar chart:

1. We start by creating a subset of the `poverty` DataFrame, named `df`. This will be a subset where the `year` values are equal to an arbitrarily selected year. We then remove the missing values, and sort the available ones using the `gini` column:

```
year = 1980
df =\
poverty[poverty['year']==year].sort_values(gini).
dropna(subset=[gini])
```

2. We can now easily create our Gini index bar chart with Plotly Express. The code also dynamically generates the title by joining the name of the indicator to the selected year:

```
import plotly.express as px
px.bar(df,
        x='Country Name',
        y=gini,
        title=' - '.join([gini, str(year)]))
```

Running the preceding code produces the chart in *Figure 5.1*:

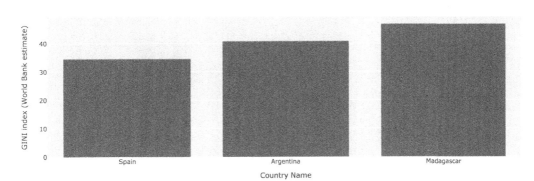

Figure 5.1 – A bar chart of the Gini index for the year 1980

For the year 1980, it seems we only have data for three countries, and having them displayed vertically seems fine, easily readable, and clear. Let's now repeat the same process for the year 1990, and see the result in *Figure 5.2*:

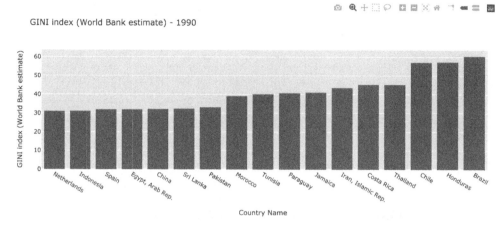

Figure 5.2 – A bar chart of the Gini index for the year 1990

We can read the country names, but not as naturally as we would if they were displayed horizontally as in *Figure 5.1*. Now, if users were reading the same chart on a narrower screen, the country names would be displayed vertically, and it becomes even more difficult to read them, as you can see in *Figure 5.3*:

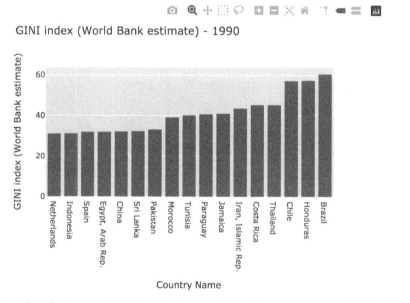

Figure 5.3 – A bar chart of the Gini index for the year 1990 with country names displayed vertically

In more recent years, we have data for many more countries, and in those cases, there is not enough horizontal space to fit them. Some names are not even displayed, unless you hover over the respective bar, or zoom in to that part of the chart. As an example, you can see the same chart for the year 2010 in *Figure 5.4*:

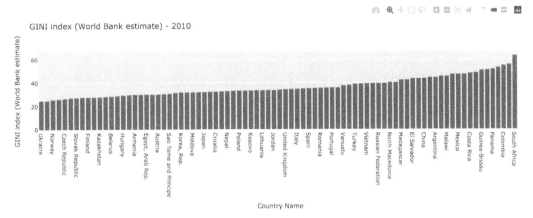

Figure 5.4 – A bar chart of the Gini index for the year 2010 with some country names not displayed

Based on the charts we just saw, we now have a better understanding of the challenge of making an interactive bar chart dynamically generated for the Gini index. If we want to let users select the year they are interested in, then we have a few points to deal with.

First, the number of available values for this metric varies from 3 to more than 150, which is a very large range. Second, it would be better, and safer, to use horizontal orientation, because in all cases country names would be displayed horizontally, and no matter how long the names are, they would be easy to read. These issues can be easily solved by setting `orientation='h'` in our call to `px.bar`, but one challenge remains. We need to determine the optimal height of the chart, based on the number of available countries in the chosen year, knowing how big the range is, as we just saw. Let's first see what the bar chart looks like when displayed horizontally, and then design the solution for an interactive one. We will run the same code, but with two principal differences. The x and y arguments need to be swapped, as they will each take the opposite axis, and we also need to set the appropriate value for the `orientation` parameter, h for "horizontal" in this case:

```
year = 2000
px.bar(df,
        x=gini,
        y='Country Name',
        title=' - '.join([gini, str(year)]),
        orientation='h')
```

The preceding code produces the chart in *Figure 5.5* for the year 2000:

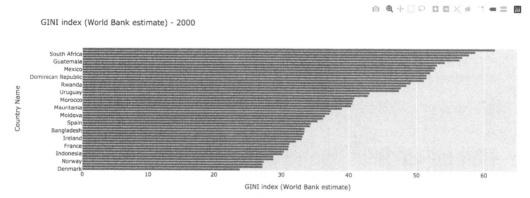

Figure 5.5 – A horizontal bar chart of the Gini index for the year 2000 for all available countries

Now the countries are very easily readable (the ones that are displayed at least), but the bars are too narrow and crowded. The chart looks unnecessarily wide (especially knowing that the minimum and maximum values are in the interval [20.2, 65.8]). We can manually set the width of the chart in our function call if we require, but we need to figure out a way to dynamically set the height of the chart, which can be set using the `height` parameter.

One way to do this is to set a fixed height in pixels. Then, based on the number of countries in `df`, we can add 20 pixels per country. For example, if we have 10 countries in `df`, then our height would be 200 + (10x20) = 400 pixels. Once `df` has been created, we can easily count the number of countries it contains, and assign it to a variable, `n_countries`. The modified code to produce this looks like this:

```
year = 2000
df =\
poverty[poverty['year']==year].sort_values(gini).
dropna(subset=[gini])
n_countries = len(df['Country Name'])
px.bar(df,
       x=indicator,
       y='Country Name',
       title=' - '.join([gini, str(year)]),
       height=200 + (20*n_countries),
       orientation='h')
```

Running the preceding code over three years that have a different number of countries produces the charts in *Figure 5.6*:

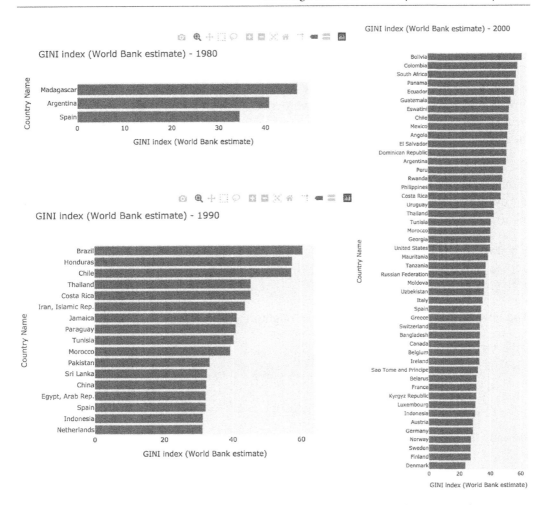

Figure 5.6 – Various horizontal bar charts with a dynamic height based on the number of countries

The long chart on the right was resized to fit on the page, but it is pretty much the same as the others in terms of the height of the bars and the readability of country names. All countries are visible, easy to read, and nothing is hidden.

With this solution, we took care of the dynamic number of countries that can be selected by dynamically setting the total height of the figure, based on the number of countries.

This approach can be thought of as a discovery approach. Users don't know exactly what they are looking for; they select a year and see whatever data is available for that year. After they select a few options, they might be interested in digging deeper to learn more about specific countries. For example, they might be interested in how a certain country's Gini index has progressed over time. We will do this next.

Creating vertical bar charts with many values

When we want to let users visualize how a country's Gini index (or any other indicator) has progressed over the years, we can do so with vertical bars. Because years represent a sequence of events, displaying them side by side is natural, because it shows a trend over time. And since years are numbers in a sequence, we don't have the readability issue that we had with country names. Even if the bars end up much thinner, and even if some of them weren't displayed, users can easily mentally "fill in the blanks" where required.

The code to produce such a chart is very similar to the last one, and actually simpler, because we don't need to worry about dynamically setting the height. Instead of `year` as our dynamic variable, we will have `Country Name`. The definition of `df` will depend on the rows in our dataset that contain the chosen country:

```
country = "Sweden"
df = poverty[poverty['Country Name']==country].
dropna(subset=[gini])
```

And now we can generate the chart in a straightforward way with the following code:

```
px.bar(df,
       x='year',
       y=gini,
       title=' - '.join([gini, country]))
```

Running the preceding code produces the chart in *Figure 5.7* for Sweden:

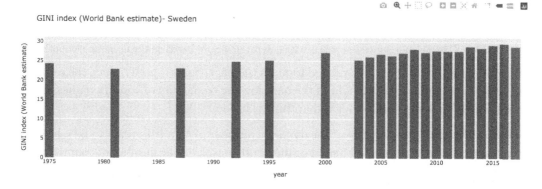

Figure 5.7 – A vertical bar chart with years on the x axis

Note that the years with missing values are still available on the *x* axis, even though there are no bars representing their value for those years. This is important because it shows where the gaps are in our data. It would be misleading otherwise if we only displayed years that contained data, giving the false impression of continuous data for all years.

We have familiarized ourselves a bit with the Gini index data, and tested how to make two types of dynamic charts. We are now ready to create a "Gini Index" section and add it to our app, which we will be doing next.

Linking bar charts and dropdowns

We now want to put together everything that we've done so far. The plan is to have two dropdowns, side by side, with a chart underneath each. The first will provide years as options that will generate a horizontal bar chart. The second will generate a vertical bar chart, based on the selected country. The end goal is to produce a new section in our app that looks like *Figure 5.8*:

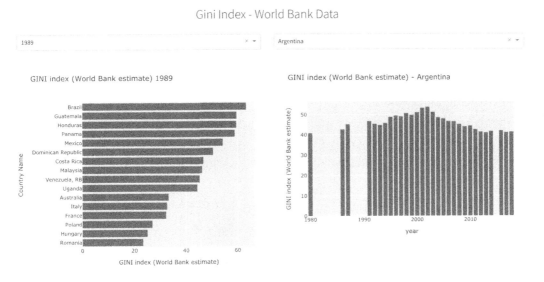

Figure 5.8 – The Gini Index section in the app with two drop-down components and two bar charts

Let's start by building this as a complete and independent app in JupyterLab, and make sure it works as expected:

1. We first run the necessary imports and instantiate the app. We already covered all these imports, except for the `PreventUpdate` exception. This is a useful tool when there is no value selected in a component that is handled by a callback function; for example, when a user first loads the app, or when there are no default values. In this case, the input value coming from `Dropdown` would be `None` and would most likely raise exceptions. In those situations, we can use this exception to freeze things, so to speak, until a proper input is passed to the callback function:

   ```python
   from jupyter_dash import JupyterDash
   import dash_html_components as html
   import dash_core_components as dcc
   import dash_bootstrap_components as dbc
   from dash.dependencies import Output, Input
   from dash.exceptions import PreventUpdate

   app = JupyterDash(__name__)
   ```

2. Create `gini_df`, which is a subset of `poverty` that doesn't have missing values in the Gini index column:

   ```python
   gini_df = poverty[poverty[gini].notna()]
   ```

3. Create the app's layout using one top-level div, within which we will place all other components:

   ```python
   app.layout  = html.Div()
   ```

4. Inside the div we just created, we want to add a section title, as well as a dbc.Row component. This row will then contain two dbc.Col elements, which would, in turn, contain a dropdown and a chart each. Here is a list of elements that will be inserted in the div:

```
[
    html.H2('Gini Index - World Bank Data',
            style={'textAlign': 'center'}),
    dbc.Row([
        dbc.Col([
            dcc.Dropdown(id='gini_year_dropdown',
                        options=[{'label': year,
'value': year}
                        for year in gini_df['year'].
drop_duplicates().sort_values()]),
            dcc.Graph(id='gini_year_barchart')
]),
        dbc.Col([
            dcc.Dropdown(id='gini_country_dropdown',
                        options=[{'label': country,
'value': country}
    for country in gini_df['Country Name'].unique()]),
    dcc.Graph(id='gini_country_barchart')
    ])
])
]
```

5. The preceding code should take care of the layout once we insert it in the top-level div. Now we can create the first callback, which takes a year as input and returns the appropriate chart. Note how the PreventUpdate exception is used at the beginning of the function:

```
@app.callback(Output('gini_year_barchart', 'figure'),
              Input('gini_year_dropdown', 'value'))
def plot_gini_year_barchart(year):
    if not year:
        raise PreventUpdate
    df =\
```

```
gini_df[gini_df['year'].eq(year)].sort_values(gini).
dropna(subset=[gini])
    n_countries = len(df['Country Name'])
    fig = px.bar(df,
                 x=gini,
                 y='Country Name',
                 orientation='h',
                 height=200 + (n_countries*20),
                 title=gini + ' ' + str(year))
    return fig
```

6. We can also do the same thing and create the other callback function that handles the second part of the Gini Index section:

```
@app.callback(Output('gini_country_barchart', 'figure'),
              Input('gini_country_dropdown', 'value'))
def plot_gini_country_barchart(country):
    if not country:
        raise PreventUpdate
    df = gini_df[gini_df['Country Name']==country].
dropna(subset=[gini])
    fig = px.bar(df,
                 x='year',
                 y=gini,
                 title=' - '.join([gini, country]))
    return fig
```

7. Finally, we run the app:

```
if __name__ == '__main__':
    app.run_server(mode='inline')
```

This should create a running app as shown in *Figure 5.8*.

We now want to incorporate this new functionality into our existing app. All we have to do is insert the visual components wherever we want them to appear. The callbacks can be added below the app's `layout` attribute. You can go ahead and make a copy of the latest version of the app that we created in *Chapter 3, Working with Plotly's Figure Objects*. You can insert the new components as a list between `dcc.Graph(id='population_chart')` and `dbc.Tabs`, as you can see in the following code snippet:

```
...
dcc.Graph(id='population_chart'),
html.Br(),
html.H2('Gini Index - World Bank Data', style={'textAlign':
'center'}),
html.Br(),
dbc.Row([
    dbc.Col([
...
        dcc.Graph(id='gini_country_barchart')
    ]),
]),
dbc.Tabs([
    dbc.Tab([
...
```

Using one indicator, we created two dynamic charts, the first allowing users to explore the data for a given year, showing all available countries, and the other allowing them to explore data for all years, for a certain country. We also explored the two ways of displaying bars, horizontally and vertically, and discussed when it can be better to use each of the orientations.

We'll now move on to exploring how to plot multiple bar charts on the same figure, and see different ways of doing so. We will also explore a new set of indicators using those new techniques.

Exploring different ways of displaying multiple bar charts (stacked, grouped, overlaid, and relative)

When we want to display values for different countries but for the same years, we have several options for how to display multiple bars on each position of the *x* axis. *Figure 5.9* shows the different ways in which we can do that when visualizing two variables, **a** and **b**:

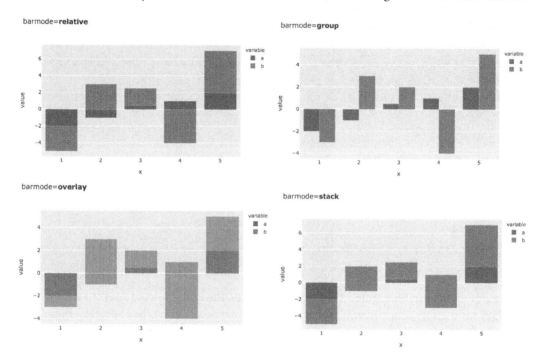

Figure 5.9 – Multiple bar charts displayed using different "barmode" options

The four bar charts in the preceding diagram show the same information, but in different ways. This can be set using the `barmode` parameter. With **relative**, bars are displayed on top of one another, with negative values below, and positive values above, the zero line. If you set it to **group**, then bars will be displayed next to one another. With **overlay**, bars are displayed in front of one another, and by default, we get some transparency in order to see both bars. Finally, if you set it to **stack**, you get them on top of one another, like relative, but in this case, the negative values cancel out the positives, as you can see for values 2 and 4 in the last chart. This is great if you want to compare proportions of each value to the total, especially if they all add up to the same total. This is what we will do with the income share indicators that are available in our dataset.

Creating the income share DataFrame

Let's take a look at the five columns that show the share of income for each of the five quintiles of countries' populations. We first create a subset of the `poverty` DataFrame, and call it `income_share_df`. This is done by filtering the columns using the regular expression shown here. We also drop missing values:

```
income_share_df =\
poverty.filter(regex='Country Name|^year$|Income share.*?20').
dropna()
income_share_df
```

Running the preceding code shows us a sample of rows from the newly created `income_share_df`, as you can see in *Figure 5.10*:

	Country Name	year	Income share held by fourth 20%	Income share held by highest 20%	Income share held by lowest 20%	Income share held by second 20%	Income share held by third 20%
67	Albania	1996	23.3	36.1	9.2	13.7	17.7
73	Albania	2002	22.2	40.4	8.4	12.6	16.5
76	Albania	2005	22.5	39.2	8.4	12.9	17.0
79	Albania	2008	22.2	39.0	8.9	13.1	16.8
83	Albania	2012	22.8	37.8	8.9	13.2	17.3
...	...	...	...	...	...	...	...
8229	Zambia	2006	19.1	59.5	3.5	6.8	11.1
8233	Zambia	2010	17.9	61.1	3.8	6.8	10.5
8238	Zambia	2016	19.3	61.3	2.9	6.0	10.6
8279	Zimbabwe	2011	21.0	49.7	5.8	9.5	14.0
8285	Zimbabwe	2017	20.6	51.1	6.0	9.1	13.2

1674 rows × 7 columns

Figure 5.10 – Sample rows showing income share quintiles per country

For every country and year combination, we have five values. Each value shows the percentage of income of the respective group's share of the total for that country and year. We want to let users select a country and, as a result, display a chart showing how the split of those five values changes across all available years. To get an idea of the end result, take a look at *Figure 5.11* showing those values for the United States:

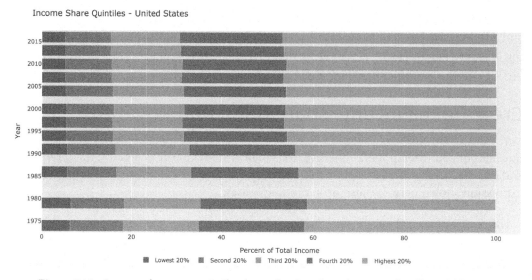

Figure 5.11 – Income shares per quintile, shown for the selected country for all available years

Since these values all add up to 100 (with minor rounding errors), we can have clearly comparable bars across the years, because they all have the same total length. Since these are proportions, we are interested in seeing the split for a particular year, and also how that split changed across years.

As you can see, it is very easy to see how things change for the rightmost and leftmost parts of the bars because they have the same baseline, whether at the beginning or the end. However, for the values in the middle, it's not easy to do so. The reason is that their size changes, as well as their baselines. So, the more divisions you add, the more difficult it gets to compare them across years. But since Plotly's charts are interactive, users can easily hover over the bars, get their exact values, and compare them.

Producing this chart should be straightforward. We already created our DataFrame, and have our values. We can just set the x and y values, and set `orientation='h'`, but the problem is that the categories are ordered alphabetically in the DataFrame, and we want them to be ordered according to their numeric meaning, from the lowest to the highest, so that their relative position can be easily understood by users. As usual, this is mainly a data manipulation challenge. So, let's do it:

1. We first need to rename the columns and order them by their value, from "lowest" to "highest." One way to do that is to prepend the column names with numbers and sort accordingly. This can easily be done using the `rename` method. After that, we sort the columns by using the `sort_index` method, and setting `axis=1`, which means the columns (as opposed to the index of the DataFrame):

```
income_share_df = income_share_df.rename(columns={
    'Income share held by lowest 20%': '1 Income share
held by lowest 20%',
    'Income share held by second 20%': '2 Income share
held by second 20%',
    'Income share held by third 20%': '3 Income share
held by third 20%',
    'Income share held by fourth 20%': '4 Income share
held by fourth 20%',
    'Income share held by highest 20%': '5 Income share
held by highest 20%'
}).sort_index(axis=1)
```

2. Check to see that our work is correct:

```
income_share_df.columns


Index(['1 Income share held by lowest 20%',
       '2 Income share held by second 20%',
       '3 Income share held by third 20%',
       '4 Income share held by fourth 20%',
       '5 Income share held by highest 20%',
       'Country Name', 'year'],
      dtype='object')
```

3. We now want to remove the redundant part of the columns and keep the position indicator together with "20%." We can use the standard library's `re` module for that. We replace any digit followed by `Income share held by` with an empty string. After that, we change the casing of the resulting string to title case:

```
import re
income_share_df.columns = [\
re.sub('\d Income share held by ', '', col).title() for
col in income_share_df.columns
]
```

4. We now create a variable, `income_share_cols`, to refer to the columns that we are interested in:

```
income_share_cols = income_share_df.columns[:-2]
income_share_cols
Index(['Lowest 20%', 'Second 20%', 'Third 20%', 'Fourth
20%', 'Highest 20%'], dtype='object')
```

5. Now, our DataFrame is ready for plotting with suitable and short names. We first create a `country` variable to use in filtering the DataFrame:

```
country = 'China'
```

6. Create the bar chart using `px.bar`. Note that when setting the value of the `x` parameter, we are using a list. Plotly Express can also work with wide format data, which is very convenient in such cases. We could have melted the DataFrame and used the approach we used in the previous chapter as well. We also set `orientation='h'` and `barmode='stack'`. The title will dynamically insert the country name, as you can see here:

```
fig = \
px.bar(income_share_df[income_share_df['Country
Name']==country].dropna(),
                x=income_share_cols,
                y='Year',
                hover_name='Country Name',
                orientation='h',
                barmode='stack',
                height=600,
                title=f'Income Share Quintiles - {country}')
fig.show()
```

7. You probably noticed that I assigned the result to a variable figure, and that is because we have a few minor details to improve. Running the preceding code produces the chart in *Figure 5.12*:

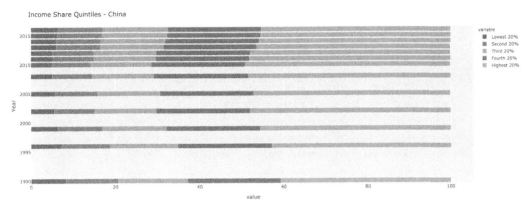

Income Share Quintiles - China

Figure 5.12 – Income shares per quintile, shown using the default options

8. The titles of the *x* axis, **value**, and the legend, **variable**, are not really informative. We will modify them, and place the legend keys right under the chart, using their logical ascending sequence. This can make it easier for readers to associate the values, and for readers on a grayscale interface, it can slightly improve things as well. As discussed in *Chapter 3, Working with Plotly's Figure Objects*, all these attributes belong under `fig.layout`, and setting them is straightforward. Note that the legend has the x and y attributes to set its position in the figure. We set the legend's x attribute to 0.25 to indicate that we want the legend to start at quarter the distance from the origin of the figure:

```
fig.layout.legend.orientation = 'h'
fig.layout.legend.title = None
fig.layout.xaxis.title = 'Percent of Total Income'
fig.layout.legend.x = 0.25
```

9.   Running the preceding code for Indonesia produces the final chart in *Figure 5.13*:

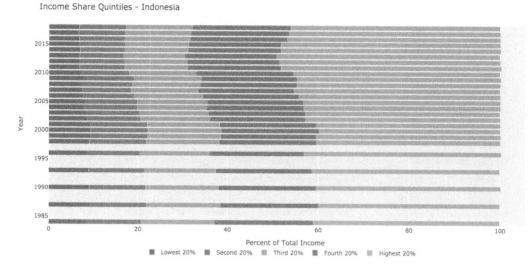

Figure 5.13 – Income shares per quintile, shown using customized options

Let's now put everything together and add the new features to our app.

Incorporating the functionality into our app

We are now ready to again add the new functionality to our app using the function and chart we just created. At this stage, not much explanation is required since we have done this enough times, but I will go through the main steps, and you can always refer to the code repository to check your work:

1.   At the top of the module, we first make the DataFrame definitions, as well as column changes, as we did. Make sure that the following code is placed after creating the `poverty` DataFrame because it depends on it:

```
income_share_df =\
poverty.filter(regex='Country Name|^year$|Income
share.*?20').dropna()
income_share_df = income_share_df.rename(columns={
    'Income share held by lowest 20%': '1 Income share
held by lowest 20%',
    'Income share held by second 20%': '2 Income share
held by second 20%',
```

```
    'Income share held by third 20%': '3 Income share
held by third 20%',
    'Income share held by fourth 20%': '4 Income share
held by fourth 20%',
    'Income share held by highest 20%': '5 Income share
held by highest 20%'
}).sort_index(axis=1)

income_share_df.columns =\
[re.sub('\d Income share held by ', '', col).title() for
col in income_share_df.columns]
income_share_cols = income_share_df.columns[:-2]
```

2. For the layout part, we require an h2 element as a title for the new section, a Dropdown component for countries, and a Graph component, right under the last charts we created for the Gini Index section:

```
dcc.Dropdown(id='income_share_country_dropdown',
             options=[{'label': country, 'value':
country}
                      for country in income_share_
df['Country Name'].unique()]),
dcc.Graph(id='income_share_country_barchart')
```

3. The callback function can be easily constructed using the code we just worked with, and it ends up as follows:

```
@app.callback(Output('income_share_country_barchart',
'figure'),
              Input('income_share_country_dropdown',
'value'))
def plot_income_share_barchart(country):
    if country is None:
        raise PreventUpdate
    fig =\
px.bar(income_share_df[income_share_df['Country
Name']==country].dropna(),
        x=income_share_cols,
        y='Year',
        barmode='stack',
```

```
            height=600,
            hover_name='Country Name',
            title=f'Income Share Quintiles - {country}',
            orientation='h')
    fig.layout.legend.title = None
    fig.layout.legend.orientation = 'h'
    fig.layout.legend.x = 0.25
    fig.layout.xaxis.title = 'Percent of Total Income'
    return fig
```

Adding this code in the right places should add the new functionality to our app. We now have multiple indicators that our users can interact with, and several of them provide different ways of looking at the data.

The four ways of displaying bar charts can be interesting, but in our case, if we want to allow users to compare more than one country, it would quickly become almost impossible to read. Going back to our Gini index country chart, for example, each selected country typically displays 20 to 30 bars, depending on how much data is available. For four countries, we are talking about around 100 bars, on half a page, which is really difficult to read.

How about allowing users to select as many countries as they want, and for each selected country, a separate chart is produced, so they can see the countries on multiple charts?

This is what faceting is all about, which we will explore next.

Using facets to split charts into multiple sub-charts – horizontally, vertically, or wrapped

This is a very powerful technique that allows us to add a new dimension to our analysis. We can select any feature (column) from our dataset to split the chart by. If you are expecting a long explanation of how it works, and what you need to learn to master it, don't. Just like most other things in Plotly Express, if you have a long-form (tidy) dataset, all you have to do is select a column and use its name for the `facet_col` or `facet_row` parameter. That's it.

Let's take a quick look at the available options for facets by looking at the relevant facet parameters:

- `facet_col`: This means you want to split the chart into columns, and the selected column name will be used to split them. This results in the charts being displayed side by side (as columns).

- `facet_row`: Similarly, if you want to split the chart into rows, you can use this parameter, which will split the chart into sub-charts displayed on top of one another.

- `facet_col_wrap`: This is really useful when you have a dynamic number of facets to produce. If you know your users will be generating multiple charts, after how many charts should the following chart be displayed on the next row in the resulting grid of charts? The answer should be an integer, and Plotly Express makes sure that after that number, the charts are displayed in the next row of charts. This ensures that for every row, we have a maximum number of columns of charts.

- `facet_row_spacing` and `facet_col_spacing`: As their names suggest, you can control the spacing between rows and columns by setting these values in the range [0, 1] as a fraction of the total figure size, horizontally or vertically.

Let's run a quick example to make sure this is clear:

1. Create a list of countries to filter by:

   ```
   countries = ['Algeria', 'Japan']
   ```

2. Modify the definition of `df` to filter the rows where `'Country Name'` is in `countries`. The pandas method `isin` can be used for this:

   ```
   df =\
   gini_df[gini_df['Country Name'].isin(countries)].
   dropna(subset=[gini])
   ```

3. Run `px.bar` with the simple addition of `facet_row='Country Name'`:

   ```
   px.bar(df,
          x='year',
          y=gini,
          facet_row='Country Name')
   ```

Running this code produces the chart in *Figure 5.14*:

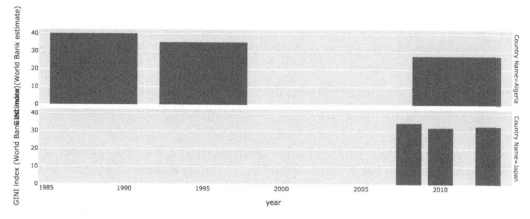

Figure 5.14 – Two bar charts generated using the facet_row parameter

4. It's very easy to extend our charts, as you can see, and we also get the sub-charts labeled for us with the correct country names. It still doesn't look as good as we would like it to be. The *y* axis titles are overlapping, and you have to look hard at the vertical titles to see which sub-chart belongs to which country. So let's improve things. Let's first start by modifying the *y* axis titles, which can be done using the `labels` parameter, by providing a dictionary and mapping the default name to the new name that we want:

```
labels={gini: 'Gini Index'}
```

5. We can also help the user to quickly identify the charts by coloring the bars by country. This will make them distinctive and will also produce a legend with colored guides, making it even easier to distinguish the charts. Again this is done by simply providing an argument to the `color` parameter, which is basically a selection of the column name that we want to use for that:

```
color='Country Name'
```

6. Another helpful thing would be to add a dynamic title to the figure as a whole. We can display the full indicator name, and underneath that, we can show a comma-separated list of the selected countries. Plotly annotations support some HTML tags, and we will use the `<br>` tag to separate the indicator name and the country list as follows:

```
title='<br>'.join([gini, ', '.join(countries)])
```

7. Having two countries on the chart is easy to read, but what if the users decide to select seven? As we did with the dynamic height of the Gini index horizontal bar chart, we also need to set a dynamic height for the faceted bar charts based on the number of selected countries. We will use the same technique, but with different values, because we are managing sub-plots, and not horizontal bars:

```
height=100 + 250*len(countries)
```

8. The full updated code can be seen here:

```
px.bar(df,
        x='year',
        y=gini,
        facet_row='Country Name',
        labels={gini: 'Gini Index'},
        color='Country Name',
        title='<br>'.join([gini, ', '.join(countries)]),
        height=100 + 250*len(countries))
```

9. The final chart can be seen in *Figure 5.15*, shown for three countries:

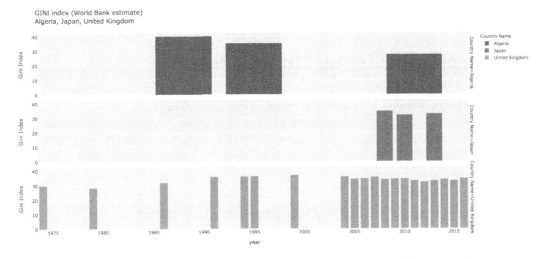

Figure 5.15 – Three bar charts generated using the facet_row parameter with customized options

The figure and function have now been updated to produce faceted charts, based on the selected countries. The only remaining change that we have to make is to set the dropdown providing the options for this, to allow multiple selections. We will do this next, as well as taking a general view of our current dashboard, and see how to improve its layout and usability.

Exploring additional features of dropdowns

The Dropdown component has an optional parameter, multi, that takes a Boolean argument, which we can set to True to allow this:

```
dcc.Dropdown(id='gini_country_dropdown',
            multi=True,
            options=[{'label': country, 'value': country}
                    for country in gini_df['Country Name'].
unique()]),
```

You can now make the changes and use the Gini country bar chart for as many countries as you like. The height of that figure on the page dynamically expands/collapses based on the dynamic height that we set, so we also don't need to worry about this aspect of the layout. The users will manage it themselves while interacting with the components. Let's now see whether it's easy for a newcomer to use those options.

Adding placeholder text to dropdowns

If you look at the Gini Index section of the app for the first time, you will see two dropdowns that allow you to make a selection, as shown in *Figure 5.16*:

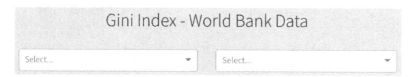

Figure 5.16 – Dropdowns without any placeholder text

But select what exactly?

The Dropdown component has an optional placeholder parameter, which can be very useful for users to know what exactly they are selecting.

We can easily update our placeholder text for both `Dropdown` components to make it clearer to users:

```
placeholder="Select a year"
placeholder="Select one or more countries"
```

We can make it even more explicit by using the `Label` component from Dash Bootstrap Components, which, as the name suggests, provides a label. These labels can be placed above the dropdowns:

```
dbc.Label("Year")
dbc.Label("Countries")
```

Adding the new options results in the updated messages as shown in *Figure 5.17*:

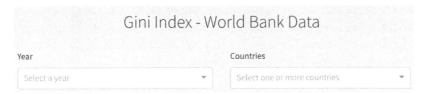

Figure 5.17 – Dropdowns with placeholder text and labels

I think it looks easier to use this way. We are also making it clear which one accepts a single option, and which accepts multiple ones. We can also do the same for the Income Share Distribution section by adding a similar label, Country, and a placeholder, Select a country.

Our app is now getting bigger, and provides many more options. It's good to take a general look and see how to improve the overall look and feel of the app, make it easier to use, and use a consistent theme across all figures.

Modifying the app's theme

We already saw how easy it is to change the theme of our app, which can be done by providing a list as an argument to the `external_style_sheets` parameter while instantiating the app. You can play around with the available ones, and we can set it to COSMO:

```
app = dash.Dash(__name__,
                external_stylesheets=[dbc.themes.COSMO])
```

This should modify several visual elements of our app.

Another thing we can consider doing is making our theme consistent with the theme of the charts that we are using. We can set the background color of the app to the same default color used in Plotly's figures. Using the `style` parameter in the top-level `html.Div`, we can set the background color to match that of the default Plotly color:

```
app.layout = html.Div([

    ...

], style={'backgroundColor': '#E5ECF6'})
```

One more change is needed to make this complete.

Plotly's `Figure` object contains two main areas, the "plot" and the "paper" areas. The plot area is the inner rectangle within the *x* and *y* axes. In all the charts that we produced, this is the area colored light blue (or gray, if you are reading the printed book).

The bigger rectangle enclosing the smaller one is the "paper" area. In the charts we have produced so far, it has been colored white. We can also set its color to the same color, making all background colors the same for our app. We simply have to add the following line to the callback functions that generate charts:

```
fig.layout.paper_bgcolor = '#E5ECF6'
```

If we run the app now, we will get some empty figures with a white background for the ones where we did not set default values. For those, we also need to create empty figures, but set the background colors to be consistent with the whole app theme. Doing this is very simple, as we did in *Chapter 3, Working with Plotly's Figure Objects*. The `dcc.Graph` component has a `figure` attribute, to which we can add the empty figures with the desired background colors. These will be modified when users make a selection. Because we have a few instances of those, it's better to create a function that can be used to create such figures whenever we want them. The following code achieves that:

```
import plotly.graph_objects as go


def make_empty_fig():
    fig = go.Figure()
    fig.layout.paper_bgcolor =  '#E5ECF6'
    fig.layout.plot_bgcolor = '#E5ECF6'
    return fig
```

Now, we can add the call to `make_empty_fig` where required, as you can see in the following example:

```
dcc.Graph(id='gini_year_barchart',
          figure=make_empty_fig())
```

With this, we have chosen a new overall theme and made sure that we have consistent background colors across all the elements of our app.

Resizing components

Another thing we need to handle is how the resizing of the browser window affects the size and placement of our different components. The figures are responsive by default, but we need to make some decisions for the figures that are placed side by side. In the Gini Index section, we have two such charts, placed in two `dbc.Col` components next to each other. All we have to do is set the desired size for those charts for large-, `lg`, as well as medium-, `md`, sized screens:

```
dbc.Col([

    ...

], md=12, lg=5),
```

When on a large screen, `lg`, the most likely scenario, each figure will have a size of 5 (out of 12), which is how the screen is split by Bootstrap. You can refer to the discussion on Bootstrap layouts, columns, and rows, as well as its grid system, in *Chapter 1, Overview of the Dash Ecosystem*, if you want a refresher. On medium-sized screens, `md`, the figures will expand to occupy 12 out of 12 columns, which means that they will take the full width of the screen at that size.

When we started learning about interactivity, we created a simple report at the top of our app. It displays the population of the selected country/region for the year 2010. We can remove this component, as it is very limited in functionality and was mainly used for illustration purposes. This can simply be done by deleting the component, together with the output area underneath it, as well as the callback that handles it.

As a result of the work we have done in this chapter, you can see in *Figure 5.18* what our app now looks like:

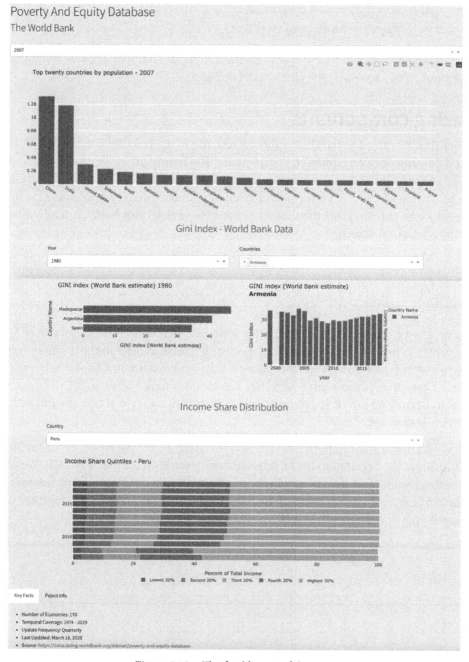

Figure 5.18 – The final layout of the app

I strongly encourage you to make these changes manually yourself, without looking at the code provided in the repository. I also encourage you to test out other layouts, play with different options, and generate lots of errors!

Making changes all the time and being in control of your code requires a consistent naming convention of the components, callbacks, and variables. It also helps if you follow a certain logical flow in the organization of your components. We will be doing these things many times, and hopefully you will master these techniques along the way.

Our app is now looking better, easier to use, and can even be shared with others if you want to. We covered many things in this chapter, taking our app to a new level, so let's recap the things that we covered.

Summary

We focused mainly on bar charts in this chapter. We also used `Dropdown` components in several ways. We saw the pros and cons of using horizontal and vertical orientation, and we actually implemented both in our app. We then analyzed the different ways in which multiple bar charts can be displayed together, and we implemented one showing the proportions of a total value. We then explored facets and saw how they enrich our figures and make them flexible and scalable. We also linked that to dropdowns, which allow multiple selections. After making sure that everything is working fine, we gave our app a facelift by choosing a new theme and making sure that all background colors are consistent. We also managed the layout for different screen sizes by setting different sizes for our figures for different screen sizes. A few helpful messages were added to make the app easier to use. Finally, we took a screenshot of the resulting app!

In the next chapter, we will explore one of the most ubiquitous chart types – the scatter plot. We will also explore how to use it together with sliders that allow users to select and modify values or ranges of values.

6
Exploring Variables with Scatter Plots and Filtering Subsets with Sliders

We are now going to tackle one of the most versatile, useful, and ubiquitous types of charts, the **scatter plot**. As its name implies, we basically scatter markers (which can be points, squares, circles, bubbles, or other symbols) on the Cartesian plane, where mainly their horizontal and vertical distances express the values they represent. Other visual attributes, such as size, color, and symbol, might be used to express other attributes, as we saw in some previous examples. As most of the fundamentals regarding figures and creating charts have been covered, we won't be spending much time on that, focusing instead on the particular details and options available to scatter plots. We will also explore and work with **sliders** as a new interactive component. Let's start right away, but first, here are the topics that we will be covering:

- Learning about the different ways of using scatter plots: markers, lines, and text
- Creating multiple scatter traces in a single plot

- Mapping and setting colors with scatter plots
- Handling over-plotting and outlier values by managing opacity, symbols, and scales
- Introducing sliders and range sliders
- Customizing the marks and values of sliders

Technical requirements

The same tools that we used in the previous chapter will be used here. We will also focus a little on Plotly's `graph_objects` module for creating scatter plots, because it provides other tools and is very useful when customizing our plots further. The packages to use are Plotly, Dash, Dash Core Components, Dash HTML Components, Dash Bootstrap Components, pandas, and JupyterLab.

The code files of this chapter can be found on GitHub at `https://github.com/PacktPublishing/Interactive-Dashboards-and-Data-Apps-with-Plotly-and-Dash/tree/master/chapter_06`.

Check out the following video to see the Code in Action at `https://bit.ly/3ancblu`.

We start by exploring the different ways, or the different things, if you want, that we can plot with scatter plots.

Learning about the different ways of using scatter plots: markers, lines, and text

We have a number of different options when using `graph_objects` to create scatter plots, as mentioned in the introduction, so we will be exploring it together with Plotly Express. To give you an idea of the versatility of the available scatter plots, the following code extracts all the `scatter` methods available to the `Figure` object, as well as those available in Plotly Express:

```
import plotly.graph_objects as go
import plotly.express as px


fig = go.Figure()
[f for f in dir(fig) if 'scatter' in f]
['add_scatter',
 'add_scatter3d',
```

```
'add_scattercarpet',
'add_scattergeo',
'add_scattergl',
'add_scattermapbox',
'add_scatterpolar',
'add_scatterpolargl',
'add_scatterternary']
```

```
[f for f in dir(px) if 'scatter' in f]
['scatter',
 'scatter_3d',
 'scatter_geo',
 'scatter_mapbox',
 'scatter_matrix',
 'scatter_polar',
 'scatter_ternary']
```

As you can see, there are some overlaps in the available methods, and there are also some methods that aren't available in both modules. We won't go into all of them, but it's good to know them, because you can easily utilize your knowledge of regular scatter plots for the other types. Let's now take a look at some of the differences between using those options.

Markers, lines, and text

One interesting option that is available in the go.Scatter object is the mode parameter. This can take any combination of markers, lines, and/or text. You can specify one, two, or all three options together. When specifying more than one option, you have to specify them as a single string, where elements are separated by the plus sign, for example, "markers+text". Let's first get to know the indicators that we are going to focus on in this chapter, and immediately explore the plotting options:

1. Run the required imports and create the poverty DataFrame:

    ```
    import pandas as pd
    import plotly.graph_objects as go
    poverty = pd.read_csv('data/poverty.csv')
    ```

2. Our dataset contains three levels of daily income at which poverty is measured. They measure "the mean shortfall in income or consumption from the poverty line – $1.90 a day". They also have the same measure for two other levels, $3.20 and $5.50. They are also available as absolute counts in different columns, but we will focus on the percentages in this chapter. Their columns start with "Poverty gap" which we can use as a pattern to extract the columns that we want:

```
perc_pov_cols =\
poverty.filter(regex='Poverty gap').columns
perc_pov_cols
Index(['Poverty gap at $1.90 a day (2011 PPP) (%)',
       'Poverty gap at $3.20 a day (2011 PPP) (% of
population)',
       'Poverty gap at $5.50 a day (2011 PPP) (% of
population)'],
      dtype='object')
```

3. To make things simple, we will be starting all related variable names and objects with `perc_pov_` to make it clear that we are dealing with the poverty percentages. Keep in mind that we now have several objects and functions in the app, and we want to make sure we keep things simple, clear, and consistent. We now use the list we just created to create three variables, one for each poverty level:

```
perc_pov_19 = perc_pov_cols[0]
perc_pov_32 = perc_pov_cols[1]
perc_pov_55 = perc_pov_cols[2]
```

4. As usual, we need to look at the description of those indicators and, most importantly, at the limitations that they may have:

```
series[series['Indicator Name']==\
perc_pov_19]['Short definition'][25]
```

```
'Poverty gap at $1.90 a day (2011 PPP) is the mean
shortfall in income or consumption from the poverty
line $1.90 a day (counting the nonpoor as having zero
shortfall), expressed as a percentage of the poverty
line. This measure reflects the depth of poverty as
well as its incidence. As a result of revisions in PPP
exchange rates, poverty rates for individual countries
cannot be compared with poverty rates reported in earlier
editions.'
```

5. The definitions are pretty much the same for the three indicators, and the
    limitations are also similar to what we saw in the previous chapter. Feel free to read
    the details, but keep in mind that these are not perfect numbers, and we have to
    be careful if we were to make any interpretations. We now create a variable for a
    country and use it to create a subset DataFrame containing the data for country
    and perc_pov_19:

```
country = 'China'
df =\
poverty[poverty['Country Name']==country][['year', perc_
pov_19]].dropna()
```

6. Create a Figure and then add a scatter plot to it, using the relevant method. The
    mode parameter should be given one of the options discussed previously, and it is
    shown here simply as mode:

```
fig = go.Figure()
fig.add_scatter(x=df['year'],
                y=df[perc_pov_19],
                text=df[perc_pov_19],
                mode=mode)
fig.show()
```

Figure 6.1 shows the effect of running the preceding code with each of the possible options for mode, with the figure titles showing how to set this option:

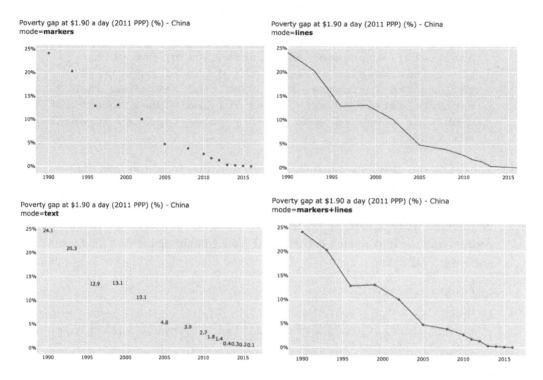

Figure 6.1 – Different ways of setting the mode parameter for scatter plots

You can also see the other options in *Figure 6.2*:

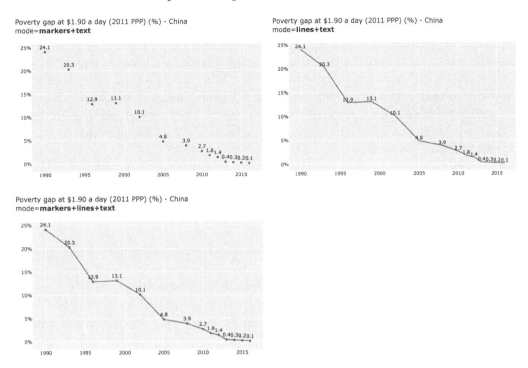

Figure 6.2 – Other ways of setting the mode parameter for scatter plots

Plotly Express has separate functions for scatter and line plots. You can plot text using the `scatter` function, which can be done by either choosing which column of your DataFrame contains the text to plot, or by providing a list of the text elements. The Plotly Express `scatter` function contains a `text` parameter that can be used for that.

Let's now take a look at how we can utilize this code to create multiple scatter plot traces.

Creating multiple scatter traces in a single plot

We will mostly be focusing on using Plotly Express as much as possible, because of its convenience, and the other advantages previously discussed in *Chapter 4, Data Manipulation and Preparation - Paving the Way to Plotly Express*. It's still very important to know how to work with `Figure` objects as you will encounter many situations where you will need to work with them, especially when you have a lot of customizations to make. Also, keep in mind that although the most important chart types are supported by Plotly Express, not all of them are.

Let's extend the preceding chart with traces of other countries and compare the two approaches. We start with the `graph_objects` module's `Figure` object:

1. Create a `countries` list to filter with:

    ```
    countries = ['Argentina', 'Mexico', 'Brazil']
    ```

2. Create a subset of `poverty`, which we will call `df`, where the values of the `Country Name` column are in the `countries` list (using the `isin` method). We then extract the `year`, `Country Name`, and `perc_pov_19` columns and drop the missing values:

    ```
    df = (poverty
         [poverty['Country Name'].isin(countries)]
         [['year','Country Name', perc_pov_19]]
         .dropna())
    ```

3. Create a `Figure` object, assigning it to a variable, `fig`:

    ```
    fig = go.Figure()
    ```

4. We now want to add a trace for each country that we want to plot. This can be done by looping over the countries and creating a sub-DataFrame that contains only data for the current country:

    ```
    for country in countries:
        df_country = df[df['Country Name']==country]
    ```

5. We now add a new trace (within the same loop, and at the same level of indentation) by using the `add_scatter` method. Note that we set `mode='markers+lines'` and we use the `name` attribute to set the title of this trace in the legend:

```
fig.add_scatter(x=df_country['year'],
                y=df_country[perc_pov_19],
                name=country,
                mode='markers+lines')
```

6. We also need to add a title for the *y*-axis, and then we can easily show the figure:

```
fig.layout.yaxis.title = perc_pov_19
fig.show()
```

Running the preceding code produces the chart in *Figure 6.3*:

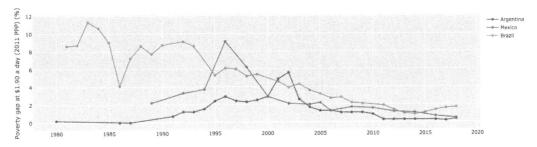

Figure 6.3 – Creating multiple scatter plots using the graph_objects module

Now, let's compare that to how we would do it with Plotly Express. The code to produce it is so short, clear, and intuitive that it barely warrants an explanation:

```
px.scatter(df, x='year', y=perc_pov_19, color='Country Name')
```

We chose the value for the data_frame parameter and selected which columns we want for the x, y, and color parameters from df. The code then produces the chart in *Figure 6.4*:

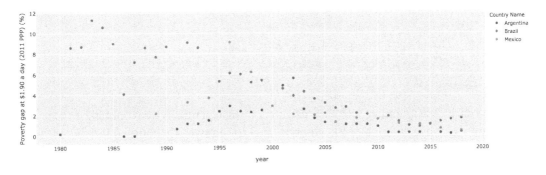

Figure 6.4 – Creating multiple scatter plots using Plotly Express

We also get the axes labeled automatically and the legend labeled properly, and we even have a title for the legend, using the column name that we selected for the color parameter.

There is a minor issue though. The disconnected points are not as easy to read as in the previous chart. This is especially important in this case because we are expressing a sequence of events, and the lines make it much clearer. With interactive dashboards, we don't know what our users are going to select, which means that they might produce charts that are even harder to read than this one. Plotly Express has separate functions for scatter and line plots, so in order to make it a "lines+markers" plot, we need to assign this to a Figure object and then add line traces. Here are the steps to do this:

1. Create a Figure object and assign it to a variable, fig:

```
fig = px.scatter(df,
                 x='year',
                 y=perc_pov_19,
                 color='Country Name')
```

2. Create another Figure object, exactly like the previous one, with a different name and chart type:

```
fig_lines = px.line(df,
                    x='year',
                    y=perc_pov_19,
                    color='Country Name')
```

3. From fig_lines, we want to add its traces to fig. If you remember, the traces can be found under the data attribute of the Figure object. The data attribute is a tuple with each element corresponding to a trace. So, we need to loop over those traces (of the data attribute) and add them to fig:

```
for trace in fig_lines.data:
    trace.showlegend = False
    fig.add_trace(trace)
fig.show()
```

Note that each new line trace will have its label on the legend. So we would have redundant line labels in the legend, which we had to remove. We handled that by setting the showlegend attribute to False for each of the traces. Running this code produces the chart in *Figure 6.5*:

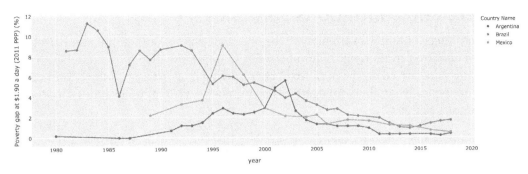

Figure 6.5 – Creating multiple scatter and line plots using Plotly Express

Comparing the mental effort and amount of code required to produce the same chart in two different approaches, we can see that there wasn't that much of a difference. This is typical when you want to produce something customized and/or something good enough for publishing. Still, for exploration purposes, Plotly Express is clearly a great starting point, and once you get a good idea of the data, you can better decide which approach to adopt.

We have seen an example of implicitly managing color on scatter plots (the colors were automatically set or us), and we are now ready to explore more options for managing color. If you are reading this on the printed grayscale version, you will see different shades of colors that might be distinguishable, but as we did previously, we will also use symbols to make it explicit and easy to understand.

Let's now explore the different options that we have for managing color.

Mapping and setting colors with scatter plots

Colors are extremely important in conveying and expressing information about our charts. It is also a very big topic, and a full discussion is beyond the scope of this book. We will focus on colors for two types of variables – discrete and continuous. We will also tackle two ways of using colors in our charts: mapping variables to colors, and manually setting our colors.

We start by exploring the differences between the two types of variables.

Discrete and continuous variables

Simply speaking, continuous variables are the ones that can take an infinite number of possible values in a certain range of numbers. For example, population is a number that can take any value, based on the number of people living in a certain country. Continuous variables are typically numbers (integers or real numbers). Height, weight, and speed are other examples as well.

Discrete variables, on the other hand, are variables that can take the value of any one of a limited set of items. Most importantly, discrete variables cannot take values in between the items. Countries are one such example. A country can either be country A or country B, but can't be 10% A and 90% B. Discrete variables are typically text variables, and usually have a relatively small number of unique items.

The way we use color to express the nature of our variables is as follows:

- For continuous variables, we use a color scale that takes on colors that gradually change between two or more colors, as the values they represent change. For example, if our color scale starts as white for the lowest value, and ends up as blue at the highest value, all values in between would take on varying shades of white and blue. A marker that has a color that contains more blue than white means that its value is closer to the maximum value of that variable and vice versa. We will try this shortly.

- Discrete variables are distinct items, and the colors we use for them need to be as distinct from each other as possible, especially the ones that appear next to each other. Examples will make this clear, and we start with continuous variables.

Using color with continuous variables

Using the same metric we started with, we want to take an arbitrary year and plot the indicator value for each of the countries. We already know how to do this. We now want to add a new dimension to our chart. We want to use color to show another value, for example, population. This will allow us to see whether there is any correlation between population and the metric we are plotting (poverty at $1.90 in this case). Let's prepare our variables and data:

1. Create variables for the indicator and year of choice:

```
indicator = perc_pov_19
year = 1991
```

2. Using the indicator and year, we create a subset of `poverty` where the year column is equal to our variable, `year`, and the `is_country` column is `True`. We then drop the missing values and sort the values according to this column. The following code achieves this:

```
df =\
poverty[poverty['year'].eq(year) & poverty['is_
country']].dropna(subset=[indicator]).sort_
values(indicator)
```

3. All we have to do is select the column we want for mapping its values to the appropriate colors, and we do this as we usually do with Plotly Express:

```
px.scatter(df,
            x=indicator,
            y='Country Name',
            color='Population, total')
```

The preceding code produces the chart in *Figure 6.6*:

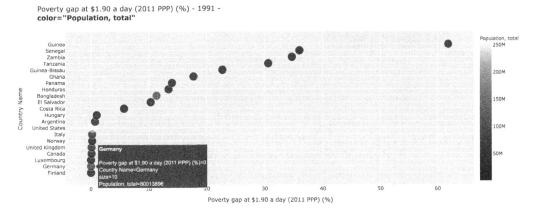

Figure 6.6 – Setting color for continuous variables with Plotly Express

We basically added a new layer to our visualization with the column that we selected. Each visual attribute adds another dimension to the chart, and makes it richer, but adding too many dimensions might make it overwhelming and difficult to read. It's up to us to strike the right balance and make sure we are presenting something meaningful and readable to our audience.

We can immediately see that the country with the highest population in the chart (the United States, in bright yellow) has one of the lowest values for our indicator. We can also see that since most other markers are closer to purple in color, this shows that the country with the highest population has quite an extreme value for that metric compared to the others. It seems to be an outlier in population, but not so, with the poverty indicator. The popup that appears when we hover over a marker also takes the same color and, being much bigger than the marker, makes it very easy to relate the color to its relative position on the color bar. The color **scale** that we have here is only one of tens of scales that we can chose from. Changing that is also very easy, and we simply need to provide the name of that scale to the parameter, `color_scale_continuous`. We can see how to do that, as well as its effect, in *Figure 6.7*, where we chose the **cividis** scale:

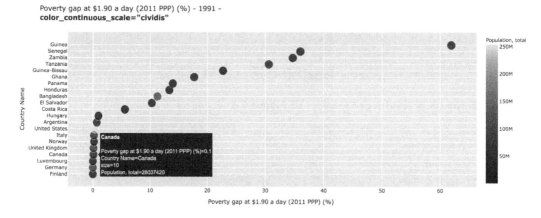

Figure 6.7 – Choosing a different continuous color scale

There is no additional information in this chart, only that we changed the color scale to a different one. It's intuitive to understand this color scale, as it moves between dark blue and bright yellow, and all combinations of colors in between. The scale is also known as a "sequential" scale, because it shows how values move from a low to a high value. You can get a full list of named color scales by running `px.colors.named_colorscales()`, which will return the names of those scales. More interesting is the option to see all those scales and compare them, so you can choose which one you want. You can produce a chart with all available scales of a certain type by running `px.colors.sequential.swatches()`, and you can see part of the output in *Figure 6.8*:

plotly.colors.sequential

Figure 6.8 – The first few sequential scales available in Plotly

Another interesting way of showing the color scales in action is by using the `swatches_continuous` functions. For example, *Figure 6.9* shows the result of running `px.colors.sequential.swatches_continuous()`:

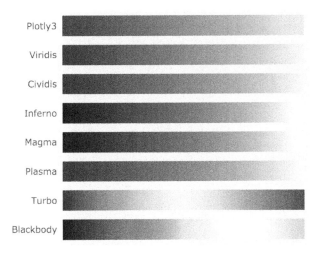

Figure 6.9 – The first few sequential scales available in Plotly as they would appear in a color bar

This gives an even better idea of how they would actually look, and shows colors with smooth transitions in between.

You can use the `swatches` functions for other types of color scales and sequences. You simply run the previous command and replace `sequential` with any of the following: `carto`, `cmocean`, `colorbrewer`, `cyclical`, `diverging`, or `qualitative`.

So far, we have mapped the data values and colors automatically by choosing which column's values we want to use for that. There is also the option of manually setting the color scales.

Manually creating color scales

One way of doing this is by providing a list of two or more colors to the `color_continuous_scale` parameter. By default, the first color you provide will be assigned to the minimum value and the last color to the maximum value. Values in between will take combinations, resulting in shades of the two colors. This shows how close the data point is to each of the extremes. We'll see an example of using more than two colors shortly. Using the same code and setting `color_continuous_scale=["steelblue", "darkorange"]` produces the chart in *Figure 6.10*:

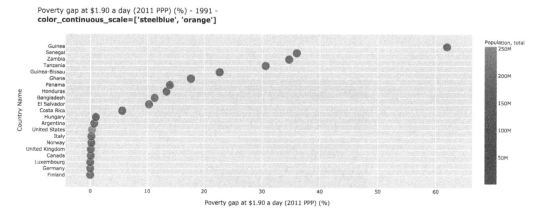

Figure 6.10 – Manually setting continuous color scales

This gives a glimpse of how granular the options are, and this is barely scratching the surface of what is available. Sometimes, you may want to rescale your data so the colors adopt a smoother progression from the minimum to the maximum. The charts we just created are a good candidate for this. We have one outlier when it comes to population, so it might be better to set the `color` parameter to a scaled version of our data if we want to do that. In general, because there are numerous scales that are well-established and tested, it is better to choose from them instead of manually setting your own colors. Another important consideration is color blindness, and trying to use scales that cater for people who have it. You don't want to use colors that are indistinguishable by some of your readers. You can run a simple check by searching online as to whether or not a color scale is colorblind-friendly.

Let's now set a scale that uses three colors. The `RdBu` (red blue) scale goes from red to blue, with mid values taking white as their color. It is one of the default scales. Let's quickly plot a simple chart with this scale:

```
y = [-2, -1, 0, 1, 2, 3, 4, 5, 6]
px.scatter(x=range(1, len(y)+1),
           y=y,
           color=y,
           color_continuous_scale='RdBu')
```

We created a list of integers in the range [-2, 6] and mapped their colors to the `RdBu` scale, which produces the chart in *Figure 6.11*:

Figure 6.11 – Manually setting a continuous diverging color scale

In this case, you can see the colors moving from red to white to blue, passing through the intermediate shades of each color. This is also known as a "diverging" scale. There is a midpoint (the white point in this case) where colors diverge, signifying two different types of values. Usually, we use this to show values above and below a certain value. In this case, we wanted to show negative values in red, zero values in white, and positive values in blue. But we didn't get that. The white midpoint was set as the midpoint of the data, which happens to be the fifth element of our list, and its value is 2.

This can be fixed by using the `color_continuous_midpoint` parameter, as you can see in *Figure 6.12*:

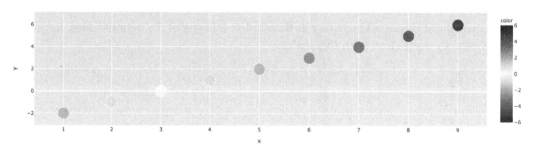

Figure 6.12 – Manually setting a midpoint for a continuous diverging color scale

We now have a more meaningful midpoint, where the divergence in color makes it easy to see positive and negative values. Another important thing this achieves is that it also shows us how skewed the data is. Note that we don't have any red markers in the chart. We have two pinkish ones, while we have more blue values. This perfectly corresponds to the list of numbers, which contains two negative, and six positive values. The color bar also makes it clear that we are only covering part of the red spectrum, while blue is fully covered.

There are many other options for setting colors, scaling the data, and expressing different values. I encourage you to learn more about this topic, and the good news is that Plotly provides options to customize colors the way you want.

Let's now see how color works with discrete variables.

Using color with discrete variables

The objective now is not to visualize the degrees of difference between values. We now want to group values based on a criterion and see the differences across those groups of values. We can immediately see what happens if we simply set the `color` parameter to a column that has text values. For example, we can set `color="Income Group"` to get the chart in *Figure 6.13*:

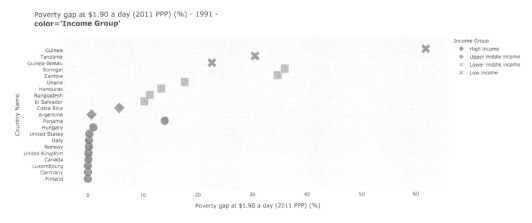

Figure 6.13 – Using color with categorical variables

Everything was automatically handled for us. Simply because we chose a column with text values, Plotly Express grouped the data according to that column, and chose a sequence of colors that are distinct from one another, so we can see how values change across the groups. We also used symbols to make it easier to see, especially on a grayscale version of the chart. This was achieved by setting `symbol='Income Group'`.

As with continuous variables, we can also set our own discrete color sequence by providing one to the `color_discrete_sequence` parameter. *Figure 6.14* shows the effect of setting this parameter, by using one of the sequences provided by Plotly:

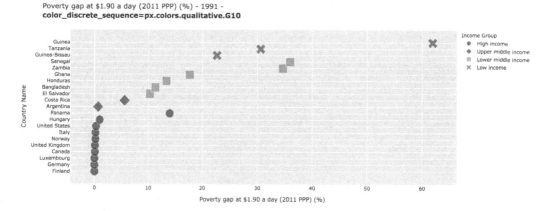

Figure 6.14 – Setting a different color sequence for categorical variables

Note that we have chosen a sequence by getting it from the available list, `px.colors.qualitative.G10`, and as you may have guessed, you can generate all the available sequences by running `px.colors.qualitative.swatches()`.

As we did with continuous variables, we can also manually set the colors of our discrete variables by providing a list of named colors. We can also use the colors' hexadecimal representation, for example, `#aeae14`, or the RGB values, for example, `'rgb(25, 85, 125)'`. Passing our chosen colors to the `color_discrete_sequence` parameter, we get the chart in *Figure 6.15*:

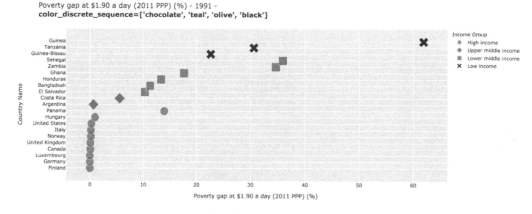

Figure 6.15 – Manually setting the colors of a sequence for categorical variables

When you manually select the colors of your choice, you need to make sure that you provide a list of colors that has the same number of elements as the unique values of the variable you are trying to visualize. Otherwise, it will cycle through the colors you provided, and this might be misleading. Again, it's usually better to select from the available established sequences, but you can set them manually if you want to. When we set the colors that we want, we didn't specify which item should take which color. We simply stated that we want the unique values to take this set of colors. Sometimes, you may want to explicitly map certain colors to certain categories. Once you know the unique values, you can provide a dictionary to the `color_discrete_map` parameter, and then map each value to the color of your choice:

```
color_discrete_map={'High income': 'darkred',
                    'Upper middle income': 'steelblue',
                    'Lower middle income': 'orange',
                    'Low income': 'darkblue'}
```

Setting this option produces the chart in *Figure 6.16*:

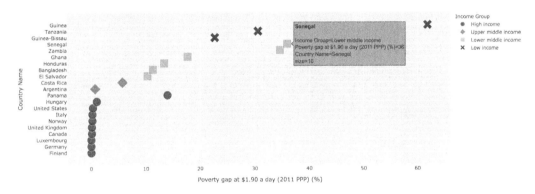

Figure 6.16 – Manually setting the colors for each value of a sequence for categorical variables

Note that most continuous variable parameters contains "scale," while the discrete ones contain "sequence." This can help in remembering and understanding the fundamental difference in the process of mapping colors to the two kinds of variables.

With continuous variables, we are giving the readers the ability to see the approximate value of the markers based on the color, as well as the relative position in the dataset. It is not clear cut, but you can tell that the population of a certain country is around twenty million, and that it looks like it's one of the highest countries in this dataset. Users can, of course, hover and get the exact value if they want. With discrete variables, we are basically more interested in grouping by those variables and seeing trends across those groups.

We covered a small subset of what can be done with colors, and now we move to consider a few other issues that might arise with scatter plots, namely, outliers and having many data points to plot.

Handling over-plotting and outlier values by managing opacity, symbols, and scales

Let's say we are now interested in seeing the relationship between our variable and population for the same year that we have been working on. We want to have `Population, total` on the *x*-axis, and `perc_pov_19` on the *y*-axis.

We first create a subset of `poverty` where `year` is equal to 2010, and `is_country` is True, and sort the values using `Population, total`:

```
df =\
poverty[poverty['year'].eq(2010) & poverty['is_country']].sort_
values('Population, total')
```

Let's now see what it looks like when we plot those two variables. Here is the code:

```
px.scatter(df,
           y=perc_pov_19,
           x='Population, total',
           title=' - '.join([perc_pov_19, '2010']),
           height=500)
```

Running this produces the chart in *Figure 6.17*:

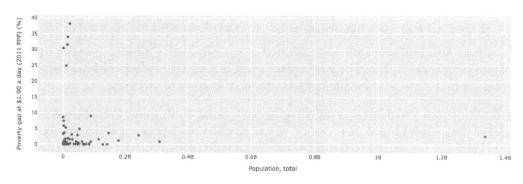

Figure 6.17 – Over-plotting and outliers in charts

The existence of one outlier, China, with a population close to 1.4 billion, forces all markers to be squeezed to a very narrow part of our chart. We also have a small cluster of values above 25 on the y-axis, but the difference is nowhere as extreme as the horizontal one. Another important issue is that there are many markers on top of one another. Having solid-colored markers means that if you plot one marker on top of another, it will not make any difference; not even a thousand markers will. The existence of the two issues together make it a very challenging chart to read.

We are going to explore a few techniques that might help with these situations, and evaluate when and how they might be useful.

Since we have many points crowded on a very small part of the chart, we are likely to have several of them overlapping. Let's see the effect of changing the opacity and size of the markers.

Controlling the opacity and size of markers

The `opacity` parameter takes values in the range [0, 1], inclusive. We can manually give it a number to control how opaque we want our markers to be. A value of 0 means completely transparent, which can also be thought of as a way to hide our markers (or a subset of them). A value of 1 means the markers will be fully opaque, taking whatever color they were assigned, and fully covering the area they are on. This also means that an `opacity` of 0.1 means that the marker will be 10% opaque. The practical implication for that is that it means that it will take 10 markers on top of one another to completely cover the area they are plotted on. If we set it to 0.5 (or 50%), this means that two markers would fully cover the area, and so on.

Since the markers are quite small, and we don't have that many values, we can also increase their size for better visibility. The `size` parameter, just like all other parameters, can take the name of a column in our DataFrame, or a list of numbers. This is another visual attribute that we can use to express the values of a certain column where the relative sizes reflect the relative value that each marker represents. It is also sometimes called a bubble chart. For this case, we want to provide a fixed size. This can easily be done by providing a list having the same length as the DataFrame we are analyzing. This would give the markers a uniform default size, which might not be what we want, so we can control it with the `size_max` parameter. Reusing the same code and setting `opacity=0.1`, `size=[5]*len(df)`, and `size_max=15`, we get the chart in *Figure 6.18*:

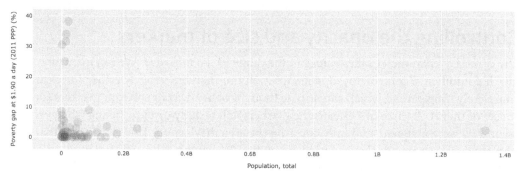

Figure 6.18 – Modifying the opacity and size of markers

This looks a little better. We have bigger markers, and with an `opacity` of `0.1`, we can better see that the majority of markers are concentrated very close to the origin. Most likely, there is more nuance than that, but because of the outlier that we have, those differences seem very small.

There will always be a trade-off between opacity and visibility. The more transparent your markers are, the clearer you can see, especially with hundreds or thousands of markers. But at the same time, they might become so transparent that you can't see anything. At `0.1` opacity, we are approaching that stage.

Let's now take a look at another technique, which involves the use of logarithmic scales for the axes.

Using logarithmic scales

Normal scales are intuitive and easy to understand. Just like physical objects, a piece of wood that is twice the length of another one contains twice as much wood, provided it is of the same width and depth. In the previous two figures, for example, the distance between 0 and 0.2 billion is the same as the distance between 0.2 and 0.4 billion. The "data distance" is also the same. On a normal scale, and in this example, every tick corresponds to an increase of a certain amount (0.2 billion in this case). On a logarithmic scale, every additional tick corresponds to a multiple of the previous one.

For example, the numbers 10, 20, 30, and 40 form a typical sequence that you might see on a normal scale. If the scale was logarithmic, we don't add 10; we would **multiply** by 10, making the sequence 10, 100, 1,000, and 10,000. Running the same code as we used previously and adding `log_x=True`, we get the updated chart in *Figure 6.19*:

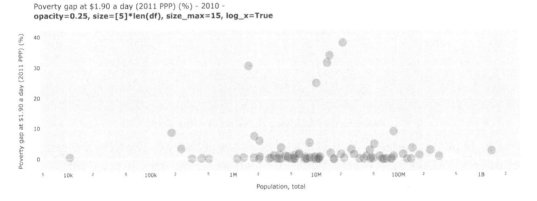

Figure 6.19 – Using a logarithmic scale

Our chart now looks quite different, but it is still actually the same chart. Note that we have changed the `opacity` to `0.25`, because `0.1` was difficult to see, and because we now have the markers a lot more dispersed than previously. We now have a much more nuanced view of how the population is distributed. We can see that the most opaque part is around the ten million mark. Compared to 1.4 billion, this is pretty much zero, which is what the previous chart told us, but now we have a better view.

Note that the major ticks are each 10 times larger than the previous one (**10k, 100k, 1M, 10M, 100M**, and **1B**), or for every major tick we are adding a zero. At the same time, we can see minor ticks, **2** and **5**, meaning that these positions represent twice and five times, respectively, the value of the previous major tick.

Let's explore another option that we might consider in such situations. We will not use any opacity this time, but we will introduce a lot of space to our markers by changing the symbol that we use. Setting symbols can be managed exactly like setting discrete colors. `symbol_sequence` is the parameter responsible for that, it will cycle through the options that we provide, and then assign one for each unique discrete value in our column. We give it a list containing one value, so all markers will have the same symbol.

We now remove the `opacity` argument and replace it with `symbol_sequence=['circle_open']` to get the new chart in *Figure 6.20*:

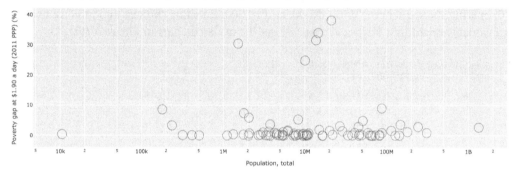

Figure 6.20 – Modifying the symbols of markers

This might be even better, as we are not sacrificing any visibility by changing the opacity. We achieved our objective of seeing where the markers are clustered, because it takes a lot of open circles to fully cover an area. The logarithmic scale spreads the markers horizontally, so it is easier to see how they are distributed. The tick labels clearly indicate the values, but we might need to make it very clear and explicit if our audience is not familiar with this kind of scale.

We can imagine providing users with all the options that we just tried. We can think of having a component that allows users to modify the opacity, another component to toggle between normal and logarithmic scales, and maybe another to change the symbols. Ideally, we shouldn't make it that difficult for users to read our charts. It's best to do the work ourselves and provide sensible defaults after having explored the data. Based on what we have explored so far, let's consider what those defaults might be.

We know that this chart plots countries, and that they cannot be more than 200. This means we can set a default opacity level that is appropriate for that number of markers. Having thousands of markers might require a much lower `opacity` level, such as `0.02`, for example. Open circles seem to have worked well for us by introducing space, so we might also choose that as the default symbol, and forget about opacity altogether. The same applies to the `size` parameter. Knowing that we are plotting population figures, and that it is most likely always going to contain outliers, as in this case, we might keep the logarithmic scale as the default.

A more general type of interactive chart might allow users to modify the indicators that they want to explore. In this case, we might give them those options. However, with more freedom and generality, our users will have to handle more of the data handling details themselves.

We have established a good understanding of our metrics and seen many examples of many countries. This exploration is crucial for building a dashboard with sensible defaults, as we just saw. Let's now explore the new interactive components of this chapter – the `Slider` components.

Introducing sliders and range sliders

The `Slider` and `RangeSlider` components are basically circles that users can drag horizontally or vertically to set or change a certain value. They are typically used for setting continuous values, as their appearance and dragging functionality are a natural fit for that. But this is not a requirement as we can use them for categorical/discrete values as well. We have seen that we have three levels of our `perc_pov_` metrics, and we know that we have all the years in our dataset to choose from. We now want to create two sliders. One allows users to select the level of poverty that they want to analyze, and the other allows them to select the year. Each combination of selections will create a different subset, and result in a different chart. *Figure 6.21* shows the top part of the end result that we will be working toward:

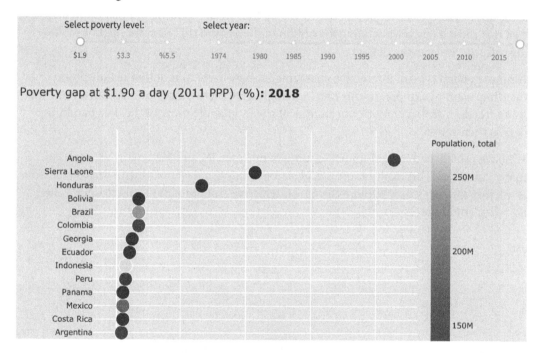

Figure 6.21 – Two sliders controlling a chart

As you can see, the new functionality requires three main components – two `Slider` components and one `Graph` component. Of course, we have a few others to control the layout, as well as labels, but the focus is mainly going to be on how to create and incorporate this new functionality.

> **Important note**
>
> The RangeSlider component is almost identical to the Slider component. The main difference is that it contains more than one handle, so users can modify the maximum and minimum points within which they want to filter data. For now, we will focus on normal Slider components, and we will tackle the RangeSlider component in later chapters.

As always, we will create this as a standalone app in JupyterLab, and once it is working fine, we will add it to the app. Let's start first by getting to know the Slider component, how it works, and then create the layout of our app.

You can create a minimal app and, within the app's layout, create the Slider component, just like you do with other components, by calling dcc.Slider():

```
app = JupyterDash(__name__)
app.layout = html.Div([
    dcc.Slider()
])
app.run_server(mode='inline')
```

This will create a simple app with a single component, as you can see in *Figure 6.22*:

Figure 6.22 – A bare-bones slider component

This is visually easy to use, and it's clear that users can slide the circle horizontally. There are no guides however, and users don't know what values they are modifying, so let's fix that. We will start by creating our first slider, containing the three poverty levels that we are analyzing. Let's take a look at the parameters that we are going to use for this:

- min: As the name suggests, this is the minimum value of the slider.

- max: This also sets the upper limit for the values.

- step: As we go (slide) from min to max, what should the increment size be? By default, it is set to 1, but you can set it to a higher or lower value. For example, if you wanted users to manage opacity, you can set min=0, max=1, and step=0.01. This would give users 100 options to choose from.

- dots: Should the slider display dots or should it be a simple line? In our case, we want users to choose between three distinct values, so it makes sense to set this option to True.

- included: Note that the slider in *Figure 6.22* is light blue to the left of the handle, and gray to its right. As you slide, the blue part expands/contracts with the handle, which is the default behavior. In our case, we are giving the user three distinct options, so we want to remove this to emphasize this fact, so we set its value to False.

- value: This is the default value that the slider should take.

Here is an example of a Slider component that ranges from 0 to 10:

```
dcc.Slider(min=0,
           max=10,
           step=1,
           dots=True,
           included=False)
```

This produces the new slider in *Figure 6.23*:

Figure 6.23 – A slider component with custom options

The dots now guide users on where they can select, and it hints that the options are distinct from one another, especially that we set included=False.

Another crucial parameter that Slider takes is the marks parameter. We need to show users what each dot corresponds to. In some cases, we might not have enough space to display all values, in which case we skip some of the values. We will do this in our years slider, but first let's create the poverty indicator slider. We first do it without the marks parameter, and then add it after that:

```
dcc.Slider(id='perc_pov_indicator_slider',
           min=0,
           max=2,
           step=1,
           value=0,
           included=False)
```

For `id`, as with other variables, we followed the rule of starting with `perc_pov_` to be consistent with other related objects in the app. The values that the callback function will receive from this component are going to be 0, 1, and 2, and this is based on the `min`, `max`, and `step` arguments we gave. Now, those values don't mean anything in our situation, because we actually want the full text of the name of the indicator. We can simply handle this by taking the value of the slider and using it as the index for the `perc_pov_cols` list that we created. In our callback function, we will use this integer value to extract the respective indicator. We will see this later when we construct our callback function. Let's now create the marks for our slider.

Customizing the marks and values of sliders

The simplest way to create these is by using a dictionary: `{0: '$1.9', 1: '$3.2', 2: '$5.5'}`. They keys will be used as the `value` attribute, and the values of the dictionary are what the user will see for each poverty level. This will suffice for our case, and we can use it as such.

We optionally have the chance to customize the style of our labels, which can take any CSS attribute as a dictionary. If you look at *Figure 6.21*, you can see that the marks (numbers) of the two sliders have a very light color, and they might give the impression that they belong to the same slider. We can improve this by setting their colors to a dark color. We can also set a bold font for the indicator slider. This will help distinguish them from the years, and it will also emphasize their uniqueness. Years are easy to immediately grasp, but users are most likely not familiar with the levels of poverty tracked in the dataset.

We want to get a color that is consistent with our charts. And since we will be using the cividis color scale, it's a good opportunity to get to know how we can extract its colors. The `px.colors.sequential` module contains, among other things, lists of the colors of the sequential color scales. We can get cividis by running the following command:

```
px.colors.sequential.Cividis
['#00224e',
 '#123570',
 '#3b496c',
 '#575d6d',
 '#707173',
 '#8a8678',
 '#a59c74',
 '#c3b369',
```

```
 '#e1cc55',
```

```
 '#fee838']
```

The list we receive contains the 10 colors that are actually used to construct this scale. Recall that we tried this manually with 2 and 3 colors. It's also interesting to know that you can get the reversed version of a scale by appending _r to its name, for example, px.colors.sequential.Cividis_r. This would give us the same scale, but the yellow would correspond to the lower values in this case.

Now, the color that we want to use for the labels of the marks is going to be the darkest one in cividis, which we can easily extract and assign to a variable as follows:

```
cividis0 = px.colors.sequential.Cividis[0]
```

Using this, we can now set our marks argument as follows:

```
marks={0: {'label': '$1.9', 'style': {'color': cividis0,
'fontWeight': 'bold'}},
        1: {'label': '$3.2', 'style': {'color': cividis0,
'fontWeight': 'bold'}},
        2: {'label': '$5.5', 'style': {'color': cividis0,
'fontWeight': 'bold'}}}
```

What we did was basically extend the dictionary, where, instead of strings as values, we added dictionaries in the following form:

```
 {'label': <label>, 'style': {<attribute_1>: <value_1>,
<attribute_2>: <value_2>}
```

> **Important note**
>
> In general, CSS attributes such as font-size and font-weight are hyphen-separated, and written in lowercase. In Dash, you can use the same attributes, but you have to remove the hyphens, and use camelCase (fontSize and fontWeight), as you can see in the previous code snippet.

Similar to what we just did, let's now create the other slider with similar customizations. First, and in order to isolate our subset, we can create a special DataFrame for these variables:

```
perc_pov_df =\
poverty[poverty['is_country']].dropna(subset=perc_pov_cols)
perc_pov_years = sorted(set(perc_pov_df['year']))
```

The important thing is that we removed any missing values from `perc_pov_cols`, and we also created a sorted list of unique years, `perc_pov_years`, using `sorted` and `set`.

The following code creates our new slider for the years:

```
dcc.Slider(id='perc_pov_year_slider',
           min=perc_pov_years[0],
           max=perc_pov_years[-1],
           step=1,
           included=False,
           value=2018,
           marks={year: {'label': str(year),
                         'style': {'color': cividis0}}
                  for year in perc_pov_years[::5]})
```

This is pretty much the same as we did for the indicators. We set the default to 2018, which is the latest year for which we have data. If this was a dynamically updated app, we can also set this value to the maximum of `perc_pov_years`. Note that we set the marks to show only one in five years. Otherwise, the slider would be very difficult to use. With this, we can see the slight difference in fonts and colors in *Figure 6.24*:

Figure 6.24 – Sliders with updated colors

The final part of our layout is going to be the `Graph` component:

```
dcc.Graph(id='perc_pov_scatter_chart')
```

As I mentioned before, we also have `Label` components, as well as `Col` and `Row` components to better manage the layout, but they weren't discussed, as we have already created several examples using them.

We are now ready to create our callback function to link the three elements that we just created:

1. We first create the decorator of the function. This is straightforward, as we did with previous examples. The slight difference is that we have two inputs in this case. In the definition of the function, the order of the parameters will correspond to the order of the Input elements, so we will name them accordingly:

    ```
    @app.callback(Output('perc_pov_scatter_chart', 'figure'),
                  Input('perc_pov_year_slider', 'value'),
                  Input('perc_pov_indicator_slider',
    'value'))
    ```

2. In the next part, we create the function's signature, as well as the first few lines. The parameters are named year and indicator. We now use the indicator value (which is an integer) to get the corresponding element from perc_pov_cols. We then create the variable df, which filters perc_pov_df to only have values from year. Then, define we dropna and sort_values. There was a year that didn't have any data, but had to be included in the values of the slider, so we need to handle the case when/if users select it. This is done using the simple check if df.empty, as you can see here:

    ```
    def plot_perc_pov_chart(year, indicator):
        indicator = perc_pov_cols[indicator]
        df = (perc_pov_df
              [perc_pov_df['year'].eq(year)]
              .dropna(subset=[indicator])
              .sort_values(indicator))
        if df.empty:
            raise PreventUpdate
    ```

3. Now that we have our DataFrame ready, we can create the Figure and return it. Most of the code should now be familiar. The hover_name parameter is used to add a title to the popup when users hover over markers. Setting it to Country Name would cause the title to take the respective country's name and display it in bold. We also utilized the same dynamic height trick that we used in the last chapter, where we set a fixed height, and added 20 pixels for each country. The ticksuffix option we added at the end should be self-explanatory, to make it clear that these are percentages:

```
fig = px.scatter(df,
                  x=indicator,
                  y='Country Name',
                  color='Population, total',
                  size=[30]*len(df),
                  size_max=15,
                  hover_name='Country Name',
                  height=250 +(20*len(df)),
                  color_continuous_scale='cividis',
                  title=indicator + '<b>: ' + f'{year}'
+'</b>')
fig.layout.paper_bgcolor = '#E5ECF6'
fig.layout.xaxis.ticksuffix = '%'
return fig
```

Adding the layout elements and callback to our app, we finally get the additional functionality in the form of two sliders that can generate more than 130 charts through their combinations. *Figure 6.25* shows the final result:

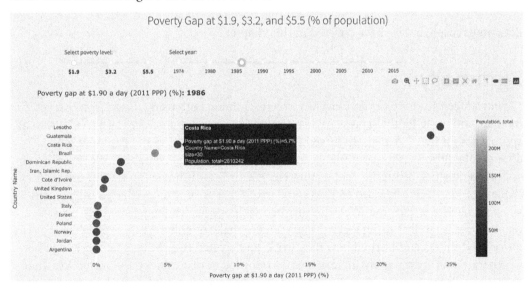

Figure 6.25 – Two sliders and a scatter plot – final result

Congratulations on yet another addition to your app! This time, we created our first multiple input callback, which enriched the options that users can generate, without being complicated or overwhelming.

From a functionality perspective, there is nothing really different between dropdowns and sliders. We could have implemented the same thing with dropdowns, and it would have worked fine. The advantage of dropdowns is that they are extremely efficient in terms of space utilization. A small rectangle can contain tens or even hundreds of hidden options that users can search. Those options can be very long strings that may be impossible to fit next to each other, on a slider, for example.

On the other hand, sliders give a better perspective. They implicitly contain metadata about the options. You can immediately see the minimum and maximum points, and how widely they are spread. When you select an option, you can easily tell how extreme your choice was relative to the other options that are available. In the case of the poverty level slider, users can see all available options immediately. And finally, sliders are more similar to how we interact with physical objects, so playing with them might be more engaging than other interactive components. So, space restrictions, the types of variables that we are analyzing, and how we want to display them are some considerations that affect our choice of interactive components that we decide to utilize.

You probably noticed that we are focusing less on how to put things together in the app, and that's intentional. We have already covered these topics several times, and it is designed to also encourage you to do them yourself and experiment with other options. You can always refer back to the code repository to check your work and for the minor details.

Let's now recap what we have covered in this chapter.

Summary

We introduced scatter plots and saw how to create them, both using the `graph_objects` module, and using Plotly Express. We saw how to create multiple traces and tried different approaches for that. We then discussed color mapping and setting and explored how different the process is for continuous and discrete (categorical) variables. We saw different scales – sequential, diverging, and qualitative. We also saw how we can set our own colors, sequences, and scales. We also tackled some issues that arise when we have outliers, and when we have over-plotting. We experimented with opacity, changing symbols, and marker sizes, as well as using logarithmic scales to make our charts more readable. We also introduced sliders and learned how they work, and created two sliders that work together to generate charts expressing three values (as opposed to two values previously). We then created a callback function that managed those interactions and integrated it into our app.

By now, and with all the examples and techniques covered, we are getting closer to the point of creating dashboards in the same way as we create slideshows and presentations. Once we master the layout elements, it's very easy to customize any size and position we want. And now that we are exploring different chart types and data visualization techniques, it will become easier to manage things and modify them the way we want.

All the charts we have explored so far used regular geometric shapes, including circles, lines, and rectangles. In the next chapter, we will explore irregular shapes, and how to visualize them, in the form of maps. Maps are very engaging, and easily recognizable, yet not so straightforward to visualize, like simple regular shapes. This will be explored next.

7

Exploring Map Plots and Enriching Your Dashboards with Markdown

In this chapter, we are going to explore how to handle maps, one of the most engaging types of charts. There are many ways of creating and handling maps, as well as many types of map plots. There are also many specialized geographic and scientific applications for maps. We will mainly be focusing on two of the most common types of map plots: **choropleth map plots** and **scatter map plots**. Choropleth maps are the type of maps we are most familiar with. These are the types of maps where geographical areas are colored to indicate a country, state, district, or any arbitrary polygon on a map, and express variations in quantity among them. Most of the knowledge we established in the previous chapter can easily be adapted to scatter map plots, as they are essentially the same, with a few differences. Similar to the x and y axes, we have longitude and latitude instead, and we also have different map projections. We will also learn about a new component, **Markdown**, from Dash Core Component.

Then, we will explore how to use **Mapbox**, which provides a rich interface with different layers, themes, and zoom levels. It also allows us to create choropleth and scatter map plots.

We will mainly cover the following topics:

- Exploring choropleth maps

- Utilizing animation frames to add a new layer to your plots

- Using callback functions with maps

- Creating a `Markdown` component

- Understanding map projections

- Using scatter map plots

- Exploring Mapbox maps

- Exploring other map options and tools

- Incorporating an interactive map into our app

Technical requirements

We will use similar tools to the ones we used in the previous chapter. We will mainly be using Plotly Express for creating our charts. The packages to use are Plotly, Dash, Dash Core Components, Dash HTML Components, Dash Bootstrap Components, pandas, and JupyterLab.

The code files of this chapter can be found on GitHub at `https://github.com/PacktPublishing/Interactive-Dashboards-and-Data-Apps-with-Plotly-and-Dash/tree/master/chapter_07`.

Check out the following video to see the Code in Action at `https://bit.ly/3sAY8z8`.

We'll start by exploring how easy it is to create choropleth maps for countries.

Exploring choropleth maps

Choropleth maps are basically colored polygons representing a certain area on a map. Plotly ships with country maps included (as well as US states), and so it is very easy to plot maps if we have information about countries. We already have such information in our dataset. We have country names, as well as country codes, in every row. We also have the year, some metadata about the countries (region, income group, and so on), and all the indicator data. In other words, every data point is connected to a geographical location. So, let's start by choosing a year and an indicator, and see how the values of our chosen indicator vary across countries:

1. Open the `poverty` file into a DataFrame and create the `year` and `indicator` variables:

```
import pandas as pd
poverty = pd.read_csv('data/poverty.csv')
year = 2016
indicator = 'GINI index (World Bank estimate)'
```

2. Create a subset of `poverty` with values from the selected year and containing countries only:

```
df = poverty[poverty['is_country'] & poverty['year'].
eq(year)]
```

3. Create a choropleth map using the `choropleth` function from Plotly Express, by choosing the column that identifies the countries and the column that will be used for the colors:

```
import plotly.express as px
px.choropleth(df, locations="Country Code",
color=indicator)
```

You can see the result of the preceding code in *Figure 7.1*:

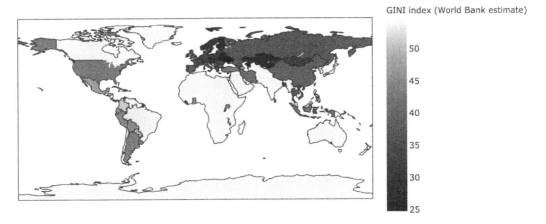

Figure 7.1 – A choropleth map of countries

The country codes we provided were already included in Plotly, and are in the three-letter ISO format. As with scatter plots, you can see that since we provided a numeric column for the color, a continuous color scale was chosen. Otherwise, we would have gotten a discrete color sequence. For example, setting color='Income Group' would produce the chart in *Figure 7.2*:

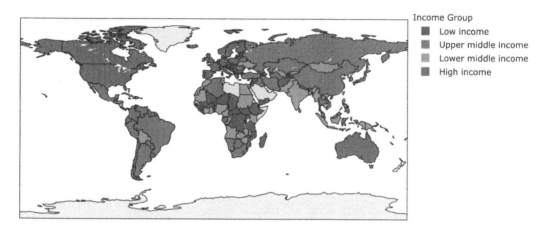

Figure 7.2 – A choropleth map of countries with a discrete color sequence

As you can see, and similar to what we saw in *Chapter 6*, *Exploring Variables with Scatter Plots and Filtering Subsets with Sliders*, the color system works in a similar way.

We can also use normal country names to plot them. To do that, we only need to set locationmode='country names' and the rest works the same. Here is an example with country names:

```
px.choropleth(df,
              locations=['Australia', 'Egypt', 'Chile'],
              color=[10, 20, 30],
              locationmode='country names')
```

This creates the chart in *Figure 7.3*:

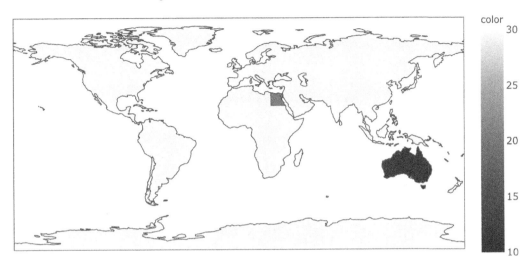

Figure 7.3 – A choropleth map of countries using country names

The title of the color bar is `color` because it is not clear what it is, and it is not a name of a column in a DataFrame. We can rename it by setting `labels={'color':` `<metric_name>}` to indicate what the metric is in our case. Let's now see how we can make the chart interactive (without using a callback).

Utilizing animation frames to add a new layer to your plots

In the last examples, we set the year as a variable and got a snapshot of the desired indicator for that year. Since the years represent sequential values, and can also be used as a grouping variable, we can use the years in the `animation_frame` parameter and make the chart interactive. This would introduce a new handle underneath the chart, where users can either drag to the desired year or press the play button to watch how the respective indicator progresses throughout the years. It would be a sequence of frames, like watching a video. What this does is that for a selected year, we will get a subset of the DataFrame where the rows in the `year` column are equal to the selected year. The chart automatically updates with colors corresponding to the values of the year that was chosen.

Here is the updated code to produce an animated chart (by year):

```
fig = px.choropleth(poverty[poverty['is_country']],|
                    color_continuous_scale='cividis',
                    locations='Country Code',
                    color=indicator,
                    animation_frame='year')
fig.show()
```

We can now see the updated chart in *Figure 7.4*:

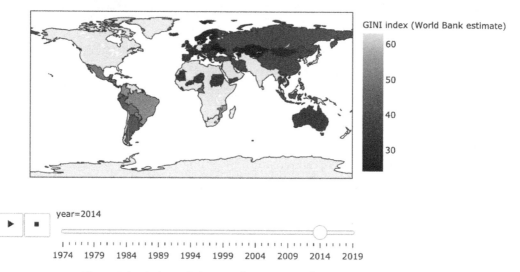

Figure 7.4 – A choropleth map of countries with an animation frame

As you can see, all we had to do is select a column name to use for `animation_frame`, and everything is handled for us. We used a DataFrame where we only have countries, which includes all years. The further sub-setting is done automatically by the argument given to `animation_frame`. We can drag the handle to a specific year or press the play button and watch how it changes over time. Note that we also changed the color scale to experiment with a different one. Both color scales used so far should also be readable on a grayscale version of the map.

Now that we have a basic map in place, let's explore what options we have to control several aspects of the map. The `layout` attribute of map charts has a sub-attribute called `geo`, under which there are several useful geographic attributes that allow us to control many aspects of our maps. These attributes work the same way as other attributes.

We basically set them by running `fig.layout.geo.<attribute> = value` to set the desired value. Let's explore some of these attributes and their effects on the previous chart:

- Remove the rectangular frame around the map:

```
fig.layout.geo.showframe = False
```

- Show the country borders, even if/when we don't have data for some countries:

```
fig.layout.geo.showcountries = True
```

- Use a different projection of the Earth. Select the `natural earth` projection type (more on this later):

```
fig.layout.geo.projection.type = 'natural earth'
```

- Limit the vertical range of the chart to focus more on countries, by setting the minimum and maximum latitude values that the map should show:

```
fig.layout.geo.lataxis.range = [-53, 76]
```

- Limit the horizontal range of the chart using the same technique:

```
fig.layout.geo.lonaxis.range = [-137, 168]
```

- Change the color of the land to `'white'` to make it clear which countries have missing data:

```
fig.layout.geo.landcolor = 'white'
```

- Set the background color of the map (the color of the oceans), as well as the "paper" background color of the figure as a whole. Use the same color that we are using for the app to have a consistent theme:

```
fig.layout.geo.bgcolor = '#E5ECF6'
fig.layout.paper_bgcolor = '#E5ECF6'
```

- Set the colors of the country borders as well as the coastlines to `'gray'`:

```
fig.layout.geo.countrycolor = 'gray'
fig.layout.geo.coastlinecolor = 'gray'
```

- Since the title of the color bar is taking up a lot of horizontal space, replace spaces with the <br> character, to split it to multiple lines:

```
fig.layout.coloraxis.colorbar.title =\
indicator.replace(' ', '<br>')
```

As a result, we get the updated chart in *Figure 7.5*:

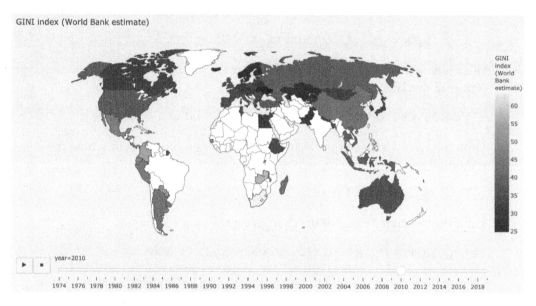

Figure 7.5 – A choropleth map of countries with custom geo options

With a few commands, we have transformed how our chart looks. We restricted the ranges to focus mainly on countries and land, as much as possible. We also set consistent background colors and displayed country borders. There are several other options that can easily be explored under the `fig.layout.geo` attribute. We are now ready to make the indicator selection dynamic; let's see how.

Using callback functions with maps

What we have done so far was done with one indicator, and we used this indicator to select the desired column from the dataset. We can easily create a dropdown to allow users to choose any of the available indicators and let them explore the whole dataset. The `year` variable is already interactive and part of the chart, as used by the `animation_frame` parameter. So, this can become the first exploratory interactive chart that users start with on our app, to help them get an overview of the available metrics and how they are changing in time.

Setting this up is straightforward, as we did several times. We will implement it, and after that, we will see how to use the Markdown component to add context around/about the map chart and the chosen indicator.

Let's do the necessary steps to implement this functionality independently in JupyterLab:

1. Create a Dropdown component, where the available options are the column names of poverty, using the columns between the third and 54th columns:

```
dcc.Dropdown(id='indicator_dropdown',
            value='GINI index (World Bank estimate)',
            options=[{'label': indicator, 'value':
indicator}
                     for indicator in poverty.
columns[3:54]])
```

2. Create an empty Graph component, right under the dropdown we just created:

```
dcc.Graph(id='indicator_map_chart')
```

3. The indicator names vary in length, and some of them are so long that they take up almost half the screen size. We can handle this in a similar way to what we did previously, by creating a simple function. The function takes a string, splits it into words, groups every three words together, and then joins them with the <br> character:

```
def multiline_indicator(indicator):
    final = []
    split = indicator.split()
    for i in range(0, len(split), 3):
        final.append(' '.join(split[i:i+3]))
    return '<br>'.join(final)
```

4. Create a callback that links the dropdown with the map chart:

```
@app.callback(Output('indicator_map_chart', 'figure'),
              Input('indicator_dropdown', 'value'))
```

5. Define the function that takes the selected indicator and returns the desired map chart. Note that we set the title of the figure by using the indicator as its value. We also used the Country Name column to set the hover name, which is the title of the box that appears when users hover over a certain country. The height was also set to 650 pixels. The remaining geo properties were omitted here to avoid repetition, but they are the same as we set them previously. We also modify the color bar title, using the multiline_indicator function we just created:

```
def display_generic_map_chart(indicator):
    df = poverty[poverty['is_country']]
    fig = px.choropleth(df,
                        locations='Country Code',
                        color=indicator,
                        title=indicator,
                        hover_name='Country Name',
                        color_continuous_scale='cividis',
                        animation_frame='year',
                        height=650)
    fig.layout.geo.showframe = False
    ...
    fig.layout.coloraxis.colorbar.title =\
    multiline_indicator(indicator)
```

Running the app in JupyterLab, you can explore the different metrics. *Figure 7.6* shows a few examples of charts produced by selecting different indicators and years:

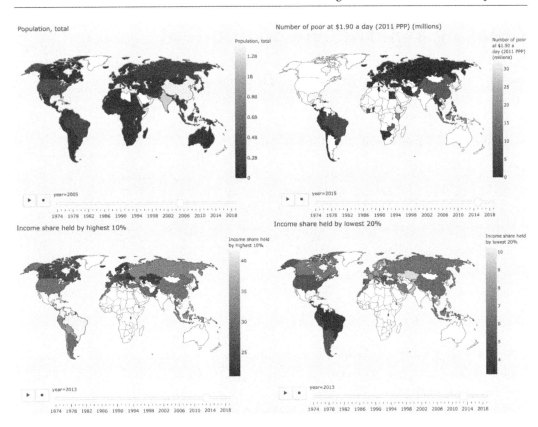

Figure 7.6 – Examples of map charts produced interactively

Once given the option, users can search the dropdown for various keywords and select what they find interesting. It is still not very clear what exactly many of these indicators refer to and what their limitations might be. This is a good opportunity for us to display those details to users, to make it clear what they are looking at. As mentioned previously, the limitations in measurement are crucial to highlight, so users are aware of them. Let's see how we can add formatted text using the `Markdown` component.

Creating a Markdown component

Markdown is a way to produce HTML in a manner that is easy to write and also easy to read. The output would be displayed as any HTML document would, but the process of writing it and reading it is much easier. Compare the following two snippets, which result in the same HTML output:

Using pure HTML, we would write the following:

```
<h1>This is the main text of the page</h1>
<h3>This is secondary text</h2>
<ul>
   <li>first item</li>
   <li>second item</li>
   <li>third item</li>
</ul>
```

The same code can be written with Markdown as follows:

```
# This is the main text of the page
### This is secondary text
* first item
* second item
* third item
```

I think it's clear that Markdown is much easier to write, as well as to read, especially when you have nested items such as the <ul> unordered list we have here.

The Markdown component works the same way. The preceding code simply has to be passed to the children argument, which would render it as the HTML shown previously. Let's create a minimal app in JupyterLab to see how the Markdown component works:

1. Make the necessary imports and instantiate an app:

```
from jupyter_dash import JupyterDash
import dash_core_components as dcc
app = JupyterDash(__name__)
```

2. Create the layout attribute of the app:

```
app.layout = html.Div([])
```

3. Pass the `Markdown` component with the preceding text to the `div` just created. Note that it is easier to use triple quotes especially when using multiline text:

```
dcc.Markdown("""
# This is the main text of the page
### This is secondary text
* first item
* second item
* third item
""")
```

4. Run the app:

```
app.run_server(mode='inline')
```

The preceding code creates a mini-app with its output shown in *Figure 7.7*:

This is the main text of the page

This is secondary text

- first item
- second item
- third item

Figure 7.7 – A sample output of the Markdown component

Markdown has several other ways of displaying text, such as numbered lists, tables, links, bold and italic text, and more. We will be covering some of these features, but they are easy to pick up in case you are not familiar with them. Keep in mind that there are various "flavors" of Markdown used by different platforms. You might come across slightly different markup/syntax rules but in general, there is a lot of overlap.

We will now add some information to the map that the user generates after selecting the metric of their choice. Basically, we will add the important information right underneath the map and slider. *Figure 7.8* shows how this will look, in order to give you an idea of what we are working toward:

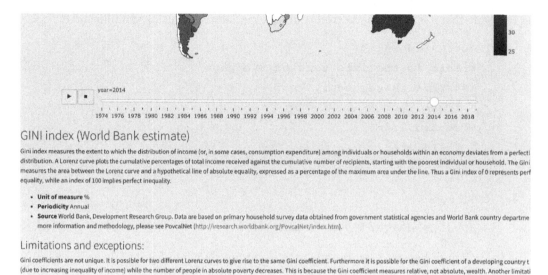

Figure 7.8 – A sample of the Markdown component

All the text and formatting you see in the figure are produced by the `Markdown` component.

In order to create a special area for it on the app, we simply add a `Markdown` component under the map, giving it a unique ID.

Producing this component will happen in the same callback we created to generate the map. The callback should now take two `Output` elements instead of one, and when returning, it should return two elements as well (the figure, as well as the Markdown generated). To get the required content for this component, we need to open the file that contains all the details about the indicators. This has been done previously, but as a reminder, we can get it by running `series = pd.read_csv('data/PovStatsSeries.csv')`. Let's now implement these steps:

1. Right under the `Graph` component, add the new `Markdown` component (note that we also set its background color to be consistent with the map, as well as the whole app). The _md suffix is for `Markdown`:

```
dcc.Markdown(id='indicator_map_details_md',
             style={'backgroundColor': '#E5ECF6'})
```

2. Update the callback function by including the new component:

```
@app.callback(Output('indicator_map_chart', 'figure'),
              Output('indicator_map_details_md',
'children'),
              Input('indicator_dropdown', 'value'))
```

3. After finishing the definition of the `fig` variable in the callback function, we now run the necessary steps for creating the `Markdown` output. Create the appropriate subset of `series`, by getting the row where the `Indicator Name` column is equal to the selected indicator:

```
series_df =\
series[series['Indicator Name'].eq(indicator)]
```

4. Extract the value of the `Limitations and exceptions` columns from `series_df`. Note that since some values are missing and since missing values are not strings, we fill them with the string `N/A`, and we also replace any instances of two newline characters, `\n\n`, with a single space, if any. We then extract the first element under its `values` attribute:

```
limitations =series_df['Limitations and\
exceptions'].fillna('N/A').str.replace('\n\n',\
' ').values[0]
```

5. Now that we have defined two variables, `series_df` and `limitations`, we will use Python's f-string formatting to insert variables where they belong using curly braces: f'{<variable_name>}'. We first insert the indicator name using an <h2> element. Headings in Markdown correspond to their HTML equivalents, where the number of hash signs corresponds to the heading level. Here we use two signs for <h2>:

```
## {series_df['Indicator Name'].values[0]}
```

6. Now we add the long description in regular text, without any hash signs before it:

```
{series_df['Long definition'].values[0]}
```

7. Next, we add the bullet points for `Unit of measure`, `Periodicity`, and `Source`. Bullet points can be created by adding a star at the beginning of the line for each bullet point. This is a simple process of getting the right element from the right column. Note that we fill missing values for `Unit of measure` by using the word `count`, which will replace the missing values where the indicator is a simple count and not a percentage. Population is one such example. In the case of `Periodicity`, we simply replace it with `N/A` wherever the respective value is missing. The stars before and after any text make it bold, similar to running `<b>text</b>`:

```
* **Unit of measure** {series_df['\
Unit of measure'].fillna('count').values[0]}
* **Periodicity**\
{series_df['Periodicity'].fillna('N/A').values[0]}
* **Source** {series_df['Source'].values[0]}
```

8. Add the `Limitations and exceptions` subtitle in `<h3>`:

```
### Limitations and exceptions:
```

9. Next, we add the already created `limitations` variable in regular text:

```
{limitations}
```

Putting the preceding code together, here is the full code that creates our `Markdown` component, with its relative position in the callback function. Note that in some cases, there are a few indicators that don't have details in the `series` DataFrame. In this case, we set the `Markdown` variable to a string, indicating the lack of such details. This condition can be seen in the following code as well, in the check to `series_df.empty`; otherwise, everything runs as previously:

```
...
fig.layout.coloraxis.colorbar.title =\
multiline_indicator(indicator)
series_df = series[series['Indicator Name'].eq(indicator)]

if series_df.empty:
    markdown = "No details available on this indicator"
else:
    limitations = series_df['Limitations and exceptions'].
fillna('N/A').str.replace('\n\n', ' ').values[0]
```

```
    markdown = f"""
    ## {series_df['Indicator Name'].values[0]}
    {series_df['Long definition'].values[0]}


    * **Unit of measure** {series_df['Unit of measure'].
fillna('count').values[0]}
    * **Periodicity**
{series_df['Periodicity'].fillna('N/A').values[0]}
    * **Source** {series_df['Source'].values[0]}
    ### Limitations and exceptions:
    {limitations}
    """

return fig, markdown
```

We finally return a tuple of `fig, markdown` instead of only `fig` as we did in the previous version. Adding this code to the app would add the respective Markdown to the map and give it much better context, as well as pointing out the limitations that our users need to keep in mind.

We will now turn to see the different projections that maps can be displayed in, and how we can change them.

Understanding map projections

We used an example of one projection type in our map, and now we'll explore this topic in more detail. When we try to draw the Earth (or part of it) on a flat rectangle, the shape is inevitably distorted somehow. So, there are different ways, or projections, available that can be used. No projection is perfect, and there are trade-offs between accuracy in shape, area, relative position, and so on. The details of which projection is more appropriate depends on the application and is beyond the scope of this book. We will, however, explore how to change the projection being used and see how to get the available projections.

With Plotly Express, we have a `projection` parameter in the map functions, which takes a string and can be used to set the desired projection type. Alternatively, we can also set it by assigning a value to `fig.layout.geo.projection.type` as we did previously.

Figure 7.9 shows a few of the available options together with their respective names in the titles:

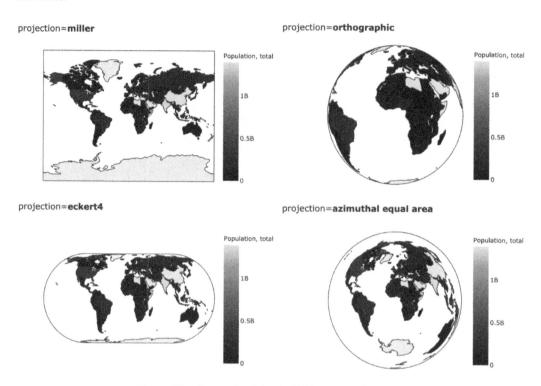

Figure 7.9 – A sample of the available map projections

As you can see, there are different ways of displaying the Earth. While **orthographic** might seem more realistic in its shape, its problem is that we can only see part of the Earth, so we lose perspective. The **azimuthal equal area** projection is actually quite realistic when you use it interactively and zoom into certain areas. Feel free to experiment with different projections and select what works for you.

We have experimented with polygon or choropleth maps so far, and now we will be exploring another type of map, with which we are already generally familiar: the scatter map.

Using scatter map plots

The main difference between the *x* and *y* axes and longitude and latitude is due to the shape of the Earth. As we approach the equator, the vertical meridians are as far away from each other as possible, and as we approach the North and South poles, they are as close as possible to each other. *Figure 7.10* shows this:

Figure 7.10 – A map of the Earth, showing longitude and latitude lines

In other words, as we approach the equator, we have a more rectangular shape, because a unit of longitude is close to a unit of latitude. Close to the poles, the proportions are completely different, and the rectangles start to approximate triangles. This is in contrast to a rectangular plane, where a vertical unit of distance corresponds to the same horizontal unit of distance, regardless of where you are on the plane. This assumes a linear scale on both axes, of course. An exception to this is the logarithmic axis, which we covered in *Chapter 6, Exploring Variables with Scatter Plots and Filtering Subsets with Sliders*. Map projections handle this for us, and we don't have to worry about this issue. So, we can simply think of them as we think about the *x* and *y* axes and select the projection that we want.

Let's see how we can make a scatter map plot with Plotly Express using the `scatter_geo` function.

We start with a very simple example:

```
df =\
poverty[poverty['year'].eq(2010) & poverty['is_country']]
px.scatter_geo(df, locations='Country Code')
```

First, we created `df`, where the year is equal to 2010, and we filtered out non-countries. Then, just like we did with choropleth maps, we selected the column to use for the `locations` parameter. This generates the simple chart in *Figure 7.11*:

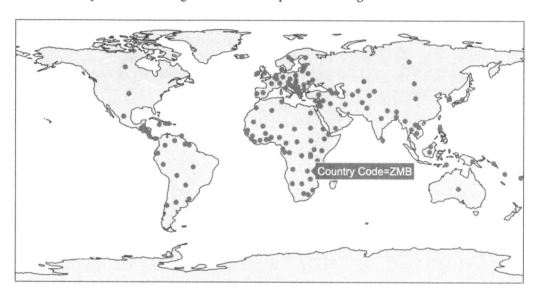

Figure 7.11 – A scatter map using the scatter_geo function

You can see how easy it is to do so. There is not much information in this chart, other than markers on countries, showing the **Country Code** value.

The country names are supported by default by Plotly. Another interesting application might be to use the `lat` and `lon` parameters to plot arbitrary locations on the map, as you can see in the following code and *Figure 7.12*:

```
px.scatter_geo(lon=[10, 12, 15, 18], lat=[23, 28, 31, 40])
```

This results in the following output:

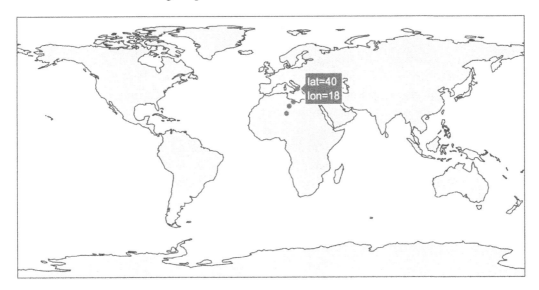

Figure 7.12 – A scatter map using latitude and longitude data

You can easily apply the concepts we covered in *Chapter 6, Explore Exploring Variables with Scatter Plots and Filtering Subsets with Sliders*, to modify the size and map colors, set the opacity, and so on.

We will now explore these options by introducing another richer way of producing maps, using Mapbox.

Exploring Mapbox maps

Mapbox is an open source library for maps. It is backed by a company with the same name that also provides additional services, layers, and themes to produce rich mapping applications. The options we will be using here can be used immediately with Plotly, but there are some other styles and services that require you to register for an account and use a token every time you generate a map.

An example should make it easy to start with, as we are already very familiar with scatter plots:

```
px.scatter_mapbox(lon=[5, 10, 15, 20],
                  lat=[10, 7, 18, 5],
                  zoom=2,
                  center={'lon': 5, 'lat': 10},
```

```
            size=[5]*4,
    color_discrete_sequence=['darkred'],
    mapbox_style='stamen-watercolor')
```

The preceding code should be straightforward. The `lon` and `lat` parameters are the equivalents of the `x` and `y` parameters for scatter plots. The `size` and `color_discrete_sequence` parameters have already been covered. An interesting new parameter is the `zoom` parameter, which we set to 2 here. This can take an integer value from 0 (the whole world) to 22 (building-level zoom), inclusive. We can also see how easy it is to set the center of a map, which we did using the first point's coordinates (5, 10). Finally, the `mapbox_style` parameter provides a set of interesting options to display maps in different styles. The `stamen-watercolor` style gives it an artistic look and can be seen in *Figure 7.13*:

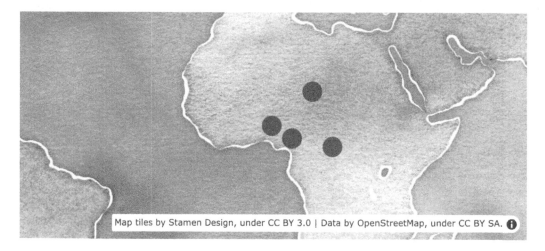

Map tiles by Stamen Design, under CC BY 3.0 | Data by OpenStreetMap, under CC BY SA.

Figure 7.13 – A scatter map using Mapbox and a custom style

Hovering over the **i** on the map displays the sources of the tiles and data. As you can see, there are so many layers and work condensed into this simple function. Let's now use the same approach to plot some data from our dataset.

Because `scatter_mapbox` mainly works with latitude and longitude data, and our dataset does not include any such data about the countries, we will obtain the data, merge it, and then plot the markers where they belong.

There are many sources for such data, and a quick online search will lead to some good sources. We can use the pandas `read_html` function for that. It takes a URL, downloads all the `<table>` elements at that URL, and returns a list of DataFrame objects. We simply have to take the one that we want. In this case, it is the first one. The following code achieves this, and creates the `lat_long` variable, which is a DataFrame:

```
lat_long =\
pd.read_html('https://developers.google.com/public-data/docs/
canonical/countries_csv')[0]
```

If you remember our discussion in *Chapter 4, Data Manipulation and Preparation - Paving the Way to Plotly Express*, where we went through several data manipulation operations, we will utilize the `merge` function from `pandas` to merge `lat_long` into `poverty` using a left merge operation.

We first take a look at the structure of the `lat_long` DataFrame by simply printing it in JupyterLab, and you can see the top and bottom five rows in *Figure 7.14*:

	country	latitude	longitude	name
0	AD	42.546245	1.601554	Andorra
1	AE	23.424076	53.847818	United Arab Emirates
2	AF	33.939110	67.709953	Afghanistan
3	AG	17.060816	-61.796428	Antigua and Barbuda
4	AI	18.220554	-63.068615	Anguilla
...	...	...	...	...
240	YE	15.552727	48.516388	Yemen
241	YT	-12.827500	45.166244	Mayotte
242	ZA	-30.559482	22.937506	South Africa
243	ZM	-13.133897	27.849332	Zambia
244	ZW	-19.015438	29.154857	Zimbabwe

245 rows × 4 columns

Figure 7.14 – The lat_long DataFrame containing latitude and longitude data for countries

The **country** column contains country codes using two letters for each. The `poverty` DataFrame also has a column called `2-alpha code`, which contains country codes using the same two-letter standard, so we merge using those columns as follows:

```
poverty = pd.merge(left=poverty, right=lat_long, how='left',
                   left_on='2-alpha code', right_on='country')
```

This will add the columns of `lat_long` to `poverty`, aligning the rows where they belong, as well as duplicating them where necessary. Remember, we are merging using the `left` method, which means the `left` argument is the basis for the merge. You can see a random sample of rows together with the important columns after merging in *Figure 7.15* to make it clear:

	Country Name	longitude	latitude	2-alpha code
5849	Paraguay	-58.443832	-23.442503	PY
2755	Greece	21.824312	39.074208	GR
7145	Tajikistan	71.276093	38.861034	TJ
554	Belize	-88.497650	17.189877	BZ
6958	Suriname	-56.027783	3.919305	SR
6895	Sub-Saharan Africa	NaN	NaN	ZG
467	Belarus	27.953389	53.709807	BY
5828	Papua New Guinea	143.955550	-6.314993	PG
7159	Tajikistan	71.276093	38.861034	TJ
6850	St. Lucia	-60.978893	13.909444	LC

Figure 7.15 – A subset of the poverty DataFrame merged with lat_long

Note that in the case where we didn't have values for the longitude and latitude, we have **NaN**. In the cases where the same country name exists, for example, **Tajikistan**, the longitude and latitude values are simply duplicated, to keep the mapping of those values to their respective country, regardless of which rows we choose.

We are now ready to create a bubble chart (a scatter plot with the marker sizes reflecting a certain quantity). We just have to create a subset of `poverty` that contains only countries and removes any missing values for the required indicator, `Population, total`, in this case. This can be done with the following code:

```
df =\
poverty[poverty['is_country']].dropna(subset=['Population,
total'])
```

Creating a bubble chart requires you call to the `scatter_mapbox` function, but we will go through the given arguments one by one:

1. Call the function with the subset just created:

    ```
    px.scatter_mapbox(df, …)
    ```

2. Select the columns that will be used for the longitude and latitude values:

    ```
    lon='longitude', lat='latitude'
    ```

3. Set the desired zoom level, to show the whole Earth:

    ```
    zoom=1
    ```

4. Map the value of the indicator to the size of the markers and set a suitable maximum size:

    ```
    size='Population, total', size_max=80
    ```

5. Map the income group that the respective country belongs to, to the color of the marker (discrete variables in this case):

    ```
    color='Income Group'
    ```

6. Choose the `year` column as the one used to animate the chart:

    ```
    animation_frame='year'
    ```

7. Set a suitable opacity level, because we will definitely have overlapping markers:

    ```
    opacity=0.7
    ```

8. Set a suitable height for the figure as a whole, in pixels:

    ```
    height=650
    ```

9. Add more information to the hover box, by including two more columns' data to appear when users hover over markers:

    ```
    hover_data=['Income Group', 'Region']
    ```

10. Select a custom color sequence to differentiate the income groups that the countries belong to:

    ```
    color_discrete_sequence=px.colors.qualitative.G10
    ```

11. Set a custom style for the map:

```
mapbox_style='stamen-toner'
```

12. Set a title for the hover box, using the country name:

```
hover_name=df['Country Name']
```

13. Set a title for the figure:

```
title="Population by Country"
```

Running the preceding code produces the interactive chart in *Figure 7.16*:

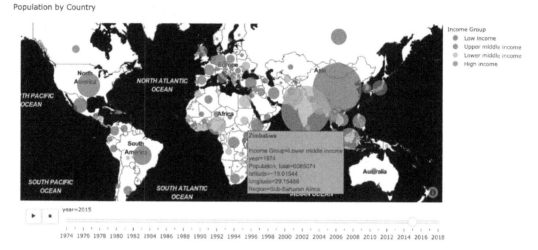

Figure 7.16 – A scatter_mapbox bubble chart for population by country using years as animation frames

Here is the full code that we just discussed to make it clear:

```
px.scatter_mapbox(df,
                  lon='longitude',
                  lat='latitude',
                  zoom=1,
                  size='Population, total',
                  size_max=80,
                  color='Income Group',
                  animation_frame='year',
                  opacity=0.7,
```

```
                height=650,
                hover_data=['Income Group', 'Region'],
                color_discrete_sequence=px.colors.
qualitative.G10,
                mapbox_style='stamen-toner',
                hover_name=df['Country Name'],
                title='Population by Country')
```

You can see how straightforward it is to set all the options, and how little code is involved. We only have to know the options and how they work.

Because this is an interactive chart, and users can zoom in and out, it is easy to handle the overlaps that we have, simply by zooming in one level. *Figure 7.17* shows the same chart after zooming (by the user):

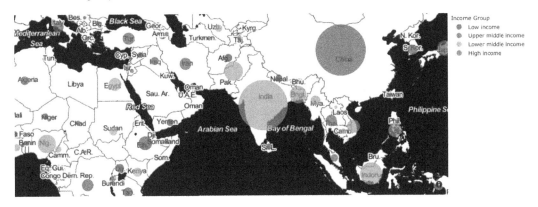

Figure 7.17 – A scatter_mapbox chart zoomed in for a better view

One advantage of bubble charts over choropleth charts is that they show how the value relates to the geographic area of the country (or any location) visualized. For example, *Figure 7.16* shows three interesting cases of Canada, Russia, and Australia, which seem to have a population that is relatively small compared to their area. In other words, their population density is low. This gives more perspective on this metric.

As you can see, there are so many options and ways to display and interact with maps, and we have barely scratched the surface of what can be done. We will now take a look at a few other options that are available, in case you are interested in learning more.

Exploring other map options and tools

The following are a few pointers on what you can explore further with mapping, without getting into too much detail.

You've probably thought about having custom polygons or areas to visualize as choropleth maps. What we have covered so far are standard countries only. Of course, you have the option of visualizing a custom area with arbitrary points.

There is a standard GeoJSON format for representing such information. It mainly consists of points, lines, and polygons. Points are simply locations on the map, similar to what we used for scatter map plots. Lines are groups of connected points, in a certain sequence, where the first and last points are not the same. And as you can guess, a polygon is similar to a line, but with the condition that the first and last points are the same. Note that many countries consist of more than one polygon. Most Plotly map functions support GeoJSON, and you can use it for custom map plotting.

This can be useful when you have custom data for custom locations and you need to obtain the relevant data.

Another important and useful project to consider learning about is `geopandas`. As the name clearly suggests, it is a specialized library that works like `pandas`, and provides special data structures and techniques for geographic data, most notably `GeoDataFrame`. It is worth learning if you have more specialized mapping requirements, or if you frequently need to customize maps further.

Let's now add the functionality we created to the app.

Incorporating an interactive map into our app

The map that we created, together with the `Dropdown` and `Markdown` components, can become the first exploratory tool in our app. We can remove the population bar chart now, and in its place, we can place the components we just created, for users to explore all the indicators, see them on the map, and scroll through the years, and for each indicator, get the full details, as well as seeing the limitations and potential issues. Once something catches the user's eye, they can then find another chart that gives more detail about the indicator they want if it exists.

In order to fully incorporate the new functionality into our app, we need to go through the following steps:

1. Add the definition of `series` at the top of the `app.py` module:

```
series = pd.read_csv('data/PovStatsSeries.csv')
```

2. Add the definition of the `multiline_indicator` function, anywhere before `app.layout`:

```
def multiline_indicator(indicator):
    final = []
    split = indicator.split()
    for i in range(0, len(split), 3):
        final.append(' '.join(split[i:i+3]))
    return '<br>'.join(final)
```

3. Add the `Dropdown`, `Graph`, and `Markdown` components at the top of the app, right under the top headings, where we previously had the population bar chart. The following code shows how, including the component IDs to make it clear, but the full definitions have been omitted. Note also the addition of a `Col` component as well as setting the width of another `Col` component, both using the `lg` (large) parameter. The first one introduces an empty column before displaying the content, and the second controls the width of the content in this column:

```
app.layout = html.Div([
    dbc.Col([
        html.Br(),
        html.H1('Poverty And Equity Database'),
        html.H2('The World Bank'),
    ], style={'textAlign': 'center'}),
    html.Br(),
    dbc.Row([
        dbc.Col(lg=2),
        dbc.Col([
            dcc.Dropdown(id='indicator_dropdown', ...),
            dcc.Graph(id='indicator_map_chart', ...),
            dcc.Markdown(id='indicator_map_details_md',
 ...)
        ], lg=8)
    ]),
    html.Br()
```

We have explored several new options in this chapter, so let's summarize what we did.

Summary

We started by exploring how to create choropleth maps, which are a type of map that we are all used to seeing. We also saw how to animate those maps if we have a sequential value, which in our case was viewing a certain indicator as it progressed throughout the available years. We then created a callback function and made the maps work with all the possible indicators that we have, so users could explore them all and then decide what they wanted to explore next.

After that, we learned how to use Markdown to generate HTML content, and how to add it to a Dash app. We then explored the different ways of displaying maps, or projections, and saw how to select the projection that we want.

We went through another type of map, which is a scatter map plot. Building on the knowledge we established in the previous chapter, it was fairly straightforward to adapt that knowledge to scatter maps. We also learned about the rich options that Mapbox provides and explored a few other topics for further exploration with maps. Finally, we integrated the new functionality into our app, which now contains a lot of explanatory text about almost all of the indicators, so users have a much better view of what they are analyzing.

In the next chapter, we will tackle a different type of chart, one that helps in counting values and showing how they are distributed in our dataset, the **histogram**. We will also explore a new component, the Dash **DataTable**, which allows us to display tabular data in a rich way, with many options to filter, visualize, download, and more.

8
Calculating the Frequency of Your Data with Histograms and Building Interactive Tables

All the chart types that we've explored so far displayed our data as is. In other words, every marker, whether it was a circle, a bar, a map, or any other shape, corresponded to a single data point in our dataset. **Histograms**, on the other hand, display bars that correspond to a summary statistic about *groups* of data points. A histogram is mainly used to count values in a dataset. It does so by grouping, or "binning," the data into bins and displaying the count of observations in each bin. Other functions are possible, of course, such as working out the mean or maximum, but counting is the typical use case.

The counts are represented like a bar chart, where the heights of the bars correspond to the counts (or other function) of each bin. Another important result is that we also see how data is distributed, and what shape/kind of distribution we have. Are the observations concentrated around a certain point or more than one point? Are they skewed to the left or the right? This can give us an overview of this aspect of our data.

Probability distributions are fundamental in statistics and crucial in getting an overview of our data. It is important to know how data values are spread in our sample or dataset, and where they are concentrated. If a dataset looks normally distributed, we might make different assumptions and have different expectations than if it were exponentially distributed. Histograms help in revealing the shape of the distribution of our data.

We will also explore Dash's **DataTable** component in this chapter. This is a flexible, powerful, and feature-rich component that helps us with, among other things, displaying, filtering, and exporting tables of data.

We will go through the following topics in this chapter:

- Creating a histogram
- Customizing the histogram by modifying its bins and using multiple histograms
- Adding interactivity to histograms
- Creating a 2D histogram
- Creating a DataTable
- Controlling the look and feel of the table (cell width, height, text display, and more)
- Adding histograms and tables to the app

Technical requirements

We will use similar tools to the ones we used in the previous chapter with one addition. We will be using Plotly Express as well as the `graph_objects` module for creating our charts. The packages to use are Plotly, Dash, Dash Core Component, Dash HTML Components, Dash Bootstrap Components, pandas, and the new `dash_table` package. You don't need to install this separately (although you can), as it is installed together with Dash when you install it.

The code files of this chapter can be found on GitHub at `https://github.com/PacktPublishing/Interactive-Dashboards-and-Data-Apps-with-Plotly-and-Dash/tree/master/chapter_08`.

Check out the following video to see the Code in Action at `https://bit.ly/3sGSCes`.

Creating a histogram

We want to see how we can get the distribution of a sample of data and get an idea of where values are concentrated, as well as how much variability/spread it has. We will do this by creating a histogram.

As always, we'll start with the simplest possible example:

1. We open the `poverty` DataFrame and create a subset of it, containing only countries and data from the year 2015:

    ```
    import pandas as pd
    poverty = pd.read_csv('data/poverty.csv')
    df = poverty[poverty['is_country'] & poverty['year'].
    eq(2015)]
    ```

2. Import Plotly Express and run the `histogram` function with `df` as the argument to the `data_frame` parameter and the indicator of our choice for the x parameter:

    ```
    import plotly.express as px
    gini = 'GINI index (World Bank estimate)'
    px.histogram(data_frame=df, x=gini)
    ```

    As a result, we get the histogram that you can see in *Figure 8.1*:

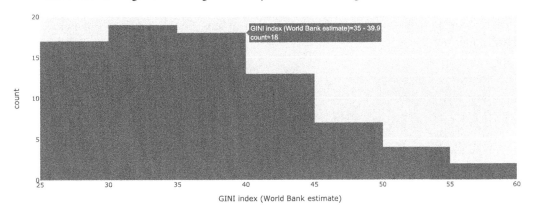

Figure 8.1 – A histogram of the Gini indicator

The *x* axis was named using the indicator we chose, and the *y* axis was given the title count. This is the default function that the histogram function uses, and it is clear also from the hover box that we see when hovering over any of the bars. Here we learn that there are 18 countries whose Gini index was in the interval (**35, 39.9**) in the year 2015. We have previously visualized this indicator by country (visualizing each and every country), but this time, we are getting an idea of how many values are available in each bin and how those values are distributed. We can see that the majority of countries have a Gini index between 25 and 40 and that the numbers get progressively lower the higher the Gini index becomes. This is valid for this particular year only, of course.

We are using the default number of bins, but we can modify it if we want. This is something that you typically want to interactively modify until you get a good view. In an interactive setting, such as in a dashboard, it's probably a good idea to allow users to modify the number of bins, especially if you don't know which metric they will choose and how the values are distributed for that metric. This is exactly our case in the dataset we are working with.

Let's see the effect of changing the number of bins, as well as other available modifications.

Customizing the histogram by modifying its bins and using multiple histograms

We can change the number of bins through the nbins parameter. We will first see the effect of using two extreme values for the number of bins. Setting nbins=2 generates the chart in *Figure 8.2*:

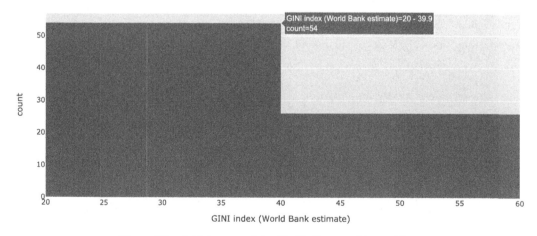

Figure 8.2 – A histogram of the Gini indicator with two bins

As you can see, the values were split into two equal bins, (**20, 39.9**) and (**40, 59.9**), and we can see how many countries are in each bin. It's quite simple and easy to understand, but not as nuanced as the histogram in *Figure 8.1*. On the other hand, setting `nbins=500` produces the chart in *Figure 8.3*:

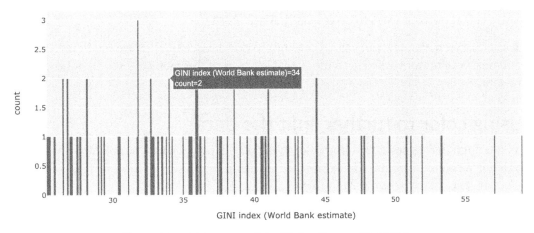

Figure 8.3 – A histogram of the Gini indicator with 500 bins

It is now much more detailed, maybe more detailed than useful. When you set too many bins, it is almost like looking at the raw data.

The default number of bins resulted in the bin size being intervals of five. Now that we know that our values range between 25 and 60 (45), we might want to see how the data is distributed across 45 bins. This makes the size of each bin 1. *Figure 8.4* shows the result of setting `nbins=45`:

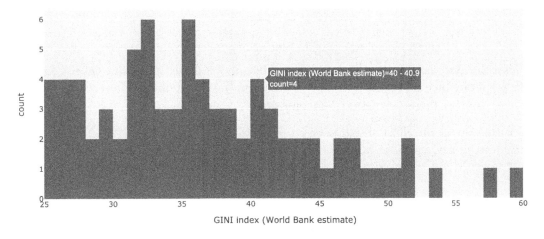

Figure 8.4 – A histogram of the Gini indicator with 45 bins

All the figures we created in this chapter so far were for the same dataset. You can see how different the distribution looks based on the selected number of bins. You can also think of it as looking at the distribution of the data with varying resolutions. There is usually an optimal resolution for your use case that can be manually tweaked until you find the most useful/insightful one for you. This is a major advantage of making histograms interactive, where you allow your users to explore as they see fit.

Recall that we have a few categorical columns in our dataset and that we might use those columns to color our bars to get a more detailed view of the data. Let's see how this can be done.

Using color to further split the data

As you might have guessed, adding color to a Plotly Express chart is simply done by selecting a column from the DataFrame we are using. Setting `color='Income Group'` generates the chart you can see in *Figure 8.5*:

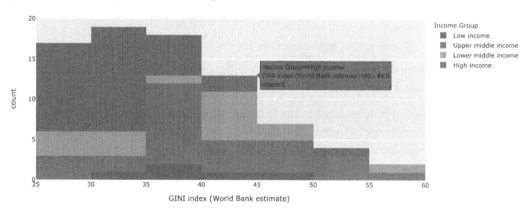

Figure 8.5 – A histogram of the Gini indicator colored by Income Group

This is the exact same histogram but enriched by another dimension of the dataset. Each bar is split by **Income Group** and colored accordingly. We can now see for each bin how many countries there are from each income group.

You can also see the effect of setting `color='Region', color_discrete_sequence=px.colors.qualitative.Set1` in *Figure 8.6*:

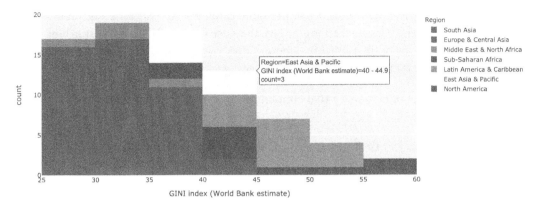

Figure 8.6 – A histogram of the Gini indicator colored by Region

Again, we have the same histogram, but colored using a different column, **Region** in this case. If you remember our discussion of bar charts in *Chapter 5, Interactively Comparing Values with Bar Charts and Dropdown Menus*, we saw that there are different ways of displaying bars. This can also be achieved using the barmode parameter. Let's explore how this applies to histograms.

> **Tip**
>
> You might have noticed that the bars in histograms are displayed in a connected manner, without any spaces between them as is the case in bar charts. This is a visual cue, to indicate the connected nature of histograms. The bins are arbitrary separation points that separate a group of observations from one another. As we saw, those can be selected differently, and result in quite different shapes. Bar charts are typically used for discrete or categorical variables and are typically displayed with some space between them to express this fact.

Exploring other ways of displaying multiple bars in histograms

The two previous histograms displayed the sub-bars in each bin stacked on top of one another. This makes sense, as those sub-bars represent a grouping of the data under the respective bin. In other words, they show the distribution of groups of countries for each bin.

In some other cases, we might want to do the same thing but for two different years. In this case, having the bars stacked might give the false impression that the sub-bars correspond to portions of the same bin, whereas they correspond to the same bin but for different years. An example can show this more easily:

1. Create a subset of `poverty` that contains only countries and the range of years is [2010, 2015]:

```
df = poverty[poverty['is_country'] & poverty['year'].
isin([2010, 2015])]
```

2. Run the `histogram` function for the Gini index, coloring by `year` and setting `barmode='group'`:

```
px.histogram(df, x=gini, color='year', barmode='group')
```

This results in the following output:

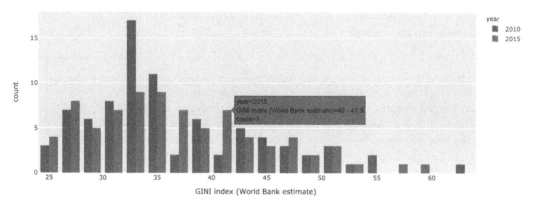

Figure 8.7 – A histogram of the Gini indicator colored by year, with barmode set to "group"

Because years represent a "before and after" view of the same metric and the same bin, I think it makes more sense to display them next to each other, so we can see how each bin value increased or decreased for the two, or more, selected years.

There is another approach to the same issue if we are more interested in highlighting the change in the distribution as a whole. We can run the same function we just ran, but use facets in addition to color to split the histogram in two. The code is also straightforward and contains one more argument, as follows:

```
px.histogram(df, x=gini, color='year', facet_col='year')
```

This results in the following output:

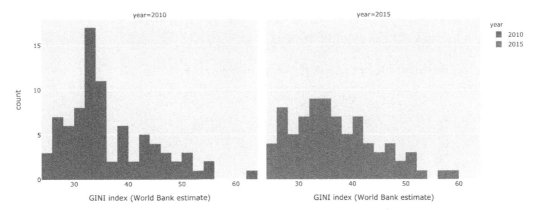

Figure 8.8 – A histogram of the Gini indicator colored and split by year

Again, the last two charts display the same information in two different ways. In *Figure 8.7*, it's very easy to compare how the count of countries for each bin changed from year to year. But it's a bit more difficult to see how the *distributions* have changed between the first and second years. The opposite is true for *Figure 8.8*. Note that we could also use `facet_row` as well, and this would have displayed the charts on top of one another. But we chose to display them next to each other because we are interested in comparing the heights of the bars, and it's much easier to do so when they are next to each other. Had we set `orientation='h'` (for horizontal), then it would have been easier to use `facet_row` in this case.

Sometimes we might be more interested in the percentage of the number of values in a certain bin, as opposed to the absolute count for each bin. Getting this is also very simple. We just need to set `histnorm='percent'`. We start by creating a `fig` object and add the new option:

```
fig = px.histogram(df, x=gini, color='year', facet_col='year',
```

We can also make it more explicit that we are displaying percentages by adding a tick suffix to the *y*-axis ticks. This can be achieved with the following code:

```
fig.layout.yaxis.ticksuffix = '%'
```

We might also want to set a more descriptive title for the *y* axis, which can also be easily achieved using the following code:

```
fig.layout.yaxis.title = 'Percent of total'
```

Running this modified code produces the chart in *Figure 8.9*:

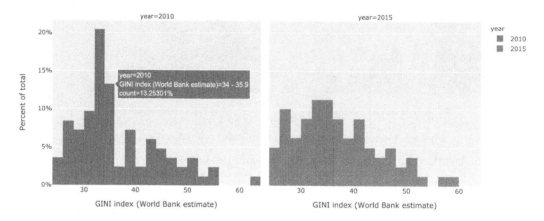

Figure 8.9 – A histogram of the Gini indicator colored and split by year, showing percentages

This chart looks identical to the one in *Figure 8.8*. The main difference is that the height of the bars represents the percentage and not the absolute count. This was also made clearer with tick suffixes and a *y*-axis title.

We have explored quite a few options with histograms. Let's now make our histograms interactive and add a few other options.

Adding interactivity to histograms

Just like we did in *Chapter 7, Exploring Map Plots and Enriching Your Dashboards with Markdown*, we can do the same with histograms. We can allow users to get a better idea about the distribution of a certain indicator in a certain year or more. The difference is that we want to allow them to customize the number of bins. Since we are now comfortable with handling multiple inputs and outputs, let's also add some more options for our users. We can also allow users to select multiple years and display multiple years on multiple sub-plots using faceting. *Figure 8.10* shows what we will be working toward to make it clear:

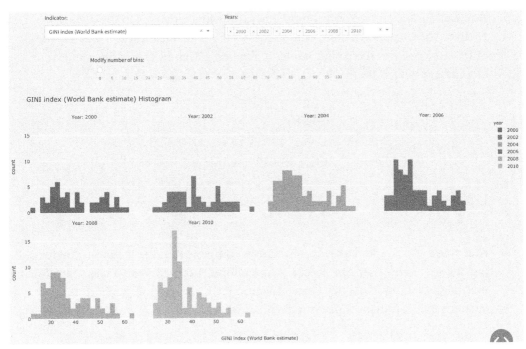

Figure 8.10 – A histogram app allowing the selection of indicator, year(s), and bins

Let's start building right away. We won't be discussing the layout elements such as color and width, but you can always refer to the code repository for the exact solution. We will focus on building the interactivity for this. Later on, we will add it to our app:

1. Make the necessary imports:

```
from jupyter_dash import JupyterDash
import dash_core_components as dcc
import dash_html_components as html
import dash_bootstrap_components as dbc
from dash.dependencies import Output, Input
```

2. Create an app object and its `layout` attribute:

```
app = JupyterDash(__name__)
app.layout = html.Div([])
```

3. Add `Label` and `Dropdown` components as the first elements to the div just created. The `Dropdown` component displays the available indicators, and is the exact same one we created in *Chapter 7, Exploring Map Plots and Enriching Your Dashboards with Markdown*:

```
html.Div([
    dbc.Label('Indicator:'),
    dcc.Dropdown(id='hist_indicator_dropdown',
                 index (World Bank estimate)',
                 indicator, 'value': indicator}
 for indicator in poverty.columns[3:54]]),
 ])
```

4. Add a `dbc.Label` and a `dcc.Dropdown` component to the list in the div for indicating that the user can select a year and the actual years to be selected, allowing multiple selections. Note that since this dropdown allows multiple selection, its default value, if provided, needs to be provided as a list:

```
dbc.Label('Years:'), dcc.Dropdown(id='hist_multi_year_
selector',
            value=[2015],
            one or more years',
            year, 'value': year}
                  for year in poverty['year'].drop_
duplicates().sort_values()]),
```

5. Again, to the same list in the div, we add another `dbc.Label` component and a `dcc.Slider` component that will allow users to modify the number of bins in the resulting histogram(s). Note that by not setting a default value, Plotly will provide the default number of bins based on the data being analyzed. It would show as **0** in the slider. Users are then free to modify it if they wish to do so:

```
dbc.Label('Modify number of bins:'),
dcc.Slider(id='hist_bins_slider',
           min=0,
           step=5,
           marks={x: str(x) for x in range(0, 105, 5)}),
```

6. Finally, we add a `Graph` component, and this will complete our layout:

```
dcc.Graph(id='indicator_year_histogram')
```

Running these steps creates our app's visible part (the layout) without any functionality. The default looks as in *Figure 8.11*, and I'll leave it to you to modify the colors, alignment, and relative positioning, using the knowledge we built in *Chapter 1, Overview of the Dash Ecosystem*:

Figure 8.11 – The default view of the histogram app with no functionality

We'll now go on to build the interactivity. In this case, we need to build a function that takes three inputs (the indicator dropdown, the years dropdown, and the bins slider). It will return a `Figure` object, which will modify the chart at the bottom of the figure:

1. Create the callback. There is nothing special here; we just make sure to have the IDs show that they are related to the histogram:

```
@app.callback(Output('indicator_year_histogram',
'figure'),
                Input('hist_multi_year_selector', 'value'),
                Input('hist_indicator_dropdown', 'value'),
                Input('hist_bins_slider', 'value'))
```

2. Create the function that generates our histogram using the inputs just created. We first check that neither `year` nor `indicator` is provided, in which case we `raise` `PreventUpdate`:

```
def display_histogram(years, indicator, nbins):
    if (not years) or (not indicator):
        raise PreventUpdate
```

3. Create a sub-set, `df`, by selecting countries only, as well as getting rows where the year is in the provided `years` argument:

```
df = poverty[poverty['year'].isin(years) & poverty['is_
country']]
```

4. We are now ready to create the figure, which is done by calling the `histogram` function. As we saw in this chapter, we provide `df` to the `data_frame` parameter, `indicator` for the x parameter, and `year` to `color`. The title of the figure will be set by concatenating the indicator with the `Histogram` string. The `nbins` parameter will take the `nbins` value selected by the user from the slider. For facets, we use the `year` column. Since we don't know how many years users will select, and we don't want them to end up creating a difficult-to-read chart, we set `facet_col_wrap=4`. This will ensure that each row of charts will contain no more than four, and the following one will be added to the next row of charts:

```
fig = px.histogram(df,
                   color='year',
                   + ' Histogram',
                   facet_col='year',
                   height=700)
```

5. A new and interesting option that we haven't covered so far is the `for_each_xaxis` attribute. Note that this is only one of several `for_each_` attributes, which you can explore separately. This is useful in situations where the number of x-axis attributes is not known, such as in this case, or simply when multiple attributes exist. By default, every facet (or sub-plot) will have its own x-axis title. As you know, there are many indicator names that are very long and will overlap in this case. To eliminate this, we set all `xaxis` titles to an empty string:

```
fig.for_each_xaxis(lambda axis: axis.update(title=''))
```

6. To replace the deleted *x*-axis titles, we can create an annotation instead. The annotation is a simple string that can easily be added with the `add_annotation` method. Because we want the X position of the annotation to be at the center of the figure, we set its x value to `0.5`. Also, because we want the Y position to be slightly below the plot area, we set the y value to `-0.12`. Now, it's important to indicate to Plotly the meaning of those numbers we provide, or their reference. We can use the `xref` and `yref` parameters to indicate that these values should take `paper` as their reference. This means to take these points as fractions of the plot and not as data points, like in scatter plots, for example. This is useful because those annotations will serve as axis titles, and so we want their position to be fixed. By default, annotations come with arrows pointing to the point selected. We can remove that by setting `showarrow=False`, as follows:

```
fig.add_annotation(text=indicator,
                   y=-0.12,
                   yref='paper',
```

The following is the full code of the function to make it clearer:

```
@app.callback(Output('indicator_year_histogram', 'figure'),
              Input('hist_multi_year_selector', 'value'),
              Input('hist_indicator_dropdown', 'value'),
              Input('hist_bins_slider', 'value'))
def display_histogram(years, indicator, nbins):
    if (not years) or (not indicator):
        raise PreventUpdate
    df = poverty[poverty['year'].isin(years) & poverty['is_
country']]

    fig = px.histogram(df,
                       color='year',
                       + ' Histogram',
                       facet_col='year',
                       height=700)

    fig.for_each_xaxis(lambda axis: axis.update(title=''))
    fig.add_annotation(text=indicator,
                       y=-0.12,
                       yref='paper',
                       fig
```

With this, we have created an independent app that can run in JupyterLab. I encourage you to fully run it and see whether you come across issues, and to also customize and make some changes to it.

So far, we have explored how to visualize the counts and distributions of values for a single set of observations. There is also an interesting way to explore two sets of observations at the same time, which can be done using a 2D histogram.

Creating a 2D histogram

In the first case, we basically counted the observations in each bin of our dataset. In this case, we will do the same but for *combinations* of bins for both datasets. The bins for each variable will end up creating a matrix. A simple example can make this easy. Let's create one and see:

1. Create a subset of `poverty` containing only countries, where the year is equal to 2000:

```
df = poverty[poverty['year'].eq(2000) & poverty['is_
country']]
```

2. Create a `Figure` object and add a `histogram2d` trace (at the time of writing, this chart type is not available in Plotly Express). We simply select any two indicators that we would like to plot together and pass them to x and y:

```
fig = go.Figure()
fig.add_histogram2d(x=df['Income share held by fourth
20%'],
                    y=df['GINI index (World Bank
estimate)'],
                    colorscale='cividis')
```

3. Add titles for the *x* and *y* axes:

```
fig.layout.xaxis.title = 'Income share held by fourth
20%'
fig.layout.yaxis.title = 'GINI index (World Bank
estimate)'
fig.show()
```

Running the preceding code generates the chart in *Figure 8.12*:

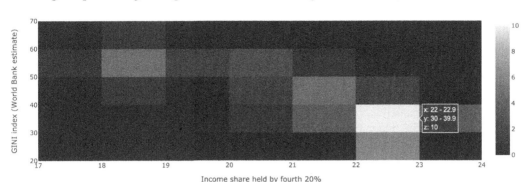

Figure 8.12 – A 2D histogram

The frequency of values is expressed in a different way here. With a 1D histogram, the height of the bars represents the frequency of values in the respective bin. In a 2D histogram, the "height" is expressed using a continuous color scale. We can see from the color bar that the counts range from 0 to 10, and that the bin combination with the most values is the **x** interval (**22, 22.9**) and the **y** interval (**30, 39.9**), with a **z** value (height) of **10**. Generally, z is used to refer to the third dimension, and so this can also be thought of as the height of this rectangle.

Note that this is different from using a scatter plot for two variables. In that case, we would be interested in seeing a correlation between the two variables, or at least how they both vary. In this case, we are trying to identify where the most frequent observations are, across two variables, and under which combination of bins.

There are still many options that you can explore with histograms, or visualizing distributions and counts in general. We have explored many of those options, and now we'll turn to explore another interactive component that is available in Dash, the DataTable.

Creating a DataTable

Technically, dash_table is a separate package, as mentioned at the beginning of the chapter, and can be installed separately. It is installed automatically with Dash, the correct, up-to-date version, which is the recommended approach.

Many times, displaying tables, especially if they are interactive, can add a lot of value to users of our dashboards. Also, if our dashboards or data visualizations are not sufficient for users, or if they want to run their own analysis, it is probably a good idea to allow them to get the raw data for that. Finally, the DataTable component allows its own data visualization through custom coloring, fonts, sizes, and so on. So, we have another way to visualize and understand our data through tables. We will explore a few options in this chapter, but definitely not all of them.

Let's see how we can create a simple DataTable in a simple app using a DataFrame:

1. Create a subset of poverty containing only countries, from the year 2000, and containing columns that have Country Name or have the income share of the top and bottom 10% of the population. We use the filter method with a regular expression to achieve that:

    ```
    df = poverty[poverty['year'].eq(2000)&poverty['is_
    country']].filter(regex='Country Name|Income share.*10')
    ```

2. Create an app in JupyterLab with a layout attribute:

    ```
    app = JupyterDash(__name__, external_stylesheets=[dbc.
    themes.COSMO])
    ```
    ```
    app.layout = html.Div([])
    ```

3. Pass a DataTable object to the div just created. As a minimum, a table requires values for the data parameter, as well as the columns parameter. One of the easiest ways to do this is by providing a dictionary converted from a DataFrame, using the to_dict('records') method. columns needs to be a list of dictionaries, where each dictionary contains the name and id keys. The name is what appears to users, and the ID is the value that will actually be used:

    ```
    DataTable(data=df.to_dict('records'),
                columns=[{'name': col, 'id': col}
                          col in df.columns])
    ```

Running this simple app with app.run_server() produces a table as you can see in *Figure 8.13*, showing the first few rows:

Country Name	Income share held by highest 10%	Income share held by lowest 10%
Afghanistan		
Albania		
Algeria		
Angola	40.2	1
Argentina	37.7	0.9
Armenia		
Australia		
Austria	22.7	3.4
Azerbaijan		
Bangladesh	27.9	3.7
Belarus	24	3.1
Belgium	28.3	3.3
Belize		

Figure 8.13 – A simple DataTable

Many times, your tables or column headers might not fit neatly in the container they are placed in. For example, in our case, many indicator names are extremely long, and their columns contain numbers that don't take much horizontal space. Let's explore some of the available options to handle this.

Controlling the look and feel of the table (cell width, height, text display, and more)

There are numerous options available to modify how your tables look, and it's always good to consult the documentation for ideas and solutions. The potentially tricky part is when you have combinations of options. In some cases, these might modify each other and not be displayed exactly the way you want. So, it is always good to isolate the options as much as possible when debugging.

In *Figure 8.13*, we displayed only three columns and the first few rows. We will now see how to display more columns and enable users to explore more rows:

1. Modify df to include all columns that contain Income share:

    ```
    df = poverty[poverty['year'].eq(2000)&poverty['is_
    country']].filter(regex='Country Name|Income share')
    ```

2. Place the DataTable in a `dbc.Col` component with the desired width, 7 in this case. The table automatically takes the width of the container it is in, so this would set its width implicitly:

```
dbc.Col([], lg=7)
```

3. We now want to determine how the column headers will behave, especially as they have quite long names. This can be achieved with the `style_header` parameter. Note that there are several `style_` parameters for headers, cells, and tables, and they also have `_conditional` variants, for example, `style_cell_conditional`, to conditionally set the style of cells. We now specify the header style with the following option, to allow text to overflow into multiple lines when/if needed:

```
style_header={'whiteSpace': 'normal'}
```

4. We now want to make sure that while scrolling, the headers remain fixed in place:

```
fixed_rows={'headers': True}
```

5. In order to control the height of the table as a whole, we can simply do so with the following parameter:

```
style_table={'height': '400px'}
```

6. In cases where we have thousands of rows, it might be heavy and affect the performance of the page, so we can use `virtualization`. In our case, it is a very small table, but we can set `virtualization` to demonstrate its usage:

```
virtualization=True
```

Putting the code together, here is the full code to generate the table:

```
dbc.Col([
    DataTable(data=df.to_dict('records'),
              columns=[{'name': col, 'id': col}
                       col in df.columns],
              style_header={'whiteSpace': 'normal'},
              fixed_rows={'headers': True},
              virtualization=True,
              style_table={'height': '400px'})
], lg =7),
```

Running this modified code produces the table in *Figure 8.14*:

Country Name	Income share held by fourth 20%	Income share held by highest 10%	Income share held by highest 20%	Income share held by lowest 10%	Income share held by lowest 20%	Income share held by second 20%	Income share held by third 20%
Cyprus							
Czech Republic							
Denmark	22.6	20.1	34.2	4.4	10.4	14.7	18.
Djibouti							
Dominican Republic	20.1	40.2	56.2	1.2	3.7	7.7	12.
Ecuador	18.1	45.9	60.7	0.9	3	7	11.
Egypt, Arab Rep.							
El Salvador	20.5	39	55.8	1	3.2	7.8	12.
Equatorial Guinea							
Eritrea							
Estonia							
Eswatini	17.5	44.1	59.5	1.8	4.5	7.5	10.

Figure 8.14 – A DataTable with custom options for width, height, scrolling, and virtualization

The scroll bar is only visible if the cursor is pointing there. It was kept for demonstration, and to make it clear that scrolling is enabled. Now users can see all the available rows by scrolling as much as they want. We will now see how to incorporate some interactivity with tables and add this to our app. We'll also use this as an opportunity to demonstrate a few other options available to the DataTable component.

Adding histograms and tables to the app

We are now ready to incorporate the table functionality into our app and add it to the callback function that we already created. What we will do is display the data that is used to generate the histograms right under the histogram figure. Since the histograms don't show data points as we discussed (only aggregates), it might be interesting for users to see for themselves if they wish.

Let's add this functionality right away:

1. Add a new div right underneath the histogram figure:

    ```
    html.Div(id='table_histogram_output')
    ```

2. Add this as an Output to the callback function:

```
@app.callback(Output('indicator_year_histogram',
'figure'),
                Output('table_histogram_output',
'children'),
                Input('hist_multi_year_selector', 'value'),
                Input('hist_indicator_dropdown', 'value'),
                Input('hist_bins_slider', 'value'))
```

3. Right after we finish the definition of our Figure object, we add the definition of
    our DataTable. We will be using the same options as before and adding a few new
    ones. We first add the ability to sort columns:

```
sort_action='native'
```

4. Now, we add the ability to filter columns. This will add an empty box right under
    each column header. Users can enter text and hit *Enter* to get a filtered table:

```
filter_action='native'
```

5. Add the ability to export the table to CSV format:

```
export_format='csv'
```

6. We set a minimum width for cells to keep it consistent and avoid any formatting
    issues due to different columns' headers:

```
style_cell={'minWidth': '150px'}
```

7. Finally, add the table to the return statement at the end of the function, so it
    returns two items instead of one:

```
return fig, table
```

As a result of adding this functionality, our updated app will contain the table that is being
used to generate the histograms, and users can export it or interact with it if they want.
Figure 8.15 shows our app with the additional customized DataTable:

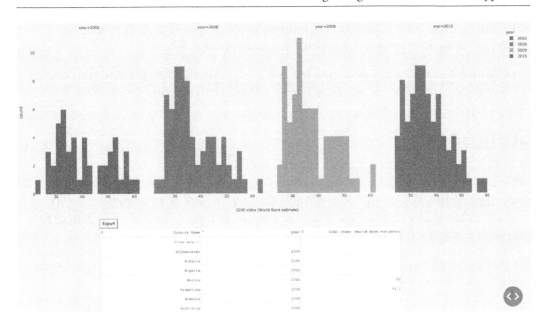

Figure 8.15 – A DataTable showing the data used to generate the histograms

We now have an **Export** button, which is clear and immediately triggers the download functionality in the browser. Header names now have arrows that allow users to sort, in an ascending or descending manner. You can also see the filtering option, with the **filter data…** placeholder text, which users can filter by.

Now, in order to incorporate this functionality into our app, we simply have to copy the components where we want them to appear. As this can be thought of as exploratory functionality (users are still not digging deep into an indicator), it's probably good to have it under the map chart.

To add the interactivity, we only have to add the callback function that we created, as we always do, after the layout of the app.

We have already done this many times, and it should be straightforward for you to do so.

Our app is now getting really rich. We have two main exploratory interactive charts at the top. The maps allow users to select a metric and see its variation across countries on the map. They can also select the year and/or allow it to play like a video. The selected indicator triggers the display of descriptive text about it, for more context to users. Under that, we have the option of selecting an indicator and one or more years, to see how this indicator is distributed with histograms. Users can modify the number of bins to get an optimal view. This also updates the table they can interact with and export.

After having explored the indicators of interest, users can go on to explore specific indicators using the three specialized charts that we created.

Congratulations! We have now completed *Part 2* of the book, so it's good to review what we have done in the chapter, as well as *Part 2*, and get ready for *Part 3*.

Summary

In this chapter, we first learned about the main difference between histograms and the other types of charts we have covered so far. We saw how easy it is to create them, and more importantly, we saw how customizable they can be with bins, `barmode`, colors, and facets. We then explored how to add interactivity to histograms by connecting them to other components with a callback function.

We then explored the 2D histogram and saw how it can provide an even richer view of two columns visualized against each other.

We introduced a new interactive component, the DataTable. We barely scratched the surface of what can be done with tables. We used them to make it easier for users to obtain, interact with, or simply view the raw data behind our histograms. We also explored the different ways to control the look and feel of our tables.

Finally, we incorporated the table functionality with the callback function we created and added the interactivity to our app.

Let's now take a quick look at what we have covered so far in the book and prepare for *Part 3*.

What we have covered so far

In the first part of the book, we covered the basics of Dash apps. We first explored how they are structured and how to manage the visual elements. Then, we explored how interactivity is created, which is mainly by using callback functions. This allowed us to create fully interactive apps. We then explored the structure of the `Figure` object and learned how to modify and manipulate it to generate the charts we desire. After that, we saw how important data manipulation and preparation are for data visualization. We went through a reshaping of our dataset, to make things more intuitive to work with. This paved the way for easily learning and using Plotly Express.

Part 2 was about getting thoroughly familiar with several types of charts, as well as interactive components. We implemented all the knowledge we built in *Part 1*, but most importantly, we did this in a practical setting. We gradually added more and more charts, components, and functionality to one app. At every step, we had to consider how it will affect the whole app and had to make sure we did so with a holistic view. You are now very familiar with making changes to many types of functionality. Although we didn't cover every type of chart and component, the general principles are similar, and you can easily adapt the knowledge you have to new situations.

Part 3 will move on to more general topics about apps, URLs, advanced callbacks, and deployment. But the next chapter will explore a few **machine learning** options. Our dataset contains many countries, years, and indicators, and the number of possible combinations to explore is massive. So, we will explore a few techniques that can help uncover trends or correlations in our data.

Section 3: Taking Your App to the Next Level

This section explores further options regarding fine-tuning, improving, and extending your app. It shows you several new strategies and techniques for modifying and pushing your app to the cloud.

This section comprises the following chapters:

9
Letting Your Data Speak for Itself with Machine Learning

While making histograms we got a glimpse of a technique that visualizes aggregates, and not data points directly. In other words, we visualized data about our data. We will take this concept several steps further in this chapter, by using a machine learning technique to demonstrate some options that can be used to categorize or cluster our data. As you will see in this chapter, and even while using a single technique, there are numerous options and combinations of options that can be explored. This is where the value of interactive dashboards comes into play. It would be very tedious if users were to explore every single option by manually creating a chart for it.

This chapter is not an introduction to machine learning, nor does it assume any prior knowledge of it. We will explore a clustering technique called **KMeans clustering** and use the `sklearn` machine learning package. This will help us in grouping our data into clusters of observations that are similar to one another, and yet distinct from observations in other clusters. We will build a very simple model with a single-dimensional dataset, and then see how this can be applied to clustering countries in our `poverty` dataset.

If you are familiar with machine learning, then this chapter will hopefully give you some ideas of how to empower your users and allow them to tune and explore several aspects of the models used. If not, you should be able to complete the chapter, and it will hopefully inspire you to explore more machine learning concepts and techniques.

We will go through the following topics in this chapter:

- Understanding clustering

- Finding the optimal number of clusters

- Clustering countries by population

- Preparing data with `scikit-learn`

- Creating an interactive K-Means clustering app

Technical requirements

We will be exploring a few options from `sklearn`, as well as `NumPy`. Otherwise, we will be using the same tools we have been using. For visualization and building interactivity, Dash, JupyterDash, the Dash Core Component library, Dash HTML Components, Dash Bootstrap Components, Plotly, and Plotly Express will be used. For data manipulation and preparation, we will use `pandas` and `NumPy`. JupyterLab will be used for exploring and building independent functionality. Finally, `sklearn` will be used for building our machine learning models, as well as for preparing our data.

The code files of this chapter can be found on GitHub at `https://github.com/PacktPublishing/Interactive-Dashboards-and-Data-Apps-with-Plotly-and-Dash/tree/master/chapter_09`.

Check out the following video to see the Code in Action at `https://bit.ly/3x8PAmt`.

Understanding clustering

So, what exactly is clustering and when might it be helpful? Let's start with a very simple example. Imagine you have a group of people for whom we want to make T-shirts. We can make a T-shirt for each one of them, in whatever size required. The main restriction is that we can only make one size. The sizes are as follows: [1, 2, 3, 4, 5, 7, 9, 11]. Think how you might tackle this problem. We will use the `KMeans` algorithm for that, so let's start right away, as follows:

1. Import the required packages and models. `NumPy` will be imported as a package, but from `sklearn` we will import the only model that we will be using for now, as illustrated in the following code snippet:

    ```
    import numpy as np
    from sklearn.cluster import KMeans
    ```

2. Create a dataset of sizes in the required format. Note that each observation (person's size) should be represented as a list, so we use the `reshape` method of NumPy arrays to get the data in the required format, as follows:

```
sizes = np.array([1, 2, 3, 4, 5, 7, 9, 11]).reshape(-1,
1)
sizes
array([[ 1],
       [ 2],
       [ 3],
       [ 4],
       [ 5],
       [ 7],
       [ 9],
       [11]])
```

3. Create an instance of the `KMeans` model with the required number of clusters. An important feature of this model is that we provide the desired number of clusters for it. In this case, we were given a constraint, which is that we can only make T-shirts in one size, so we want to discover a single point that would be the center of our discovered cluster. We will explore the effect of the chosen number of clusters after that. Run the following code:

```
kmeans1 = KMeans(n_clusters=1)
```

4. Fit the model to the data using the `fit` method. This means that we want the model we just created to "learn" the dataset based on this particular algorithm, and with the provided parameters/options. This is the code you will need:

```
kmeans1.fit(sizes)
KMeans(n_clusters=1)
```

We now have a model that has been trained on this dataset, and we can go on to check some of its attributes. As a convention, the resulting attributes of the fitted models have a trailing underscore to them, as we will see now. We can now ask for the clusters that we asked for. The `cluster_centers_` attribute provides the answer to this. The centers (in this case, one center) are basically the means of the clusters of our data points. Let's check the result, as follows:

```
kmeans1.cluster_centers_
array([[5.25]])
```

We received the attribute in the form of a list of lists. The center of our cluster is 5.25, apparently. You might be thinking that this is a convoluted way of calculating the mean of our dataset, and you would be right. Have a look at the following code snippet:

```
sizes.mean()
5.25
```

Indeed, our cluster center happens to be the mean of our dataset, which is exactly what we asked for. To visualize this, the following screenshot shows the relative position of the cluster center, related to our data points:

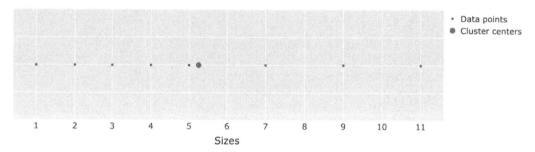

Figure 9.1 – The Sizes data points, with the cluster center provided by KMeans

The chart depicted in the previous screenshot is very simple—we simply plot the sizes on the x axis, and an arbitrary constant value for the y axis.

In order to evaluate the performance of our model and how well it fits the data, there are several ways to do this—one way is by checking the `inertia_` attribute. This is an attribute of the instance we created and can be accessed after fitting it to the data, using dot notation, as follows:

```
kmeans1.inertia_
85.5
```

The `inertia_` metric is the sum of squared distances of samples, to their closest cluster center. If the model performs well, the distances of the samples to the provided cluster centers should be as short as possible (data points are close to the cluster centers). A perfect model would have an inertia rate of 0. Also, looking at it from the other side, we also know that asking for one cluster would give us the worst possible outcome because it is just one cluster, and to be the average point it has to be very far from the extreme data points.

Accordingly, we can improve the performance of the model simply by adding more clusters, because their distances to the centers would be reduced.

Now, imagine that I called you and shared some good news. We have an additional budget for one more size, and now we want to make T-shirts in two sizes. Translating to machine learning language, this means we need to create a new model with two clusters. We repeat the same steps and modify the n_clusters argument, as follows:

```
kmeans2 = KMeans(n_clusters=2)
kmeans2.fit(sizes)
kmeans2.cluster_centers_
array([[3.],
       [9.]])
```

We now have two new centers, as specified.

It's not enough to know the centers of our clusters. For each point, we need to know which cluster it belongs to, or we want to know the size of T-shirt that we will give to each person in our group. We can also count them and check the number of points in each cluster.

The labels_ attribute contains this information, and can be seen here:

```
kmeans2.labels_
array([0, 0, 0, 0, 0, 1, 1, 1], dtype=int32)
```

Note that the labels are given using integers starting at 0. Also note that the numbers don't mean anything quantitative. Points that have a zero label are not from the first cluster; nor are points with the label 1 "more" than the others in any way. These are just labels, such as calling them group A, group B, and so on.

We can map the labels to their respective values by using the zip function, as follows:

```
list(zip(sizes, kmeans2.labels_))
[(array([1]), 0),
 (array([2]), 0),
 (array([3]), 0),
 (array([4]), 0),
 (array([5]), 0),
 (array([7]), 1),
 (array([9]), 1),
 (array([11]), 1)]
```

This will be very important later when use those labels in our charts.

Let's also visualize the two centers to get a better idea of how this works. The following screenshot shows where the cluster centers are located relative to other data points:

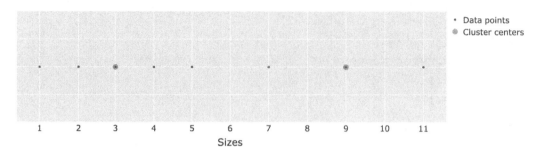

Figure 9.2 – The Sizes data points, with two cluster centers provided by KMeans

The centers make sense visually. We can see that the first five points are close to each other and that the last three are distinct and far from them, with larger gaps. Having 3 and 9 as cluster centers makes sense, because each of them is the mean of the values of its own cluster. Let's now numerically validate that we have improved the performance of our model by checking the inertia rate, as follows:

```
kmeans2.inertia_
18.0
```

Indeed, the performance was tremendously improved and reduced from 85.5 to 18.0. Nothing surprising here. As you can expect, every additional cluster would improve the performance until we reach the perfect result with an inertia rate of 0. So, how do we evaluate the best options available for the number of clusters?

Finding the optimal number of clusters

We will now see the options we have in choosing the optimal number of clusters and what that entails, but let's first take a look at the following screenshot to visualize how things progress from having one cluster to eight clusters:

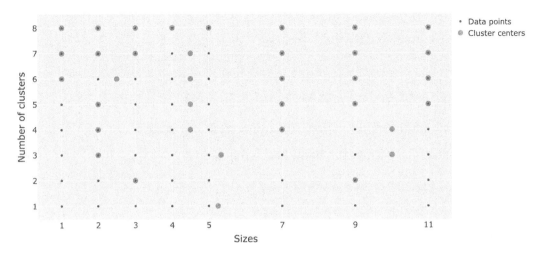

Figure 9.3 – Data points and cluster centers for all possible cluster numbers

We can see the full spectrum of possible clusters and how they relate to data points. At the end, when we specified 8, we got the perfect solution, where every data point is a cluster center.

In reality, you might not want to go for the full solution, for two main reasons. Firstly, it is probably going to be prohibitive from a cost perspective. Imagine making 1,000 T-shirts with a few hundred sizes. Secondly, in practical situations, it usually wouldn't add much value to add more clusters after a certain fit has been achieved. Using our T-shirt example, imagine if we have two people with sizes 5.3 and 5.27. They would most likely wear the same size anyway.

So, we know that the optimal number of clusters is between one and the number of unique data points we have. We now want to explore the trade-offs and options of figuring out that optimal number. One of the strategies we can use is to check the value of additional—or incremental—clusters. When adding a new cluster, does it result in a meaningful reduction (improvement) in inertia? One such technique is called the "elbow technique." We plot the inertia values against the number of clusters and see where there is a sharp change in the direction of the curve. Let's do this now.

We loop through the numbers from 1 to 8, and for each number we go through the same process of instantiating a KMeans object and getting the inertia for that number of clusters. We then add that value to our inertia list, as illustrated in the following code snippet:

```
inertia = []
for i in range(1, 9):
    kmeans = KMeans(i)
```

```
    kmeans.fit(sizes)
    inertia.append(kmeans.inertia_)
inertia
```

```
[85.5, 18.0, 10.5, 4.5, 2.5, 1.0, 0.5, 0.0]
```

As expected, our inertia improved from 85.5 to a perfect zero at the end.

We now plot those to see where the elbow lies, as follows:

```
import plotly.graph_objects as go
fig = go.Figure()
fig.add_scatter(x=list(range(1, 9)), y=inertia)
fig.layout.xaxis.title = 'Number of clusters'
fig.layout.yaxis.title = 'Inertia'
fig.show()
```

Running the preceding code produces the chart shown in the following screenshot:

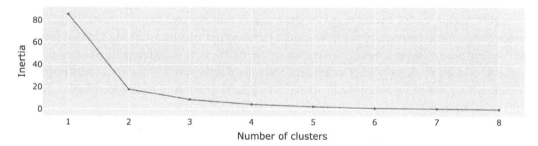

Figure 9.4 – The "elbow" method, showing inertia values for all possible cluster numbers

You can clearly see a sudden drop when moving from 1 to 2 and that inertia keeps decreasing, but at a lower rate as we move toward the final value. So, three or maybe four clusters might be the point where we start to get diminishing returns, and that could be our optimal number of clusters. We also cheated a little by including one cluster, because we already knew that it would be the worst-performing number of clusters. You can see the same plot without the first value in the following screenshot:

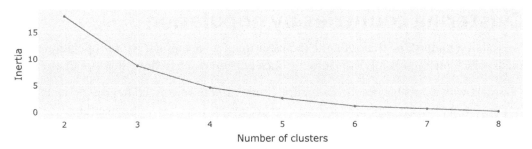

Figure 9.5 – The "elbow" method, showing inertia values for all possible cluster numbers excluding 1

This looks quite different and also shows that we cannot mechanically make a decision without knowing more about the data, the use case, and whatever constraints we might have.

The example we explored was extremely simple in terms of the number of observations, as well as the number of dimensions, which was one dimension. KMeans clustering (and machine learning in general) usually handles multiple dimensions, and the concept is basically the same: we try to find centers of clusters that minimize the distance between them and the data points. For example, the following screenshot shows what a similar problem might look like in two dimensions:

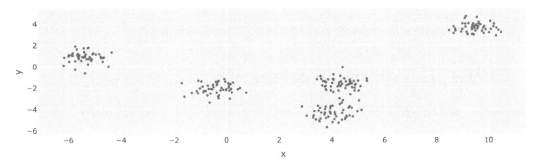

Figure 9.6 – Clustered points in two dimensions

This could correspond to additional measurements relating to our group of people. So, we might have their height on the *x* axis and their weight on the *y* axis, for example. You can imagine what KMeans would give us in this case. Of course, in real life, data is rarely so neatly clustered. You can also see how much accuracy we might lose by selecting the wrong number of clusters. If we specify three clusters, for example, the three blobs in the middle would probably be considered a single cluster, even though we can see that they are quite distinct from one another and that their points are quite close to each other. Also, if we specify seven or eight clusters, we could get unnecessary divisions between clusters, or we would have passed the elbow on the elbow chart in this case.

We are now ready to use this understanding of clustering in our dataset.

Clustering countries by population

We will first understand this with one indicator that we are familiar with (population), and then make it interactive. We will cluster groups of countries based on their population.

Let's start with a possible practical situation. Imagine you were asked to group countries by population. You are supposed to have two groups of countries, of high and low populations. How do you do that? Where do you draw the line(s), and what does the total of the population have to be in order for it to qualify as "high"? Imagine that you were then asked to group countries into three or four groups based on their population. How would you update your clusters?

We can easily see how KMeans clustering is ideal for that.

Let's now do the same exercise with KMeans using one dimension, and then combine that with our knowledge of mapping, as follows:

1. Import pandas and open the poverty dataset, like this:

    ```
    import pandas as pd
    poverty = pd.read_csv('data/poverty.csv')
    ```

2. Create variables for the year and desired indicators, as follows:

    ```
    year = 2018
    indicators = ['Population, total']
    ```

3. Instantiate a KMeans object with the desired number of clusters, like this:

    ```
    kmeans = KMeans(n_clusters=2)
    ```

4. Create a df object, which is the poverty DataFrame containing only countries and data from the selected year only. Run the following code to do this:

    ```
    df = poverty[poverty['year'].eq(year) & poverty['is_
    country']]
    ```

5. Create a data object, which is a list of columns that we choose (in this case, we only chose one). Note in the following code snippet that we get its values attribute, which returns the underlying NumPy array:

    ```
    data = df[indicators].values
    ```

6. Fit the model to the data, as follows:

    ```
    kmeans.fit(data)
    ```

We have now trained the model on our data and are ready to visualize the results. Remember our discussion in *Chapter 7, Exploring Map Plots and Enriching Your Dashboards with Markdown*, that in order to create a map, we simply need a DataFrame with a column containing country names (or codes)? This is enough to produce a map. If we want to color our countries, we need another column (or any list-like object) containing corresponding values.

The kmeans object we just trained contains the labels of the countries and would tell us which country belongs to which cluster. We will use that to color countries, so we do this with one function call. Note that we can convert the labels to strings, which would cause Plotly Express to treat them as categorical and not continuous variables. The code is shown in the following snippet:

```
px.choropleth(df,
              locations='Country Name',
              locationmode='country names',
              color=[str(x) for x in  kmeans.labels_])
```

This code produces the chart shown in the following screenshot:

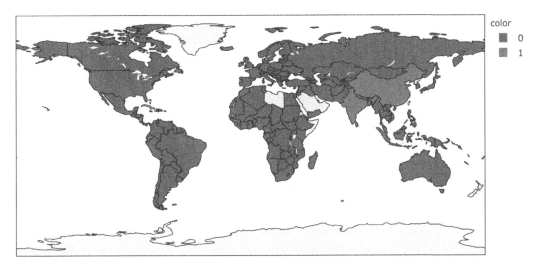

Figure 9.7 – Countries clustered by population

Since we have already developed a template of options for maps, we can copy this and use it to enhance this map and make it consistent with the theme of our app. Let's use that and see the effect of having **1**, **2**, **3**, and **4** clusters on the same map, and discuss the details. The following screenshot shows four maps, each with a different number of clusters:

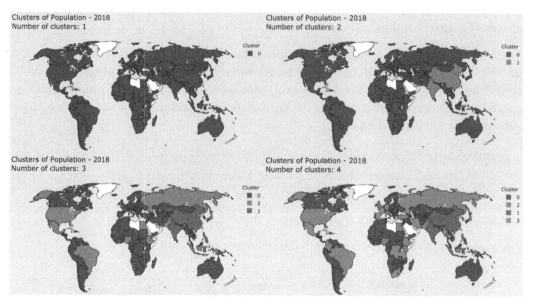

Figure 9.8 – Countries clustered by population using different numbers of clusters

> **Important note**
>
> The colors may not be easy to distinguish on these maps if you are reading the grayscale version, and I encourage you to check out the online version and repository.

As you can see, coloring the map with one cluster (one label for all countries) produces a map with a single color. Things start to get interesting when there are two clusters involved, and this also makes intuitive sense. The two countries forming the cluster with a higher population (namely, China and India) have very large populations that are also close to each other—1.39 billion and 1.35 billion, in this case. The third country, the **United States (US)**, has a population of 327 million. This is exactly what KMeans is supposed to do. It gave us two groups of countries where countries in each cluster are very close to each other and far from countries in the other cluster. Of course, we introduced an important bias by selecting two as the number of clusters, and we saw how that might not be the optimal case.

When we chose three clusters, we can see that we have a medium-population cluster, with the US being one of them. Then, when we chose four, you can see that Russia and Japan were moved to the third category, even though they were in the second category when we had three clusters.

We now have enough code and knowledge to take this to the next level. We want to give our users the option to select the number of clusters and indicator(s) that they want. We need to address some issues in our data first, so let's explore that.

Preparing data with scikit-learn

`scikit-learn` is one of the most widely used and comprehensive machine learning libraries in Python. It plays very well with the rest of the data-science ecosystem libraries, such as `NumPy`, `pandas`, and `matplotlib`. We will be using it for modeling our data and for some preprocessing as well.

We now have two issues that we need to tackle first: missing values and scaling data. Let's see two simple examples for each, and then tackle them in our dataset. Let's start with missing values.

Handling missing values

Models need data, and they can't know what to do with a set of numbers containing missing values. In such cases (and there are many in our dataset), we need to make a decision on what to do with those missing values.

There are several options, and the right choice depends on the application as well as the nature of the data, but we won't get into those details. For simplicity, we will make a generic choice of replacing missing data with suitable values.

Let's explore how we can impute missing values with a simple example, as follows:

1. Create a simple dataset containing a missing value, in a suitable format, as illustrated in the following code snippet:

   ```
   data = np.array([1, 2, 1, 2, np.nan]).reshape(-1, 1)
   ```

2. Import the `SimpleImputer` for `scikit-learn`, as follows:

   ```
   from sklearn.impute import SimpleImputer
   ```

3. Create an instance of this class with a `mean` strategy, which is the default. As you might have guessed, there are other strategies for imputing missing values. The code is shown in the following snippet:

```
imp = SimpleImputer(strategy='mean')
```

4. Fit the model to the data. This is where the model learns the data, given the conditions and options we set while instantiating it. The code is shown in the following snippet:

```
imp.fit(data)
```

5. Transform the data. Now that the model has learned the data, it is able to transform it according to the rules that we set. The `transform` method exists in many models and has a different meaning, depending on the context. In this case, transforming means imputing the missing data, using the `mean` strategy. The code can be seen in the following snippet:

```
imp.transform(data)
array([[1. ],
       [2. ],
       [1. ],
       [2. ],
       [1.5]])
```

As you can see, the model has transformed the data by replacing the missing value with 1.5. If you look at the other non-missing values [1, 2, 1, 2], you can easily see that their mean is 1.5, and this is the result that we got. We could have specified a different strategy for imputing missing values, such as the median or the most frequent strategy. Each has its own advantages and disadvantages; we are simply exploring what can be done with machine learning in Dash.

Next, we move on to scaling our data.

Scaling data with scikit-learn

In *Figure 9.6*, we saw how clustering might look in two dimensions. If we want to cluster our poverty data by two indicators, one of them would be on the *x* axis and the other would be on the *y* axis. Now, imagine if we had a population on one of the axes and a percentage indicator on the other axis. The data on the population axis would range from 0 to 1.4 billion, and the data on the other axis would range from 0 to 1 (or from 0 to 100). Any differences in the percentage indicator would have negligible influence on the distances, and the means would mainly be calculated using the disproportionate size of the population numbers. One solution to this problem is to scale values.

There are different strategies for scaling data and we will explore one of them—namely, standard scaling. The `StandardScaler` class assigns z-scores (or standard scores) to the data points and normalizes them. The z-score is simply calculated by subtracting each value from the mean and dividing by the standard deviation. There are other ways of calculating this but we will focus on a simple example to better illustrate this concept, as follows:

1. Create a simple dataset, like this:

    ```
    data = np.array([1, 2, 3, 4, 5]).reshape(-1, 1)
    ```

2. Import `StandardScaler` and create an instance of it, like this:

    ```
    from sklearn.preprocessing import StandardScaler
    scaler = StandardScaler()
    ```

3. Fit `scaler` to the data and transform it. For convenience, many models that have a `fit` and a `transform` method and also have a `fit_transform` method, which we will use now, as follows:

    ```
    scaler.fit_transform(data)
    array([[-1.41421356],
           [-0.70710678],
           [ 0.        ],
           [ 0.70710678],
           [ 1.41421356]])
    ```

We have now transformed our numbers to their equivalent z-scores. Note that the mean value 3 has now become 0. Anything higher than 3 is positive, and anything lower is negative. The numbers also indicate how far (high or low) the corresponding value is from the mean.

This way, when we have multiple features in our dataset, we can normalize them, compare them, and use them together. At the end of the day, what we care about is how extreme a certain value is and how close it is to the mean. A country with a Gini index of 90 is a very extreme case. It's as extreme as a country with a population of 1 billion. If we use those two together, the 1 billion will dominate and distort the calculation. Standardization helps us achieve a better way of dealing with data at different scales. It's still not perfect but is a very big improvement over using data in different scales. Now, we are able to use more than one feature while clustering our data.

Creating an interactive KMeans clustering app

Let's now put everything together and make an interactive clustering application using our dataset. We will give users the option to choose the year, as well as the indicator(s) that they want. They can also select the number of clusters and get a visual representation of those clusters, in the form of a colored choropleth map, based on the discovered clusters.

Please note that it is challenging to interpret such results with multiple indicators because we will be handling more than one dimension. It can also be difficult if you are not an economist and don't know which indicators make sense to be checked with which other indicators, and so on.

The following screenshot shows what we will be working toward:

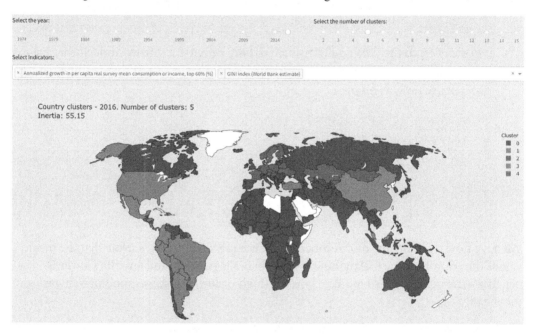

Figure 9.9 – An interactive KMeans clustering application

As you can see, this is a fairly rich application in terms of the combinations of options that it provides. As I also mentioned, it's not straightforward to interpret, but as mentioned several times in the chapter, we are simply exploring what can be done with only one technique and using only some of its options.

We have created many sliders and dropdowns so far in the book, so we won't go into how to make them. We will simply make sure we have descriptive IDs for them, and I'll leave it to you to fill in the blanks. As shown in the preceding screenshot, we have two sliders, one dropdown, and one graph component, so let's set ID names for them. As usual, the following components should go wherever you want them to be in app.layout:

```
dcc.Slider(id='year_cluster_slider', …),
dcc.Slider(id='ncluster_cluster_slider', …),
dcc.Dropdown(id='cluster_indicator_dropdown', …),
dcc.Graph(id='clustered_map_chart', …)
```

We will now go through creating our callback function step by step, as follows:

1. Associate the inputs and outputs in the callback, as follows:

    ```
    @app.callback(Output('clustered_map_chart', 'figure'),
                  Input('year_cluster_slider', 'value'),
                  Input('ncluster_cluster_slider', 'value'),
                  Input('cluster_indicator_dropdown',
    'value'))
    ```

2. Create the signature of the function with suitable parameter names, as follows:

    ```
    def clustered_map(year, n_clusters, indicators):
    ```

3. Instantiate a missing values imputer, a standard scaler, and a KMeans object. Note that with SimpleImputer, we also specify how missing values are encoded. In this case, they are encoded as np.nan, but in other cases they might be encoded differently, such as N/A, 0, -1, or others. The code is shown in the following snippet:

    ```
    imp = SimpleImputer(missing_values=np.nan,
    strategy='mean')
    scaler = StandardScaler()
    kmeans = KMeans(n_clusters=n_clusters)
    ```

4. Create df, a subset of poverty that has only country's data and data from the selected year, and then select the year and Country Name columns, and the selected indicators. The code is shown in the following snippet:

    ```
    df = poverty[poverty['is_country'] & poverty['year'].
    eq(year)][indicators + ['Country Name', 'year']]
    ```

5. Create `data`, a subset of `df` that only contains the selected indicators' columns. The reason we have two distinct objects is that `df` is going to be used for plotting the map and will also use the year and country name. At the same time, `data` will only contain numeric values in order for our models to work with it. The code can be seen here:

```
data = df[indicators]
```

6. In some cases, as we saw several times in the book, we might come across a situation where we have a column that is completely empty. In this case, we can't impute any missing values because we don't have a mean, and we have absolutely no clue what to do with it. In this case, I think it's best to not produce a chart and inform the user that for the selected combination of options, there is not enough data to run the models. We first check if we have such a situation. DataFrame objects have an `isna` method. When we run it, it returns the same DataFrame filled with `True` and `False` values, indicating whether or not the respective value is missing. We then run the `all` method on the resulting DataFrame. This will tell us if all values are missing for each column. Now, we have a pandas Series with `True` and `False` values. We check if any of them is `True` by using the `any` method. In this case, we create an empty chart with an informative title, as follows:

```
if df.isna().all().any():
    return px.scatter(title='No available data for the
selected combination of year/indicators.')
```

7. If everything went fine, and we don't have a column with all its values missing, we proceed by creating a variable that has no missing values (imputed if some are missing), as follows:

```
data_no_na = imp.fit_transform(data)
```

8. Next, we scale `data_no_na` using our instance of `StandardScaler`, like this:

```
scaled_data = scaler.fit_transform(data_no_na)
```

9. Then, we fit the model to our scaled data, as follows:

```
kmeans.fit(scaled_data)
```

10. We now have everything we need to produce our chart—most importantly, the labels_ attribute—and we can do so with a single call to px.choropleth. There is nothing new in the options we use in this function, as you can observe in the following code snippet:

```
fig = px.choropleth(df,
                    locations='Country Name',
                    locationmode='country names',
                    color=[str(x) for x in  kmeans.
labels_],
                    labels={'color': 'Cluster'},
                    hover_data=indicators,
                    height=650,
                    title=f'Country clusters - {year}.
Number of clusters: {n_clusters}<br>Inertia: {kmeans.
inertia_:,.2f}')
```

After that, we copy the geographic attributes we already used to customize the map and make it consistent with the app as a whole.

Here is the full function, including the geographic options for your reference:

```
@app.callback(Output('clustered_map_chart', 'figure'),
              Input('year_cluster_slider', 'value'),
              Input('ncluster_cluster_slider', 'value'),
              Input('cluster_indicator_dropdown', 'value'))
def clustered_map(year, n_clusters, indicators):
    imp = SimpleImputer(missing_values=np.nan, strategy='mean')
    scaler = StandardScaler()
    kmeans = KMeans(n_clusters=n_clusters)
    df = poverty[poverty['is_country'] & poverty['year'].
eq(year)][indicators + ['Country Name', 'year']]
    data = df[indicators]
    if df.isna().all().any():
        return px.scatter(title='No available data for the
selected combination of year/indicators.')
    data_no_na = imp.fit_transform(data)
    scaled_data = scaler.fit_transform(data_no_na)
    kmeans.fit(scaled_data)
```

```
    fig = px.choropleth(df,
                        locations='Country Name',
                        locationmode='country names',
                        color=[str(x) for x in  kmeans.
labels_],
                        labels={'color': 'Cluster'},
                        hover_data=indicators,
                        height=650,
                        title=f'Country clusters - {year}.
Number of clusters: {n_clusters}<br>Inertia: {kmeans.
inertia_:,.2f}',
                        color_discrete_sequence=px.colors.
qualitative.T10)
    fig.layout.geo.showframe = False
    fig.layout.geo.showcountries = True
    fig.layout.geo.projection.type = 'natural earth'
    fig.layout.geo.lataxis.range = [-53, 76]
    fig.layout.geo.lonaxis.range = [-137, 168]
    fig.layout.geo.landcolor = 'white'
    fig.layout.geo.bgcolor = '#E5ECF6'
    fig.layout.paper_bgcolor = '#E5ECF6'
    fig.layout.geo.countrycolor = 'gray'
    fig.layout.geo.coastlinecolor = 'gray'
    return fig
```

We have made a big jump in this chapter in what can be visualized and interactively explored. We also got a minimal introduction to a single machine learning technique to cluster our data. Ideally, the options provided to your users will depend on the discipline you are working in. You might be an expert yourself in the domain you are dealing with, or you might work closely with such an expert. It is not only a matter of visualization and statistics, but domain knowledge is also a crucial aspect of analyzing data, and with machine learning this is critical.

I encourage you to learn more and see what you can achieve. Having the skills to create interactive dashboards is a big advantage for running machine learning models, as we saw, and allows you to discover trends and make decisions at a much faster rate. Eventually, you will be able to create automated solutions that provide recommendations, or make certain decisions based on certain inputs.

Let's now recap on what we learned in this chapter.

Summary

We first got an idea of how clustering works. We built the simplest possible model for a tiny dataset. We ran the model a few times and evaluated the performance and outcomes for each of the numbers of clusters that we chose.

We then explored the elbow technique to evaluate different clusters and saw how we might discover the point of diminishing returns, where not much improvement is achieved by adding new clusters. With that knowledge, we used the same technique for clustering countries by a metric with which most of us are familiar and got firsthand experience in how it might work on real data.

After that, we planned an interactive KMeans app and explored two techniques for preparing data before running our model. We mainly explored imputing missing values and scaling data.

This gave us enough knowledge to get our data in a suitable format for us to create our interactive app, which we did at the end of the chapter.

We next explored advanced features of Dash callbacks—most notably, pattern-matching callbacks. The callbacks we have run so far have been straightforward and fixed. Many times, we want to create more dynamic interfaces for our users. For example, based on the selection of a certain value in a dropdown, we might want to display a special type of chart or create another dropdown. We will explore how this works in the next chapter.

10
Turbo-charge Your Apps with Advanced Callbacks

We will now take our apps to a new level of abstraction and power by introducing new options available to callbacks. The general pattern we have followed has been that we provide users with a component that they can interact with. Based on a given set of options available to the component, users can influence certain actions, such as producing a chart, for example. We will be exploring other options such as deferring the execution of callbacks until a certain event happens, for example, clicking a "Submit" button. We will also take a look at how we can allow users to modify the layout of the app itself, by allowing them to add new dynamic components to it. We will use some of this knowledge to add a minor but important improvement to the clustering functionality that we introduced in *Chapter 9, Letting Your Data Speak for Itself with Machine Learning*.

We will first start by introducing the optional **State** parameter in our callbacks. So far, all of our callbacks fire immediately when the user makes changes to any of the inputs. In many cases, we want the users to set a few options and only then hit a "Submit" button to invoke the callback function. This becomes important when we have multiple inputs where it might be annoying or awkward if outputs change while users are still making changes. In other cases, those callbacks might take a long time to execute and/or be expensive to run. Again, in this case, we want to block the execution until the user decides to trigger it.

Once the concept of State has been established, we will explore a new type of dynamic callbacks that enable our users to make changes to the app, by adding new charts for example. So far, we have allowed the users to simply modify the input values available in the interactive components. We can take this to a new level by introducing dynamic components that are generated based on the user's interactions.

Finally, we will get an overview of **pattern-matching callbacks**, which allow us to link dynamically created and interactive components together in a streamlined way.

Here are the main topics that we will cover in this chapter:

- Understanding State

- Creating components that control other components

- Allowing users to add dynamic components to the app

- Introducing pattern-matching callbacks

Technical requirements

We will be using the same basic tools that we have used in most chapters so far, and mainly focus on some new features in callback functions. We will use Dash, Dash HTML Components, Dash Core Components, and Dash Bootstrap Components for making our apps. For data manipulation, we will use pandas. For the charts and visualizations, we will be using Plotly and Plotly Express, and finally, we will use JupyterLab to interactively explore and create new functionality independently, before incorporating it into our app.

The code files of this chapter can be found on GitHub at https://github.com/PacktPublishing/Interactive-Dashboards-and-Data-Apps-with-Plotly-and-Dash/tree/master/chapter_10.

Check out the following video to see the Code in Action at https://bit.ly/3v6ZYJw.

Let's start by getting familiar with State.

Understanding State

The typical callback function structure that we used so far contained one or more `Output` elements and one or more `Input` elements. As mentioned in the introduction, the callbacks fire immediately when users modify an `Input` element. We want to relax this option a little. We will start with a simple example demonstrating why and how to use `State`, which is an optional argument that can be given to our callbacks.

To make the problem we are trying to solve clear, take a look at *Figure 10.1*:

You chose "one" from the dropdown, and wrote "hello" in the textarea.

Figure 10.1 – An interactive app with outputs that are not properly synchronized with input values

As you can see, the output is showing the wrong values. The reason is that the app was made very slow by introducing a waiting time, to simulate a practical situation that you might face with your apps. The output was not wrong, actually; it just took too long to update, so when the input was changed, it wasn't immediately reflected in the output area. This is more important in this case because there are two inputs governing the output. The interval between modifying the first and second output might cause such confusion.

Another more important issue is that these options might take much more time and cost a lot in terms of lost computing power and/or lost analyst time. Our dataset is very small, and the types of calculations we ran on it are also very simple, so performance was not an issue. In practical situations, you will more likely deal with much larger datasets and run computations that take a considerable amount of time. For example, changing the number of clusters to update our model took a really negligible amount of time. In reality, that might take seconds, minutes, or even more. We will solve this by adding a "Submit" button and introducing `State` to our callback function.

Buttons are available as HTML components from the Dash HTML Components package. They can also be used through Dash Bootstrap Components. Using the latter has two advantages. First, they integrate well with the theme you are using, so this takes care of visual consistency. Also, and this is probably more important, they easily get one of the meaningful colors in case you want to communicate "success," "warning," "danger," or any of the other available colors/messages.

Buttons are available as dcc.Button or dbc.Button. Let's see how they can be used to control the behavior of our app.

We need to first clarify the difference between Input and State in our callbacks.

Understanding the difference between Input and State

First, keep in mind that Input is what triggers the function, and that State is simply a set of conditions that the app is in. It is up to us to decide which components functions as State and which as Input.

Let's update the guidelines for callback functions to clarify the distinction that was just introduced:

- The order of callback arguments has to always be one or more of Output, Input, and optionally State arguments, in that order. If we have multiple elements of any one of them, they all need to follow one another.

- State is optional.

- The Input element(s) is what triggers the callback to fire. Changing any or all of the State in the app would not cause the execution of the callback.

- Once an Input element is modified, the callback will be triggered with whatever State has been changed since it was last triggered.

Let's now see how to produce the code for the app shown in *Figure 10.1*, and then modify it for the desired behavior. The callback function currently looks like this:

```
@app.callback(Output('output', 'children'),
              Input('dropdown', 'value'),
              Input('textarea', 'value'))
def display_values(dropdown_val, textarea_val):
    return f'You chose "{dropdown_val}" from the dropdown, and
wrote "{textarea_val}" in the textarea.'
```

This is how we have managed all callbacks so far. Note that the callback will run if either of the two inputs were modified. The change we want to introduce will require two steps:

1. Add a button component to the page, placed under the `Textarea` component:

    ```
    import dash_bootstrap_components as dbc
    dbc.Button("Submit", id="button")


    # OR


    import dash_html_components as html
    html.Button("Submit", id="button")
    ```

2. Add the button as an `Input` argument to the callback function. We now introduce a new property that we haven't seen yet, which is `n_clicks`. As the name suggests, this corresponds to the number of clicks that were made on a certain component during its lifetime in the user session. With every click, the number gets incremented by one, and we can use that variable to check and control the callback's behavior. Note that we can also give it a default starting value, typically zero, but we can give it another number if we want:

    ```
    Input("button", "n_clicks")
    ```

3. Now that we have made the button our `Input`, we want to keep `Dropdown` and `Textarea`, but make them `State` arguments as follows:

    ```
    @app.callback(Output('output', 'children'),
                  Input('button', 'n_clicks'),
                  State('dropdown', 'value'),
                  State('textarea', 'value'))
    ```

4. With these changes, the callback now waits for `Input` to be changed. The user can change `Dropdown` and/or `Textarea` as many times as they want without being interrupted, and when they are ready, they can hit the "Submit" button to get the desired result.

5. When the app loads for the first time, the default value of the n_clicks property
    is None. Also, we have nothing in the Textarea component and there are
    no options selected from the dropdown yet. So, we do as usual: we use raise
    PreventUpdate if we don't have a value for n_clicks. To update the function
    we introduced, we can simply introduce the following change to the signature of the
    function. Note the addition of the corresponding n_clicks argument, as well as
    its relative order:

```
def display_values(n_clicks, dropdown_val, textarea_val):
    if not n_clicks:
        raise PreventUpdate
    return …
```

If we update the code, we can see that things will work as expected and the user will be
more in control of the process. *Figure 10.2* shows the updated functionality:

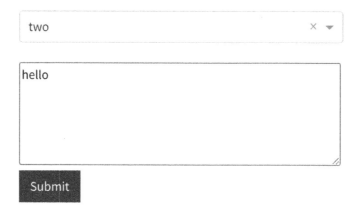

You chose "two" from the dropdown, and wrote "hello" in
the textarea.

Figure 10.2 – An interactive app with outputs now properly displaying the expected input values

We can improve this experience even more by providing the user with a visual cue,
indicating that some processing is underway.

With this new knowledge fresh in mind, let's use it to modify the behavior of our
clustering functionality that we discussed in the introduction to this chapter. *Figure 10.3*
shows the desired outcome that we want to achieve:

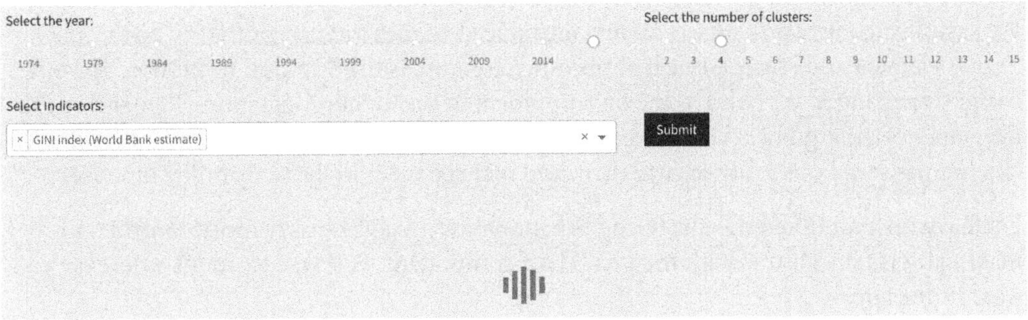

Figure 10.3 – The clustering functionality with a Submit button and a visual progress indicator

As you can see, we have introduced two new features. The first is the button that we have already discussed and implemented in our independent small app. The second is the Dash Core Components `Loading` component. This component is responsible for displaying the symbol that is seen moving, or sometimes spinning, where the output is expected to appear. Using it is extremely simple, but it's also crucial in such cases as this. It's always good to confirm to users that their selection (or any other interaction) has been acknowledged and is under process. Actually, I think it's good to use the `Loading` component on all outputs to give this confirmation to users. It's very easy to implement, and this is how we can update the app to reflect this functionality:

```
import dash_core_components as dcc
dcc.Loading([
    dcc.Graph(id='clustered_map_chart')
])
```

The `Graph` component already exists in our app; we just need to add it as the `children` argument to the `Loading` component as you can see in the preceding code. This will cause the animated symbol to remain animated until the underlying object appears in its place.

Let's now modify the callback function to make the desired change:

```
@app.callback(Output('clustered_map_chart', 'figure'),
              Input('clustering_submit_button', 'n_clicks'),
              State('year_cluster_slider', 'value'),
              State('ncluster_cluster_slider', 'value'),
              State('cluster_indicator_dropdown', 'value'))
def clustered_map(n_clicks, year, n_clusters, indicators):
```

We basically made two changes. We first introduced `clustering_submit_button` as an `Input` element and renamed each of the other arguments from `Input` to `State`. The other change is passing `n_clicks` as the first argument to the function signature. Remember that the names of the arguments can be anything, and what matters is their order. We gave them clear names so we can easily refer to them and manage them in the body of the function.

You have now modified the clustering functionality, giving the user more control and making it visually clearer with the `Loading` component. Feel free to add it wherever you want in the app.

Now we can take our callbacks to another interesting level.

Creating components that control other components

How about we provide an interactive component on the page where its values (set by the user) serve as inputs to another function, which is in turn responsible for the final output? *Figure 10.4* shows what the result looks like, and following that is a discussion of the details and implementation:

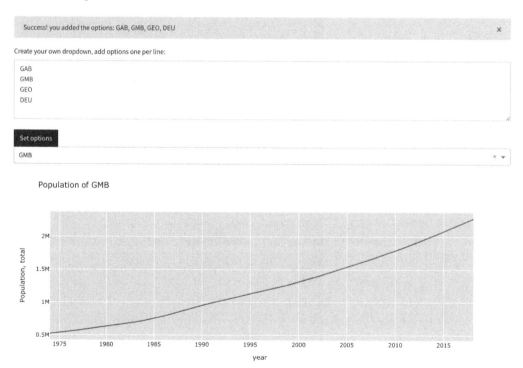

Figure 10.4 – An app with a component that dynamically determines the values of another component

Let's go through the visual elements of this app's layout, one by one:

1. **Success message**: The green strip at the top doesn't appear when the app loads. It only appears after the user adds the options to the dropdown and hits the **Set options** button. Note that there is a dynamic message showing the user the values that they added. Also, note that the alert message is "dismissable." We have the **x** symbol on the right, allowing the user to remove this message.

2. **Instruction line**: A simple message telling the user that they can add text in the `Textarea` component, which will be used to feed into the `options` property of the `Dropdown` component underneath it. At this point in the app, `Dropdown` is empty and has no options to choose from, and the `Graph` component also shows an empty chart.

3. **The Set options button**: Once the user adds a set of options to `Textarea` and hits this button, those lines will become options in `Dropdown`.

4. **The resulting chart**: We have used the three-letter country codes here. The user inputs whichever country codes they want, and these become options to the `Dropdown` component. After that, choosing a certain country code filters the dataset by getting rows where the country code is equal to the user's selection. It then uses the resulting DataFrame to create the chart at the end.

There is not much practical value in such an app, as it would have been much easier to simply provide the options in a `Dropdown` component and produce the chart. We are simply doing this to demonstrate the new options that we can utilize and doing so with a dataset with which we are familiar. There is also a big potential for errors. What if the user doesn't know the code for a certain country? What if they make a typo? Again, this is just for demonstration purposes.

This app can be written in around 30 lines of code and gives us two layers of options, where one depends on the other. One set of options "waits" and depends on the others to produce its outputs accordingly.

We now code the layout of the app, and after that we create the two callback functions that make it interactive:

1. Run the necessary imports:

```
from jupyter_dash import JupyterDash
import dash_core_components as dcc
import dash_html_components as html
import dash_bootstrap_components as dbc
import pandas as pd
poverty = pd.read_csv('data/poverty.csv')
```

2. Create an app and its layout. All the following elements go into the app's layout:

```
app = JupyterDash(__name__,
                  external_stylesheets=[dbc.themes.
COSMO])

app.layout = html.Div([
    component_1,
    component_2
    ...
])
```

3. Create an empty div that will contain the success message:

```
html.Div(id='feedback')
```

4. Create a Label component, telling the user how to interact with the app:

```
dbc.Label("Create your own dropdown, add options one per
line:")
```

5. Create an empty Textarea component. Note that this is also available and similar to the component of the same name, belonging to Dash Core Components:

```
dbc.Textarea(id='text', cols=40, rows=5)
```

6. Add a button for generating the dropdown and its options:

```
dbc.Button("Set options", id='button')
```

7. Create an empty `Dropdown`:

```
dcc.Dropdown(id='dropdown')
```

8. Create an empty `Graph` component:

```
dcc.Graph(id=chart')
```

This should be enough for the visual elements of our app. We now need two functions to create the interactivity we want:

1. `set_dropdown_options`: This function will take the lines from `Textarea` as input and return a list of options to be fed to the `Dropdown` component.

2. `create_population_chart`: This function takes its input from the `Dropdown` component and generates a population chart below it.

We now start with the first one:

1. Create the callback with the appropriate `Output`, `Input`, and `State` arguments. We have two outputs that this function affects. The first is the `options` property of the `Dropdown` component. The second is the div containing the success message. For our `Input`, we will have the button, and our `State` will be the `Textarea` component:

```
@app.callback(Output('dropdown', 'options'),
              Output('feedback', 'children'),
              Input('button', 'n_clicks'),
              State('text', 'value'))
```

2. Create the function signature with appropriate argument names:

```
def set_dropdown_options(n_clicks, options):
```

3. Create a variable holding the text provided as a list. We achieve that by splitting the incoming text from `Textarea`. We also make sure to check for the case of not having any clicks and use `raise PreventUpdate` in that case:

```
if not n_clicks:
    raise PreventUpdate
text = options.split()
```

4. Create the success message as an `Alert` component, which is available from Dash Bootstrap Components. Note that we also color it with a "color" called "success." Naturally, you can also think of additional functionality that checks for valid inputs, and if it doesn't get one, the color of the message would be "warning" or "danger," for example. Note that the text also dynamically adds the comma-separated options that were provided by the user. We also set `dismissable=True` to allow users to remove it from the page if they want to:

```
message = dbc.Alert(f"Success! you added the options: {',
'.join(text)}",
                    color='success',
                    dismissable=True)
```

5. Create the options list that will set the `options` property of the currently empty `Dropdown` component. We use the `text` variable for that:

```
options = [{'label': t, 'value': t} for t in text]
```

6. Return the tuple of `options` and `message`:

```
return options, message
```

Let's now turn to our other function, which will take the selected country code, and use it to generate the chart:

1. Create the callback with the required `Output` and `Input`:

```
@app.callback(Output('chart', 'figure'),
              Input('dropdown', 'value'))
```

2. Create the function signature as well as the check for the availability of a value from the dropdown:

```
def create_population_chart(country_code):
    if not country_code:
        raise PreventUpdate
```

3. Create the required DataFrame subset based on the input value:

```
df = poverty[poverty['Country Code']==country_code]
```

4.   Return a chart with the appropriate values:

```
return px.line(df,
               x='year',
               y='Population, total',
               title=f"Population of {country_code}")
```

We can now run the preceding code and create the desired app.

To better understand the structure of our app, and to get used to inspecting our callback chains, we can run the app in debug mode by running app.run_server(debug=True) and see how inputs and outputs relate to one another in *Figure 10.5*:

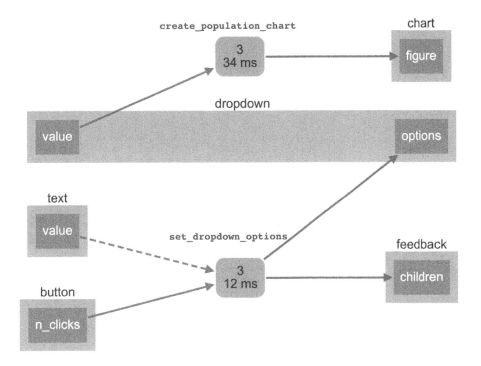

Figure 10.5 – App callback graph

You can easily see the names of the components and their IDs as specified in our code. You can easily trace the sequence of events, starting from the bottom left, following the arrows to the top right of the diagram.

We saw how we can create dynamic options in certain components that depend on other components for their values. Dash neatly handled the behavior of components and properly triggered the right functions when their inputs were available.

Let's take things to an even more abstract and powerful level. Let's now allow users to add full components by clicking a button.

Allowing users to add dynamic components to the app

Not only will users be able to add components to the app's layout, but the components' contents will also be dynamically generated. Take a look at *Figure 10.6* for the simplest example that we will start with:

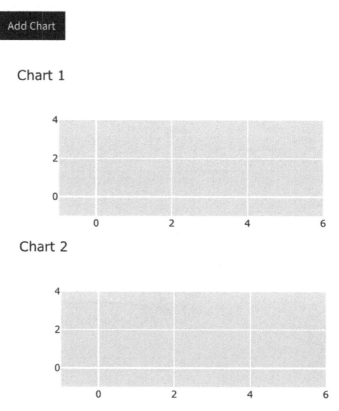

Figure 10.6 – An app allowing users to add components to the app's layout

Although extremely simple, the charts in this app have different dynamic names, as you can see in the chart titles. This was based on the dynamic value of n_clicks, which changes on every click.

The amount of code required to generate this is similar to any simple app; there isn't much complexity involved. We just need to look at it with fresh eyes. Let's start by coding the layout, which will consist of two simple components:

1. Create a button to trigger the addition of new charts:

    ```
    dbc.Button("Add Chart", id='button')
    ```

2. Create an empty div, with its `children` attribute set to an empty list. The empty list is the key element that we will be working with:

    ```
    html.Div(id='output', children=[])
    ```

When this app loads for the first time, the user only sees a button that they can use to add a chart. The area below it gets populated with an additional chart every time they click the button.

Let's now create the callback function for this app:

1. Create the `Output`, `Input`, and `State` arguments as usual. The interesting part to notice here is that the `children` property of the empty div acts both as `Output` and as `State`. We usually take some component's value and use it to influence or change another component in the app. Who said we can't take a component, make a change to it, and return it back to where it came from in its new state? This is exactly what we will do:

    ```
    @app.callback(Output('output', 'children'),
                  Input('button', 'n_clicks'),
                  State('output', 'children'))
    ```

2. Create the function signature and check for n_clicks. Note here that `children` is acting as `State` in this case:

    ```
    def add_new_chart(n_clicks, children):
        if not n_clicks:
            raise PreventUpdate
    ```

3. Create an empty bar chart with a dynamic title, using the n_clicks property:

    ```
    new_chart = dcc.Graph(figure=px.bar(title=f"Chart {n_clicks}"))
    ```

4. Append the new chart to the `children` component. If you remember, we set the initial value of `children` in the empty div as an empty list. The following line will take this list and append `new_chart` to it. There is nothing special about this; we are simply using Python's `list.append` method:

```
children.append(new_chart)
```

5. Now that our `children` list has been mutated by appending a new item to it, we simply return it. Keep in mind that the return value of the callback function will go to the div, and so now it is acting as an output:

```
return children
```

Note that this functionality was created by the application of simple principles. We aren't using any new features here. The first technique was passing `children` to our callback, and receiving it from the other side. The second one was using the `n_clicks` property to dynamically set the titles of the charts.

The diagram in *Figure 10.7* shows the relationship between the elements we created:

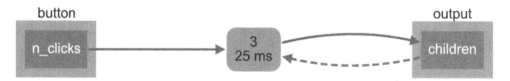

Figure 10.7 – A callback function graph where a function returned a component that it received and mutated

This diagram will remain the same regardless of the number of charts that were added to the app. This means you don't have to worry about managing as many callback functions as there are clicks.

If you are ready to take this even further, we can add another component under each chart, for example, a `Dropdown` component. And we can let the dropdown's selected value produce a chart. Each dropdown value will be independent of the others (if added by the user) and will only modify the chart it belongs to. The good news is that all this will also be managed with one additional callback function utilizing pattern-matching callbacks.

Introducing pattern-matching callbacks

Mastering this feature, and here we are dealing with a truly new feature, will allow you to take your apps to a new level of interactivity and power. The most important feature of this capability is that it allows us to handle the interactivity of components that didn't exist before. As we've done so far, when we allowed users to create new charts by clicking a button, those components did not exist before in the app. The more interesting thing is that the callback function that handles them all is as simple as any other callback that takes values from a dropdown and produces a chart. The trick is in slightly changing the id attribute of our components.

So far, we have set the id attributes as strings, and the only requirement was that they be unique. We will now introduce a new way of creating this attribute, which is by using dictionaries. Let's first take a look at the end goal, then modify the layout, the callbacks, and finally, discuss the new way of handling the id property. *Figure 10.8* shows what our app will look like:

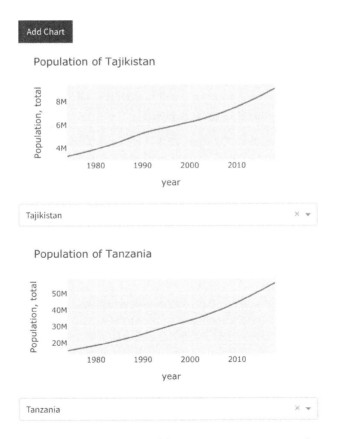

Figure 10.8 – An app allowing users to add interactive components to the app's layout

In the previous app, we were able to let the user generate new components on the fly, and their content could be dynamic as well. We demonstrated this with chart titles, using the n_clicks property to set the title dynamically. But after adding those charts, the user couldn't interact with them. In other words, they are dynamically generated, with potentially dynamic content, but once generated, they are static, and we cannot interact with them.

The improvement we are now introducing is that we are making those charts interactive (using the dropdowns) and having each of them linked to a single component, a dropdown in this case. As you can see in *Figure 10.8*, each chart comes with its own dropdown, and the user can independently generate multiple charts on top of one another and compare. After that, they can do even more, by selecting different countries on different charts. Of course, you can imagine a more involved set of apps where users can do many other things.

The new additions to create this new functionality will be done in three steps:

1. Modify the add_new_chart function: This will simply consist of adding a dropdown under each chart and appending two components, instead of one. Note that the layout is exactly the same. We simply have a button and an empty div underneath it.

2. Create a new callback function: This will link the newly generated pairs of charts and dropdowns to determine their behavior.

3. Modify the id attributes in the app: This is where we introduce the new functionality and is the main feature that allows us to manage as many additional components and their interactivity using a single callback function.

We first start by modifying the add_new_chart callback function:

1. We defined new_chart in the function, and this remains the same. Right under that, we want to add new_dropdown for users to select the country that they want to visualize:

```
new_chart = dcc.Graph(figure=px.bar(title=f"Chart {n_
clicks}"))
```

```
countries = poverty[poverty['is_country']]['Country
Name'].drop_duplicates().sort_values()
```

```
new_dropdown = dcc.Dropdown(options=[{'label': c,
'value': c}
                            for c in countries])
```

2. Append the new components. In the first example, we appended `new_chart`, but this time, we want to append the two items. The only thing to modify is to put the two new components in a new div and append the new div. This way, we are effectively appending one element (the div that contains two elements):

```
children.append(html.Div([
    new_chart,
    new_dropdown
]))
```

This is enough to cause the button to append two items for each click. As you can see, the change was very simple. However, we will later come to set the `id` attributes for these components in order to make them dynamically interactive.

Now we have pairs of components added with every click on our button. One of them has to be an `Output` element (`Graph`), and the other has to be an `Input` element (`Dropdown`). As with every other interactivity feature, they need to be linked with a callback function. We will create this now, and after that, we will take a look at how to link those dynamic IDs together and manage how the two callbacks interact with each other. The function is as simple as any callback that we have created so far. Here it is, but without the decorator, which we will discuss right after:

```
def create_population_chart(country):
    if not country:
        raise PreventUpdate
    df = poverty[poverty['Country Name']==country]
    fig = px.line(df,
                  x='year', y='Population, total',
                  title=f'Population of {country}')
    return fig
```

Figure 10.9 contains a diagram showing our pattern-matching callback function:

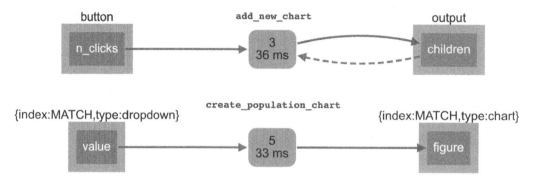

Figure 10.9 – The callback graph of a pattern-matching callback

The top graph in *Figure 10.9* is exactly the same as the one in *Figure 10.7*. It is for the simple function that adds new charts by appending them to the children of the empty div. Note that the `id` attributes are labeled above each box representing a component. Here they are **button** and **output**.

The graph for the second callback, `create_population_chart`, shows a similar structure, but the IDs are dictionaries and not strings.

Pattern-matching callbacks use those dictionaries to map the different elements together. Let's unpack those dictionaries and then see how they fit into the callbacks.

The first one is `{"index": MATCH, "type": "dropdown"}`. I believe the **type** key is clear. We use it to make it easy to identify other components whose "type" is "dropdown." It's important to note that these names could be anything, but obviously we would want meaningful and helpful names. The other dictionary has **chart** for its **type** key. Again, this is also flexible, but I think it's clear here which elements we are referring to.

Now we want to have independent functionality for each pair of components. In other words, we want the user to be able to modify the second dropdown, generating whatever chart they want, without that action affecting any other components in the app. How do we achieve that? We simply tell Dash to match them, with MATCH. This again belongs to an arbitrarily named key, **index** in this case. But MATCH is a wildcard object that is available in the `dash.dependencies` module. There are also ALL and ALLSMALLER, which work in a similar way with slight differences, but we will mainly focus on MATCH. Now let's take a look at how the updated functions need to be specified to cater to those IDs. The good news is that the only things we have to change are the `id` attributes of the relevant components and pass them to the relevant callback function arguments.

We are now ready to add the proper `id` attributes to complete the pattern-matching callbacks. The first function, `add_new_chart`, takes the new dictionary `id` attributes for the inner components that we allow the user to add to the app. Note here that the "index" key takes `n_clicks` as its value. This value, as we saw several times, is dynamic and changes every time the user clicks the button. This means that every time the user clicks the button, we have a new unique ID with which we can identify this component:

```
def add_new_chart(n_clicks, children):
    new_chart = dcc.Graph(id={'type': 'chart',
                               'index': n_clicks},
                          figure=px.bar())
    new_dropdown = dcc.Dropdown(id={'type': 'dropdown',
                                    'index': n_clicks},
                               options=[option_1, option_2,
...])
```

Now we have to map those IDs properly in the second function that is responsible for managing their interactivity. The "type" key will be used to map "chart" to "chart" and "dropdown" to "dropdown". As for `n_clicks`, since it is dynamic, we match it with MATCH:

```
@app.callback(Output({'type': 'chart', 'index': MATCH},
'figure'),
              Input({'type': 'dropdown', 'index': MATCH},
'value'))
def create_population_chart(country):
    ...
```

Here you can find the full code for the two functions as a reference to get the full picture:

```
from dash.dependencies import Output, Input, State, MATCH
@app.callback(Output('output', 'children'),
              Input('button', 'n_clicks'),
              State('output', 'children'))
def add_new_chart(n_clicks, children):
    if not n_clicks:
        raise PreventUpdate
    new_chart = dcc.Graph(id={'type': 'chart',
                              'index': n_clicks},
```

```
                              figure=px.bar(title=f"Chart {n_
clicks}"))
    countries = poverty[poverty['is_country']]['Country Name'].
drop_duplicates().sort_values()
    new_dropdown = dcc.Dropdown(id={'type': 'dropdown',
                                   'index': n_clicks},
                                options=[{'label': c, 'value':
c}
                                for c in countries])
    children.append(html.Div([
        new_chart, new_dropdown
    ]))
    return children


@app.callback(Output({'type': 'chart',
                      'index': MATCH}, 'figure'),
              Input({'type': 'dropdown',
                     'index': MATCH}, 'value'))
def create_population_chart(country):
    if not country:
        raise PreventUpdate
    df = poverty[poverty['Country Name']==country]
    fig = px.line(df,
                  x='year',
                  y='Population, total',
                  title=f'Population of {country}')
    return fig
```

You can easily imagine how flexible and extensible our apps can become with such functionality, not to mention the ease of managing callbacks. Yet they are not straightforward and might need some time to get used to, which I believe is worth it.

We introduced many new concepts around callbacks, utilized some tricks, and introduced new functionality. So, let's review what was covered in the chapter.

Summary

We first introduced the optional `State` argument to callback function decorators. We saw how by combining it with `Input`, we can defer the execution of functions until the user decides to execute them. We also ran several examples that added buttons to invoke the execution. We then created a simple app where the user's inputs to a certain component were used to dynamically populate options of another component that was "waiting." Those new options were in turn used to create another component.

Another interesting application of simple principles was allowing users to add new components having dynamic content.

We finally introduced the most powerful and flexible feature, the pattern-matching callbacks. We created an app where users are able to add as many charts as they want. Furthermore, those charts acted independently from one another, and users were empowered to customize their own dashboard.

That was a lot to cover, and we turn next to another feature that allows us to extend and expand our apps. We can only have so many components on a page until it becomes cluttered. In many cases, it makes sense to create separate pages/URLs for separate functionality, which is the topic of the next chapter.

11
URLs and Multi-Page Apps

So far, we have been building everything on one page. We kept adding new charts and interactive components to a single div and incorporated them as we saw fit. Adding new URLs can be useful for space-saving purposes, so that we don't end up having too many components on a single page. URLs also serve as a tool for classifying content and providing context, so users know "where" they are and what they are doing.

Even more interesting is the ability to programmatically generate many additional pages to your app, simply by displaying content based on the URL (or any part of it). This is what we will do in this chapter.

Once we get to know how the **Location** and **Link** components work, we will then make a slight change to the structure of the app, by making and isolating new layouts. Then, it will be clear how easy it is to make a multi-page app. We will have a general layout with an empty area in the middle, and using a simple rule, content will be displayed based on the URL.

All the functionality we have built was mainly based on indicators. We created many charts for those indicators, showing how they vary in time and across countries. Our users might also be interested in country-oriented reports. So, we will create a page for each country, where users can check whichever indicator they want for the country of interest and optionally compare with other countries. With a few simple changes, we will add 169 new pages to our app.

We will cover the following topics in this chapter:

- Getting to know the `Location` and `Link` components
- Extracting and using attributes of URLs
- Parsing URLs and using their components to modify parts of the app
- Restructuring your app to cater to multiple layouts
- Adding dynamically generated URLs to the app
- Incorporating the new URL interactivity into the app

Technical requirements

For the new components that we will introduce, we will still be using the same tools. Dash, Dash Core Components, Dash HTML Components, and Dash Bootstrap Components will be used to build our new functionality and add it to our app. We will also be using pandas for data manipulation, JupyterLab and `jupyter_dash` for experimenting with isolated functionality, and Plotly and Plotly Express for data visualization.

The main topic of this chapter will be manipulating parts of the URLs and using them as inputs to modify other components. This is the same as using any other element of our app to create the functionality that we want. Let's start by getting to know the two components that make this possible.

The code files of this chapter can be found on GitHub at `https://github.com/PacktPublishing/Interactive-Dashboards-and-Data-Apps-with-Plotly-and-Dash/tree/master/chapter_11`.

Check out the following video to see the Code in Action at `https://bit.ly/3eks3GI`.

Getting to know the Location and Link components

These components are part of Dash Core Components, and their names make quite clear what they are and what they might do. The Location component refers to the browser's location bar. It is also referred to as the address bar or the URL bar. We typically place a Location component in the app, and it doesn't produce anything visible. We mainly use it to discover where we are in the app, and based on that, we induce some functionality. Let's create a simple example to see how it can be used in its simplest form:

1. Create a simple app:

```
import dash_html_components as html
import dash_core_components as dcc
from jupyter_dash import JupyterDash
from dash.dependencies import Output, Input
app = JupyterDash(__name__)
```

2. Create a simple layout for the app containing a Location component and, right underneath it, an empty div:

```
app.layout = html.Div([
    dcc.Location(id='location'),
  html.Div(id='output')
])
```

3. Create a callback function that takes the href attribute of the Location component and prints it to the empty div:

```
@app.callback(Output('output', 'children'),
Input('location', 'href'))
def display_href(href):
    return f"You are at: {href}."
```

4. Run the app and observe its output:

```
app.run_server(mode='inline')
You are at: http://127.0.0.1:8050/.
```

It's quite straightforward and clear. We simply ask the Location component to tell us where it is, and we display it in the empty div. In this example, we asked for the href attribute, and we got the full URL of the current page. For various reasons, we might be interested in other attributes, for more nuanced functionality. Let's build another simple app to extract the other available attributes of the Location component and get to know how to use the Link component as well.

Getting to know the Link component

As the name suggests, this component produces links. Another way of creating links is by using the HTML <a> tag, which is available in the Dash HTML Components package. While <a> is more suitable for external links, Link is better suited for internal ones. A nice advantage is that it simply changes the pathname attribute and does so without refreshing the page. So, it is fast and responsive, just like changing the value in any other interactive component.

In the update to our simple app, we will add an <a> link, as well as a few Link component links, so you can experience the difference in refreshing and also get to know both types of link. Our Location component will now get the location of the current page, but we will also use it to extract all the available attributes and discuss some ideas about how they might be used. Let's create the elements that will go into our app's layout:

1. Add a Location component:

    ```
    dcc.Location(id='location')
    ```

2. Add an <a> component through Dash HTML Components, pointing to an internal page using a relative path:

    ```
    html.A(href='/path',
                children='Go to a directory path'),
    ```

3. Add a Link component pointing to a page with a search attribute (query parameters):

    ```
    dcc.Link(href='/path/search?one=1&two=2',
                children='Go to search page')
    ```

4. Add another `Link` component pointing to a page with a hash, which is also known as a fragment:

```
dcc.Link(href='path/?hello=HELLO#hash_string',
children='Go to a page with a hash')
```

5. Add an empty div where the output will be displayed:

```
html.Div(id='output')
```

This is similar to the previous app, as you can see; we only added a few links. These will be displayed as regular links on the page. We will now extract and display the parts that we are interested in, using a new callback function:

1. Create the decorator of the function, adding a separate `Input` element for each attribute of the `Location` component. As you will see, the location is the full URL, but each part gets automatically extracted for us depending on what we specify:

```
@app.callback(Output('output', 'children'),
              Input('location', 'pathname'),
              Input('location', 'search'),
              Input('location', 'href'),
              Input('location', 'hash'))
```

2. Create the signature of the callback function, taking each of the `Location` component's attributes as `Input` elements. Note that we append an underscore to the `hash` argument, to make it clear that we are not using the built-in Python function of the same name:

```
def show_url_parts(pathname, search, href, hash_)
```

3. Return the different attributes of the URL we are in, in the empty div:

```
return html.Div([
    f"href: {href}",
    f"path: {pathname}",
    f"search: {search}",
    f"hash: {hash_}"
])
```

Running the preceding code and clicking on the links we have created shows different URL attributes shown in the div, as you can see in *Figure 11.1*:

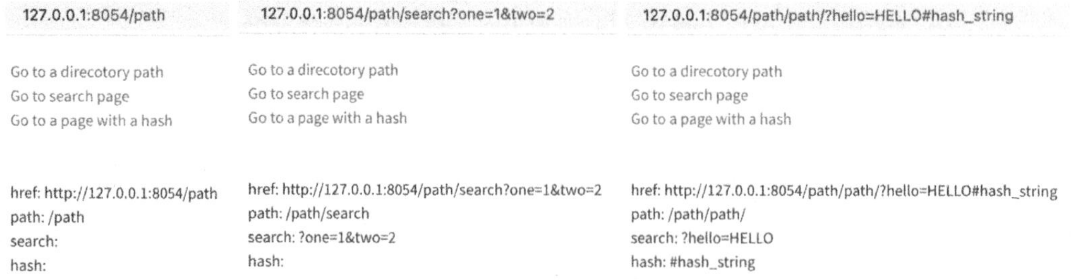

127.0.0.1:8054/path	127.0.0.1:8054/path/search?one=1&two=2	127.0.0.1:8054/path/path/?hello=HELLO#hash_string
Go to a direcotory path	Go to a direcotory path	Go to a direcotory path
Go to search page	Go to search page	Go to search page
Go to a page with a hash	Go to a page with a hash	Go to a page with a hash
href: http://127.0.0.1:8054/path	href: http://127.0.0.1:8054/path/search?one=1&two=2	href: http://127.0.0.1:8054/path/path/?hello=HELLO#hash_string
path: /path	path: /path/search	path: /path/path/
search:	search: ?one=1&two=2	search: ?hello=HELLO
hash:	hash:	hash: #hash_string

Figure 11.1 – The Location component showing various URL parts for different URLs

As you can see, we have used the `Link` component to change the URL and used `Location` to extract whichever attribute we wanted. You can easily see how this might be used in other types of callback functions that do more than just display those attributes. Let's take a look at how we can parse and extract query parameters and their values using Python's `parse_qs` (parse query string) function:

```
from urllib.parse import parse_qs
parse_qs('1=one&2=two&20=twenty')
{'1': ['one'], '2': ['two'], '20': ['twenty']}
```

We can now do whatever we want with those values. A more practical application, taking our dataset as an example, is that you can create specific and shareable URLs, where users can share a specific chart with a certain set of options, simply by providing a URL for it:

```
parse_qs('country_code=CAN&year=2020&inidcator=SI.DST.02ND.20')
{'country_code': ['CAN'], 'year': ['2020'], 'inidcator': ['SI.
DST.02ND.20']}
```

Once you get a country name, a year, and an indicator, you can easily take this as an input to a callback function and produce the desired chart based on those selections. You can also imagine making it easier for your users, where the selections they make in the interactive components change the `Location` component, making it very easy to share those URLs. The great thing about this, as mentioned already, is that it works without refreshing the page, so it won't slow down the process in any way.

Let's see how this works in a practical application, using our dataset.

Parsing URLs and using their components to modify parts of the app

Having established some working knowledge about how Location and Link components work, we want to use this in our app. The plan is to add 169 new pages using three callbacks and adding a few new layout elements. The user will have a drop-down menu of countries to choose from. Selecting a country modifies the URL, which will render the country layout. This layout will include a heading, a chart, and a table about the country in the URL.

Figure 11.2 shows a sample of a country page that we will build:

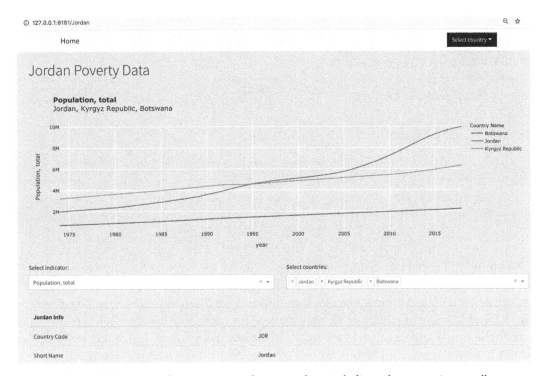

Figure 11.2 – A sample country page showing a chart including other countries as well

As you can see, we now have a template for a country page. This was triggered because the URL contained a country that is one of the available countries in the dataset. Otherwise, it will display the main app, containing all the components that we have built so far. Users can also click on the **Home** link to go there.

Let's first see how to restructure our app.

Restructuring your app to cater to multiple layouts

At this stage, we haven't moved from the basic structure that we discussed in *Chapter 1, Overview of the Dash Ecosystem*, and as a reminder, *Figure 11.3* shows a simplified representation of the current structure:

App parts	app.py

imports (boilerplate)	`import dash`
	`import dash_html_components as html`
	`import dash_core_components as dcc`

app instantiation	`app = dash.Dash(__name__)`

app layout: a list of HTML and/or interactive components	`app.layout = html.Div([`
	`    dcc.Dropdown()`
	`    dcc.Graph()`
	`    ...`
	`])`

callback functions	`@app.callback()`
	`    ...`
	`@app.callback()`
	`    ...`

running the app	`if __name__ == '__main__':` `    app.run_server()`

Figure 11.3 – The structure of a Dash app

Everything will remain the same, with the exception of the layout part. Right now, we only have one layout attribute, and everything was added to the main div. We used tabs to efficiently utilize space in some cases, and from Dash Bootstrap Components we used the Row and Col components to flexibly manage how components are displayed. To create the new layout structure, we need to create one main layout, which will serve as the skeleton of our app. In this layout, we will have an empty div, which will get populated with the appropriate content, depending on the URL we are on. *Figure 11.4* shows how this skeleton might look. This is just to make it easy to visualize; it would never show an empty page like this. Note that we also added a navigation bar, to which we can add several other elements, and this can be thought of as another addition to our app:

Figure 11.4 – The new skeleton layout of the app showing an empty main content area

> **Tip**
>
> As you can see on the skeleton page with the empty body, you can use Dash for very fast prototyping and designing apps. Before you start coding, you can quickly build the layout you want, share with other stakeholders, get feedback, and only then start coding the interactivity.
>
> As we did with the same figure, you can also isolate or remove certain elements, to make it easier for your audience to understand the structure of the app you are building.

Let's now code the different parts that we need to upgrade our app with country URLs and a navigation bar. We start by first creating a few separate layouts:

1. **Main layout**: This will function as the main skeleton of our app. It will contain the navigation bar together with the country drop-down menu. For now, we will simply declare a `NavbarSimple` component and discuss its details in the following section. Our layout will also contain the footer that has tabs, which we previously created. The body of this layout, like our simple app at the beginning of the chapter, will have a `Location` component, as well as an empty div that will display the required layout:

```
main_layout = html.Div([
                dbc.NavbarSimple([
    ...
                ]),
                dcc.Location(id='location'),
                html.Div(id='main_content'),
```

```
dbc.Tabs([

    ...

    ])

])
```

2. **Indicators dashboard**: This is basically the layout part that we have been working with so far, as is, with no changes. We just save it to a new variable and pass it to the `main_content` div when the right condition is met (if the URL does not contain a country name):

```
indicators_dashboard = html.Div([
    # all components we built so far
])
```

3. **Country dashboard**: This will also be saved to a variable and displayed when its condition is met, which is when there is a country name in the URL. The content of this layout (chart and table) will be for the country in the URL:

```
country_dashboard = html.Div([
    html.H1(id='country_heading'),
    dcc.Graph(id='country_page_graph'),
    dcc.Dropdown(id='country_page_indicator_dropdown'),
    dcc.Dropdown(id='country_page_contry_dropdown'),
    html.Div(id='country_table')
])
```

4. **Validation layout**: This will be a simple list and has to be in the form of a Dash component, containing the previous three layouts. The importance of this list is to indicate to Dash which layouts are available to the app, as a whole. When we display the contents of one of the layouts and not the others, some components will not be part of the app, and some callbacks will break. The `validation_layout` attribute solves this issue for us. It's also a nice and easy way to know and manage the layout of our app as a whole. This can come in handy with more complex apps that have many more layouts. You can think of it as the app's table of contents:

```
app.validation_layout = html.Div([
    main_layout,
    indicators_dashboard,
    country_dashboard,
])
```

We still need to specify the app's `layout` attribute, so Dash knows which one to use as the default layout. This is very simple:

```
app.layout = main_layout
```

Let's now see how to manage the content that will be displayed in the `main_layout` part.

Displaying content based on the URL

Once our layouts have been set up the way we did, we need a very simple function to manage the content.

The function checks if the path name attribute of the `Location` component is one of the available countries or not. If it is, it returns the `country_dashboard` layout. Otherwise, it returns `indicators_layout`. Note that the second condition includes anything other than a country from the available countries. Since we don't have any other functionality in this app, and to catch any URL errors, it's good to send anything else to the home page. In more elaborate apps, though, it might be better to create error pages.

We need to take note of two simple points. First, that the pathname attribute returns the path which contains `"/<country_name>"`, so we need to extract everything but the first character. Second, when we change the URL, if it contains special characters, such as spaces, they are automatically URL-encoded. This can be easily handled with the `unquote` function:

```
from urllib.parse import unquote
unquote('Bosnia%20and%20Herzegovina')
  'Bosnia and Herzegovina'
```

Choosing a country with spaces, as in this case, converts spaces to their URL-encoded equivalent `%20`, so we need to use `unquote` on the name to be able to handle it as normal text.

Here is the code that creates a `countries` list, containing all available countries, and the simple callback that manages the display of the content, based on the URL:

```
countries = countries = poverty[poverty['is_country']]['Country
Name'].drop_duplicates().sort_values().tolist()


@app.callback(Output('main_content', 'children'),
              Input('location', 'pathname'))
  def display_content(pathname):
```

```
if unquote(pathname[1:]) in countries:
    return country_dashboard
else:
    return indicators_dashboard
```

We just went through a high-level description of the new layout and structure of the app, and we now need to fill in some blanks and discuss some details about how to create the navigation bar, the drop-down menu, and its links.

Adding dynamically generated URLs to the app

We now want to complete our main layout with a navigation bar, a home page link, as well as a drop-down menu for the countries. To achieve that, we introduce the NavbarSimple component from Dash Bootstrap Components and see how we can use it.

The NavbarSimple component will take a few elements to create the structure we want as follows:

1. We first create the navigation bar and give it brand and brand_href arguments, to indicate what the name would be and where it would link to:

```
import dash_bootstrap_components as dbc
dbc.NavbarSimple([
    ...
], brand="Home", brand_href="/")
```

2. For its children argument, we will add a dbc.DropdownMenu component. We will also give it a label value so users know what to expect when they click on the menu. We will fill its children argument in the next step:

```
dbc.DropdownMenu(children=[
    menu_item_1,
    menu_item_2,
    ...
], label="Select country")
```

3.   We now need to supply a list of dbc.DropdownMenuItem components to the drop-down menu. Those items will each get children and href arguments. Both of these will be for a country from the list of countries we created in the previous section:

```
dbc.DropdownMenu([
    dbc.DropdownMenuItem(country, href=country)
    for country in countries
])
```

Putting together the code for the full NavbarSimple component, you can see it here:

```
dbc.NavbarSimple([
    dbc.DropdownMenu([
        dbc.DropdownMenuItem(country, href=country)
        for country in countries
    ], label='Select country')
], brand='Home',brand_href='/')
```

With this, we have implemented our navigation bar, and we can also add the Tabs component to the same layout, which we implemented in *Chapter 1, Overview of the Dash Ecosystem*. Now it is very easy to modify or add any navigational elements you want, whenever you want, which will take effect on the website as a whole.

Note that the children of the navigation bar contained links that act the same way as the Link component, so we also have this option when needed.

With the full layout of the whole app ready and the correct layout being loaded based on the URL, we are now ready to implement the last two callback functions that will generate the country_dashboard layout for us.

But here is the situation. I, your former colleague, wrote the code and created the functionality. I left the company without explaining anything, and you cannot get in touch with me. You need to figure out the structure for yourself, and you want to make some changes to my code.

This is a typical situation that you will probably face, so let's see how we can approach it.

Incorporating the new URL interactivity into the app

Having created a dropdown that automatically changes the URL based on the selected value, we have allowed our users to go from page to page as they please. We now need to manage the display of the right content based on the selected country.

Since the code was already written, one thing you can do is run the app in debug mode and get a visual representation of all the available components and see how they are connected with callbacks.

Figure 11.5 shows the graph of the callbacks that have been created. Let's use it to understand how this functionality was implemented:

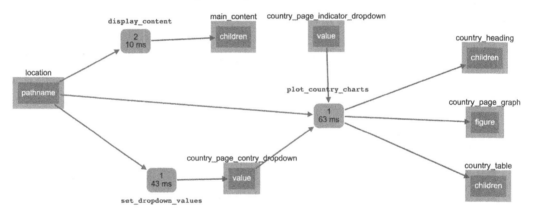

Figure 11.5 – The various components and callbacks managing the URL functionality

Let's go through the figure from left to right and see what is going on here. You can refer to *Figure 11.2* to see how this graph corresponds to visible components in the app:

- Everything starts with the **pathname** attribute of the component with the ID **location**. This can be induced by the user selecting a country from the drop-down menu, directly entering the full URL containing a country name, or clicking on a link from a web page.

- The URL (its pathname attribute) influences three components, as you can see. Most importantly, it determines what goes into the **children** attribute of the **main_content** div. If the URL happens to contain a country, then the country_dashboard layout will be displayed, using the **display_content** callback. This would display certain components that would make the two other callbacks relevant.

- Assuming a country was selected, our second callback, **set_dropdown_values**, will take this country and use it to populate the dropdown that selects the country to plot on this page.

- The **plot_country_charts** callback takes three inputs and modifies three outputs, as you can see at the right end of *Figure 11.5*. The **country_heading** is a simple <h1> component that says "<country name> Poverty Data". **country_page_graph** is the main graph that is displayed on the page, and **country_table** is a dbc. Table component showing various details about the country, extracted from the country CSV file that contains data about each country in the dataset.

After this, you get the code from the repository to see how this was implemented, and you see two callbacks that you want to review and eventually change:

```
@app.callback(Output('country_page_contry_dropdown', 'value'),
              Input('location', 'pathname'))
 def set_dropdown_values(pathname):
     if unquote(pathname[1:]) in countries:
         country = unquote(pathname[1:])
         return [country]
@app.callback(Output('country_heading', 'children'),
              Output('country_page_graph', 'figure'),
              Output('country_table', 'children'),
              Input('location', 'pathname'),
              Input('country_page_contry_dropdown', 'value'),
              Input('country_page_indicator_dropdown',
'value'))
 def plot_country_charts(pathname, countries, indicator):
     if (not countries) or (not indicator):
         raise PreventUpdate
     if unquote(pathname[1:]) in countries:
         country = unquote(pathname[1:])    df =
poverty[poverty['is_country'] & poverty['Country Name'].
isin(countries)]
     fig = px.line(df,
                   x='year',
                   y=indicator,
                   title='<b>' + indicator + '</b><br>' + ',
'.join(countries),
```

```
                    color='Country Name')
    fig.layout.paper_bgcolor = '#E5ECF6'
    table = country_df[country_df['Short Name'] ==
countries[0]].T.reset_index()
    if table.shape[1] == 2:
        table.columns = [countries[0] + ' Info', '']
        table = dbc.Table.from_dataframe(table)
    else:
        table = html.Div()
    return country + ' Poverty Data', fig, table
```

By now, it should be easy for you to figure out how to read new code, even code that contains components that you have never seen before. The general structure of apps has been covered and modified so many times, with so many components, and I think you are now comfortable with figuring this out for yourself.

This is the last coding exercise in the book, and the last functionality that we will add. It doesn't mean that the app is complete. On the contrary, there are many things that can be modified and added. One thing you might consider doing is implementing a special URL for each indicator and having a special page for it, just like we did with countries. The difference is that this may not be as straightforward as the case with countries. We have some indicators that are percentages and others that are simple numbers. Some indicators should be taken together as a group, such as the ones showing different income quantiles. You can really get creative with what you want to change and how.

Let's now recap what we covered in this chapter.

Summary

We first got to know the two main components that are responsible for modifying, reading, and parsing URLs, the **Location** and **Link** components. We created two simple apps in which we saw how to extract the part of the URL that we are interested in and experimented with several options for what can be done with them.

We then saw how to modify parts of an app by taking values from parsed URLs. With this knowledge, we were able to restructure our app. We created a skeleton layout with an empty div, in which the right content would then be displayed based on the URL.

We then incorporated the new functionality into our app. We were left with a final exercise that you can expect to go through in real life, which is a colleague handing you some code that you have to figure out and modify yourself.

Now that we have explored many options, layouts, components, and functionality, the next natural step is to deploy our app on a public server, so we can share it with the world.

This will be the topic of the next chapter.

12
Deploying Your App

We have done a lot of work, and I'm sure you are looking forward to sharing that work with the world. With the app in its current state, we will go through the process of setting up a server and deploying the app on a public address.

Essentially, what we will be doing is moving our data and code to a different computer and running the app in a similar way to what we have done so far. However, we need to set up a hosting account, a server, and a **Web Server Gateway Interface** (**WSGI**) in order for our app to be publicly available and visible. We will also need to establish a basic workflow for a development, deployment, and update cycle.

We will take a brief look at the **Git** source control management system, as well as do some basic **Linux system administration**. We will cover just enough to get our app online, and we won't even be scratching the surface of what can be done with those systems—I only mention them as a reference for further research. The approach we follow is creating a very basic installation to get our app online as fast as possible. This will not be achieved using simple tools. On the contrary—we will be using some of the most powerful tools available, but we will use a very simple setup. This will allow us to keep things simple at the beginning, and then explore how to expand our apps and setup later.

We then take a look at an alternative way of deploying our apps, which is through Dash Enterprise. This is the paid and supported version of Dash that is specifically tailored for large organizations.

The following topics will be covered in this chapter:

- Establishing the general development, deployment, and update workflow
- Creating a hosting account and virtual server
- Connecting to your server with **Secure Shell (SSH)**
- Running the app on the server
- Setting up and running the app with a WSGI
- Setting up and configuring the web server
- Managing maintenance and updates
- Deploying and scaling Dash apps with Dash Enterprise

Technical requirements

We now need a Linux server connected to the internet, the data files, and our app's code. We will be installing Gunicorn (Green Unicorn, the WSGI) and nginx (the web server), as well as our app's Python packages as dependencies. We will install Dash and its main packages, Dash Bootstrap Components, pandas, and sklearn. An account on a source code management system such as Git will be needed, and we will be using GitHub as an example for this chapter.

Our development workflow so far has been to test certain functionality on JupyterLab and run it, and once it is working fine, we incorporate it to our app. This development workflow will not change. We will simply add a few steps and components for deployment after making our changes. So, let's start by establishing the workflow that we will be working with.

Establishing the general development, deployment, and update workflow

When we discuss deployment, we are assuming that we are happy enough with what we have developed so far. This could be when we run our app for the first time, or after having introduced some changes or fixed some bugs. So, our data and code are ready to go. Our focus will be to set up the required infrastructure to enable us to run the code online.

The setup we will be going through is going to be simple and straightforward. We will be using Linode as an example for our hosting provider. An important feature of Linode is that it follows a philosophy of "open cloud." This means that the server we will be working with will be a plain Linux server, using open source components and packages that you can customize the way you want and migrate to and from with ease. The potential challenge here is that with more freedom comes more complexity and responsibility. In *Chapter 4, Data Manipulation and Preparation – Paving the Way to Plotly Express*, we discussed the trade-off involved in choosing between higher- and lower-level software, and in this case, we will be working with a lower-level system to run our app.

If you are experienced in running and managing servers, then you will have the full flexibility that you need and you can skip most of the chapter. The good news for beginners is that even though you will be "on your own," we will be running a very simple setup with simple defaults. This should enable you to easily deploy your app, and you can gradually learn more about how you might want to customize your setup, knowing that you have full access to some of the top tools.

Our deployment workflow will contain three main components, outlined as follows:

- **Your local workstation**: This has been extensively covered so far, and you should have experience with the local setup that we have been working with so far.

- **A source code management system**: You don't really need this to get your app to run but it is a very good practice to follow, especially when your app grows in size and when more people are involved in its maintenance.

- **A server with the required infrastructure and setup**: Your code and data will be running and served to the public from here.

To make things clearer, the following screenshot shows the elements we are discussing and, following that, a brief description of them and how they relate to each stage in the development and deployment cycle:

Figure 12.1 – The three main components in the development, deployment, and update cycle

One or more people write code on their local machines, and the code they write travels both ways between them and the central Git repository. Note that code does not travel between collaborators on the project—for example, by email; they only send their code changes/additions to the Git repository. There are many benefits to using a central Git repository. This is a large topic and there are special books for it, so we will only cover very basic concepts, and I encourage you to learn more. One of the most important things that Git facilitates is to have everyone collaborate on a single set of changes—this streamlines the process for everyone. There needs to be one or more administrators of the central repository, and that person(s) approves what goes into the main repository and what doesn't. Additionally, they need to be able to resolve conflicts. Two people might work on the same file separately, and they might both push changes that conflict with each other, so someone needs to decide what to do in such cases.

The approved version gets pushed from Git to the server and the website gets published. As you can see, code goes in one direction only at this stage. Even if you are working alone, it's highly advised to use Git to manage changes.

Another important benefit is that every set of changes (which are called "commits") that are made contains metadata about when the changes were made, and by who. More importantly, the commits show to which branch of changes they belong. In case you need to roll back some changes, you can also "check out" a certain commit or a branch, and take the full repository back to a certain state. You can fix your bugs and make changes while your app is running, and then re-introduce them.

This was an oversimplification of what Git does and how it works, but I think it's worth mentioning and learning more about. We will use it for deployment and introduce very basic commands. We will go through the process of making a change to one of our files in the final section of this chapter, to give an example of how a change can be introduced using Git.

At this stage, you have your code working locally with all the required data, and you want to push it to a central Git repository and then to your server for deployment. Alternatively, you might simply clone this book's repository and deploy it to your server as well.

Now that we have established the general cycle of our work and explored the main components and steps, we are ready to start our work online, and we first do so by setting up a Linode account.

Creating a hosting account and virtual server

It's straightforward to set up an account on Linode, and you can do so from the signup page at `https://login.linode.com/signup`. Once you register and provide your billing information, you can start by creating a "Linode." Virtual servers with their own **Internet Protocol (IP)** address are also called Linodes (Linux + node), similar to the name of the company.

The process is straightforward and can be done through the main dashboard that you land on when you log in.

The following screenshot shows some of the main options available to create and manage your account:

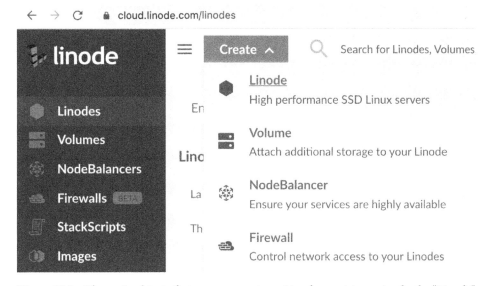

Figure 12.2 – The main objects that you can create on Linode; most importantly, the "Linode"

Once you select the **Create** option and then select **Linode**, you are given several options to choose from. We will go with **Distributions**. You can think of distributions as bundles of software based on the Linux kernel but containing different components. Each distribution is customized for a certain use case. We will be using the Ubuntu distribution for our Linode. Other options can be interesting—for example, **Marketplace** provides the option to create a full installation of popular software with a few clicks. Feel free to explore these other options as well. *Figure 12.3* shows the distribution we selected, and after that you have a few simple options to choose from. Most importantly, you need to choose a plan, and there are many to choose from, giving you a lot of flexibility. You can use the smallest one for now, and then you can decide when/if you want to upgrade. In the following screenshot, you can see the Ubuntu distribution being selected:

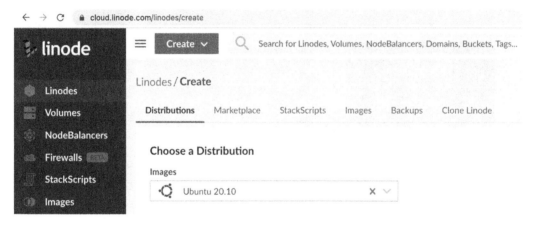

Figure 12.3 – Selecting and configuring a distribution on Linode

Once you have finalized the remaining options you can hit the **Create** button, and you should now land on the dashboard for your newly created Linode. The following screenshot shows the top of the screen for that interface:

Linodes / **dash_book**   Docs

● RUNNING   Power Off   Reboot   Launch LISH Console   •••

Summary   **IP Addresses**   **Access**

1 CPU Core   25 GB Storage   172.105.72.121   **SSH Access**   ssh root@172.105.72.121

1 GB RAM   0 Volumes   2a01:7e01::f03c:92ff:fe5a:2dd5/64 **LISH Console via SSH** ssh -t eda@lish-frankfurt.lin

Plan: Nanode 1GB   **Region:** Frankfurt, DE   **Linode ID:** 25436235   **Created:** 2021-03-22 17:07

Add a tag +

Analytics   Network   Storage   Configurations   Backups   Activity Feed   Settings

Figure 12.4 – The Linodes dashboard containing several reports and details

You can see all the relevant details about your newly created Linode on this screen, and you can refer back to it to get performance data and other information, or in case you want to make any changes. Later on, you will probably want to either upgrade your plan or add volumes for extra storage, and so on.

For us, the interesting part of this screen is the **SSH Access** part. We will now use this to log in to our server, and we won't be using the web interface from now on.

> **Important note**
>
> Linode provides several ways to interact with and manage your account. It provides an **application programming interface** (**API**) and a **command-line interface** (**CLI**), among other tools, from which you can do pretty much anything that you can do through the web interface. It's more convenient to use the web interface for simple tasks such as the one we just did. Using the API and/or the CLI becomes more useful for automating and operationalizing tasks on a large scale.

Now that we have our server running, we want to start working on it. This will mainly be done through the SSH interface.

Connecting to your server with SSH

SSH is a protocol for moving data securely, over an unsecured network. This will enable us to get access to and run code from the command line of our server, using the Terminal on our local machine.

Let's start by copying the `ssh root@127.105.72.121` command by clicking on the clipboard icon next to it, which you can see in *Figure 12.4* as well.

Now, open the terminal application on your local machine and paste the command, as follows:

```
ssh root@172.105.72.121
The authenticity of host '172.105.72.121 (172.105.72.121)'
can't be established.
ECDSA key fingerprint is SHA256:7TvPpP9fko2gTGG11W/4ZJC+jj6fB/
nzVzlW5pjepyU.
Are you sure you want to continue connecting (yes/no/
[fingerprint])? yes
Warning: Permanently added '172.105.72.121' (ECDSA) to the list
of known hosts.
root@172.105.72.121's password:
```

As you can see, we had two main responses: one asking if we want to connect and add the IP to the list of known hosts, to which we answered `yes`; and another response, after having confirmed, asking us for our password.

Once you enter your password, which you have created for this specific server (Linode) and not for your account, you get the new prompt, as follows:

```
root@localhost:~#
```

You now have root access to your server from your own terminal application. A good thing to do immediately (and frequently) is to update your system's packages. Two quick commands to do that are shown here:

```
apt-get update
apt-get upgrade
```

Later on, you will probably need to manage updates to other packages that you install separately.

Having root access is very powerful and you can do anything as the root user, which means that this could also be a security risk. If someone else were able to accidentally sign in using your root user, they could potentially add or delete any files they want, with no restrictions whatsoever.

Because of that, we will use the recommended practice of creating a limited user immediately, and only signing in using that user. Proceed as follows:

1. Create a new user using whatever name you want, as follows:

    ```
    adduser elias
    ```

2. You will be prompted to enter and re-enter a password for this user. By now, you will have three passwords: one for the Linode account, another for the root user of this Linode, and one for the limited user we just created. Optionally, you can also provide the full name, phone number, and other details. You can hit *Enter* and skip those options if you want. Even though this user is limited, we can add it to the `sudo` (superuser do!) group. This will allow this user to access root privileges temporarily, whenever we want to make some admin tasks or access sensitive files. Now that we have a new limited user, let's add it to the `sudo` group, as follows:

    ```
    adduser elias sudo
    ```

3. Having created a limited user that can temporarily use `sudo` privileges, we can now sign out of root, and log back in again with the new user, as follows:

```
exit
```

4. You should get a message that the connection to your IP address was lost, and you should see the prompt in the Terminal of your local machine. Now, we log in using the new user, the same way we did previously, as follows:

```
ssh elias@172.105.72.121
```

5. Once you log in successfully, you will be given a new prompt showing the logged-in user, as seen here:

```
elias@localhost:~$
```

We are now ready to get started with building our app on the server, but before that, let's see how we can access sensitive files and use `sudo` privileges, as follows:

1. Try to access one of the system's log files—for example, using the `cat` command, as illustrated in the following code snippet:

```
elias@localhost:~$ cat /var/log/syslog
cat: /var/log/syslog: Permission denied
```

2. We were not given permission, which is the right outcome. Now, we can ask for `sudo` access by running the same command and preceding it with the `sudo` command, as follows:

```
elias@localhost:~$ sudo cat /var/log/syslog
[sudo] password for elias:
```

3. Enter the password for this user and get access to the requested sensitive files.

You will face this situation quite frequently, and you can easily use the `sudo` command to get temporary root access.

We have a good part of our server ready to go, but we are still not there yet. We now want to get our files and data on the server, and then install the required Python packages.

Running the app on the server

What we will do in this section is exactly what we did back in *Chapter 1, Overview of the Dash Ecosystem*. We will clone the code and data repository from GitHub and get them to the server, install the dependencies, and try to run the app.

You typically have Python already installed on such servers, but it's always good to check and know how to get it, in case you don't. An easy way to check if we have it installed, and to get the version in one go, is to run `python --version` from the command line. Keep in mind that the `python` command can be interpreted to mean Python 2. The upgrade to Python 3 took a while to get fully implemented, and so, during that time, to differentiate between the two versions the `python3` command was used, to be explicit about wanting to run Python version 3. This applies to the `pip` command, which can also be run as `pip3`.

When I ran `python3 --version`, I got version 3.8.6. By the time you read this, the default version might be different. Also, at the time of this writing, Python 3.9 was launched and was considered stable. This is what I got when I tried to run it from the command line:

```
elias@localhost:~$ python3.9
Command 'python3.9' not found, but can be installed with:
sudo apt install python3.9
```

No explanation needed. We were also reminded that in order to install such a package, we need to use `sudo` as well. These are some examples of what you can use and what you might typically face, but Linux administration is another massive topic, and it's good to familiarize yourself with some of its basics.

Let's now activate a virtual environment and clone the GitHub repository, using the exact same steps we used in *Chapter 1, Overview of the Dash Ecosystem*, as follows:

1. Create a Python virtual environment in a folder called `dash_project` (or any other name you want). This will also create a new folder with the name you chose. Note that you might need to install `venv` for this to work, and you should get the command to do so, as in the previous example, as follows:

    ```
    python3 -m venv dash_project
    ```

2. Activate the virtual environment. You should now see the name of the environment in parentheses, indicating that the environment is activated, as illustrated in the following code snippet:

    ```
    source dash_project/bin/activate
    (dash_project) elias@localhost:~/dash_project$
    ```

3. Go into the environment folder by running the following command:

```
cd dash_project
```

4. We now want to clone our GitHub repository, and get all available files and code on our server. We will use the book's repository as an example, but I encourage you to run and clone your own instead. Run the following command:

```
git clone https://github.com/PacktPublishing/Interactive-
Dashboards-and-Data-Apps-with-Plotly-and-Dash
```

5. Next, we need to install the required packages, which we do by getting into the main folder and running the command for that, as follows:

```
cd Interactive-Dashboards-and-Data-Apps-with-Plotly-and-
Dash/
pip install -r requirements.txt
```

6. We can now enter into any chapter's folder to run that particular version of the app. In the following code snippet, we can see what happens if we go into the final version of *Chapter 11, URLs and Multi-Page Apps*:

```
cd chapter_11
python app_v11_1.py
```

Going through the preceding sequence of steps produces the exact same result that we are familiar with when running our apps locally, as you can see in the following screenshot:

```
Dash is running on http://127.0.0.1:8050/

 * Serving Flask app "app_v11_1" (lazy loading)
 * Environment: production
   WARNING: This is a development server. Do not use it in a production deployment.
   Use a production WSGI server instead.
 * Debug mode: on
```

Figure 12.5 – The app running on the server

Getting the preceding message means that the code is working fine, with no issues. Of course, it also gives us a big warning that we are using a development server only and that we should not use it in a production deployment.

So, we will set up our web server. But before that, we need to use the interface that makes it easy for our web framework (Flask) to work with any web server we want. This interface is called a WSGI (pronounced Wiz-ghee, or whiskey!).

Let's first establish a basic understanding of the components and phases involved in serving our app that we will be working with. The following diagram shows a simple sequence that requests and responses flow through when a user accesses our app from their browser:

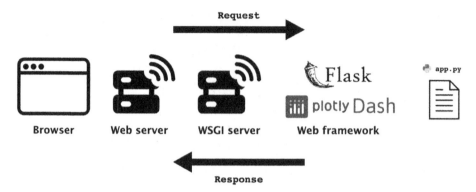

Figure 12.6 – The components of our app, on a public server

The request starts from the left (as you can see in the preceding screenshot), and then goes through several components until it reaches Dash, which runs our app.py module. Then, our app's code generates a response that goes through the same components in the opposite direction, until it reaches the user's browser.

Let's briefly discuss each of those elements, as follows:

- **Browser**: This is straightforward and can mean any **HyperText Transfer Protocol (HTTP)** client. When the user enters a **Uniform Resource Locator (URL)** and hits *Enter*, the browser makes a request to the web server.

- **Web server**: The job of the web server is to handle the requests that it receives. Our problem is that the server doesn't execute Python code, so there needs to be some way for us to get the requests, interpret them, and return responses.

- **WSGI server**: This is the middleware that does the job of speaking the server's language, as well as speaking Python. Having this set up means that our web framework (Flask, in this case) does not need to worry about handling the server or handling many requests. It can focus on creating the web app, and only needs to make sure that it conforms to the WSGI specification. This also means that with this set up, we are free to change our web server and/or WSGI server without having to make any changes to our app's code.

- **Web framework**: This is the Flask web framework with which Dash is built. A Dash app is basically a Flask app, and we have covered this quite extensively.

We don't need to know about web servers or WSGI servers any more than this for now. Let's see how simple it is to run our app using our WSGI server.

Setting up and running the app with a WSGI

We have run our app using the `python app.py` command from the command line. Alternatively, we used the `app.run_server` method when running with `jupyter_dash`. We are going to do it now with Gunicorn, our WSGI server.

The command is slightly different from the previous one and is run with the following pattern:

```
gunicorn <app_module_name:server_name>
```

We have two main differences here. First, we only use the module name, or the filename without the `.py` extension. Then, we add a colon, and then the server name. This is a simple variable that we have to define, and it can be done with one line of code, right after we define our top-level `app` variable, as follows:

```
app = dash.Dash(__name__)
server = app.server
```

Now that we have defined our sever as `server`, and assuming our app is in a file called `app.py`, we can run the app from the command line, as follows:

```
gunicorn app:server
```

That's it for the WSGI server!

Once that change has been made, we can go to the folder where our app is and run it with the preceding command. The following screenshot shows the output we get when running our app with the `gunicorn` command:

```
[2021-03-23 14:50:51 +0000] [54222] [INFO] Starting gunicorn 20.0.4
[2021-03-23 14:50:51 +0000] [54222] [INFO] Listening at: http://127.0.0.1:8000 (54222)
[2021-03-23 14:50:51 +0000] [54222] [INFO] Using worker: sync
[2021-03-23 14:50:51 +0000] [54224] [INFO] Booting worker with pid: 54224
```

Figure 12.7 – Running the app with the Gunicorn WSGI server

This output shows that our app is working fine. We can also see that it is listening at a different port. The default port for Dash is `8050`, while here it is `8000`.

We have come one step closer to the browser and the user. It seems the code is working fine with the WSGI server. Let's now set up our web server to make our app publicly available.

Setting up and configuring the web server

We will be using nginx as our web server in this example. You can now stop the app using *Ctrl* + *C* from the command line. Alternatively, you can stop your app using the `kill` command, which requires you to know the ID of the process that is running your app. This is useful if you log in later and have no idea which processes are running, and want to identify the process responsible for your app.

You can run the `ps -A` process status command from the command line to get all the currently running processes. You can either scroll to find a process whose name contains `gunicorn` or add a pipe, and search for that process in the previous command's output, as follows:

```
ps -A | grep gunicorn
```

Running the preceding command while the app is running gets us the output you see in the following screenshot:

```
elias@localhost:~$ ps -A | grep gunicorn
  54222 pts/1     00:00:00 gunicorn
  54224 pts/1     00:00:02 gunicorn
```

Figure 12.8 – How to find the process IDs for processes containing a certain text pattern

The process IDs are the same as the ones that we got when we ran with Gunicorn, which you can also see in the preceding screenshot.

To stop the app, you can use the `kill` command, as follows:

```
kill -9 54222
```

Now that we have checked that our app runs with our WSGI server, it is time to set up our web server.

As mentioned before, even though we will use the simplest possible configuration to make things easy for us, we will still be using one of the most powerful web servers available.

Let's start by installing it. From the command line, while logged in to your server, run the following command:

```
sudo apt install nginx
```

We now want to create a configuration file for our app. Installing nginx does several things, one of which is creating a `sites-enabled` folder. We want to create our configuration file there, with basic options. We can use any text editor for that; a simple one to use that you can usually find on Linux machines is the `nano` editor. Running it as a command followed by a filename opens that file for editing (or creates one if it doesn't exist).

From the command line, run the following command to open and edit our file:

```
sudo nano /etc/nginx/sites-enabled/dash_app
```

You should get an empty file, and you can copy and paste the following code, but make sure to replace the IP address after `server_name` with your own IP address:

```
server {
    listen 80;
    server_name 172.105.72.121;
    location / {
        proxy_pass http://127.0.0.1:8000;
        proxy_set_header Host $host;
        proxy_set_header X-Forwarded-For $proxy_add_x_
forwarded_for;
    }
}
```

This code contains configuration for the `server` context, as you can see. It tells it to listen on port `80`, which is the default port for web servers. It also defines the `server_name` as the IP address. Later on, you can use this to define your own domain name.

It then defines the behavior of the server for `location` / under another block. The most important thing for us is that we are making nginx a proxy server with the `proxy_pass` directive and telling it to listen to the URL and port that Gunicorn is listening to. So, now, the cycle should be complete. Our web server will be sending and receiving requests and responses through the correct URL and port, where the interface with our Python code is handled by Gunicorn.

Installing nginx creates a default configuration file, which we need to unlink with the following command:

```
sudo unlink /etc/nginx/sites-enabled/default
```

We just need to reload nginx after making this change. Keep this in mind when you make any changes in the future. You should reload nginx for any changes to take place, which you can do with the following command:

```
sudo nginx -s reload
```

Now, we can run our app with `gunicorn app:server`, and then, using our browser, we can navigate to our IP address and see the app online, as can be seen in the following screenshot:

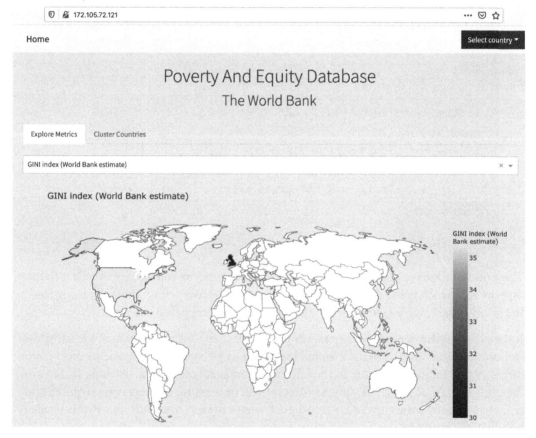

Figure 12.9 – The app deployed on a public address

Congratulations! Your app is now available to anyone with an internet connection; it is on a public server, and you can share your work with the world.

What happens after that? How do you make changes, and what if there were upgrades to the packages that you used?

We tackle some simple guidelines that might be helpful to follow for the maintenance phase, after we have deployed our app.

Managing maintenance and updates

Several things will probably need to be managed and handled after publishing your app, and we cover a few of them.

Fixing bugs and making changes

This should follow the same workflow we established at the beginning of this chapter. Any changes to our code, whether bug fixes or additions to our functionality, should be done the same way. We edit code locally, make sure it is running correctly, and then push to the central Git repository. Then, from the server, we pull the changes and rerun the app.

Updating Python packages

There are several packages that our app depends on, and you will most likely have even more in your daily work. Those packages will release updates every now and then, and you need to make sure that they are up to date. Some of those updates are security updates and need to be handled as soon as possible, while others introduce new options to packages. In general, you can run `pip install --upgrade <package_name>` to achieve this, but you will still need to check if the new functionality might change the way your app is running or whether it will break your existing code. Well-maintained packages usually publish any such breaking changes and also provide instructions for upgrading, if needed.

Once you have decided to upgrade packages, you can run the upgrade locally to first test your app and make sure it is running with the new version, as follows:

1. From the command line, go into the app's folder on your local machine, as follows:

```
cd /path/to/your/app
```

2. Activate the virtual environment, like this:

```
source /bin/activate
```

3. You should now see the name of your environment in parentheses (env_name) and you are now ready to upgrade the package of your choice, as follows:

```
pip install --upgrade  <package_name>
```

4. Assuming everything went fine, run your app, and make sure it is running as expected by executing the following command:

```
python app.py
```

5. If everything went well, you now need to update your requirements.txt file to reflect the new version of the package, and possibly modified versions of other dependencies. We first use the pip freeze command. This takes all the available packages in the current environment, as well as their dependencies, together with the right version number and prints them out to stdout. Now, we want to take this output and redirect it to the requirements.txt file to overwrite it with the updated requirements. We can do those two steps in one go, but it's good to familiarize yourself with the output of the first command first, which can be seen here:

```
pip freeze > requirements.txt
```

6. Commit the changes to the Git repository and push to GitHub. The git add command adds the file(s) to the staging area, which means they are now ready to be added to the history of the repository. The next step is to commit those additions with the git commit command, which also takes a message in which you state what has been done. We then submit the changes to the online repository with the push command, as follows:

```
git add requirements.txt
git commit -m 'Update requirements file'
git push
```

7. Now that you have the latest requirements.txt file on your central Git repository you can pull it to your server, just as we did in this chapter. After logging in to your server, moving into your project's folder, and activating its virtual environment, you can pull the changes. The git pull command does two things. First, it fetches the latest changes of the repository from the remote server. Then, it merges the changes into the local copy, and you get the updated app. The command is shown here:

```
git pull
```

8. The change we fetched and merged in this case was the updated `requirements.`
    `txt` file. We now run the following command to install our packages on the server
    using the new versions:

```
pip install -r requirements.txt
gunicorn app:server
```

This should start your app again, with the latest updates included. While we changed the
requirements file in this case, we could have also changed the app's file, or maybe added
new data. Whatever the change, this is the general cycle that we go through to incorporate
those changes.

Now that you have a new component to handle—your server—you will also be managing
and maintaining it as well.

Maintaining your server

The following list provides a very brief and oversimplified set of things that you might be
interested in, without instructions. The proper way is to learn more about Linux system
administration, but these are likely things you will want to manage and can easily find
guides and documentation for:

- **Adding a custom domain**: You probably want a nice name for your app, and not
  an IP address. This is straightforward, and you need to buy a domain name from
  a registrar and make the necessary changes to enable that. You can find many
  examples and guides on Linode's documentation on how to achieve that.

- **Setting up a security certificate**: This is important and has become straightforward
  and free to do. Many guides and examples are available for that as well.

- **Updating packages**: As we did the first time we logged in, it's good to constantly
  update your server's packages and especially make sure you have the latest
  security updates.

- **More security**: The only security measure we took was adding a limited user, which
  was added to the `sudo` group. There are other things that can be done as well, such
  as hardening your SSH access with authentication key pairs and configuring
  a firewall, among other actions.

Now that we have explored how to deploy Dash on a bare Linux server, we turn next to see how it might be deployed on the supported and fully loaded one, Dash Enterprise. We will highlight the benefits of Dash Enterprise and discuss when it might be appropriate to use it in Chapter 13, *Next Steps*.

Deploying and scaling Dash apps with Dash Enterprise

We will now explore several phases and options that go into Dash Enterprise deployment.

Initializing the app

Once you have a contract and your setup is ready, you can go to your Application Manager page to initialize your app. This can be done by clicking the **Initialize App** button, which will prompt you to name your app. The app name will determine the URL of your application, which will be accessible on the URL `https://<your-dash-enterprise-domain>/<app-name>` as you can see in *Figure 12.9*:

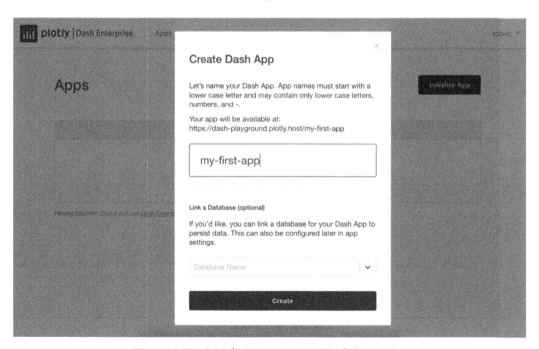

Figure 12.10 – Initializing your app on Dash Enterprise

Building your application (optional)

If you have your application already written, you can skip to the following phase. Otherwise, you can use the Dash Enterprise Development Workspaces tool to build your application.

It also contains an isolated production-like environment that allows you to author an app from creation to deployment without leaving the browser. Additionally, you can select from more than eighty app templates that cover most use cases to get you started fast. *Figure 12.10* shows sample apps:

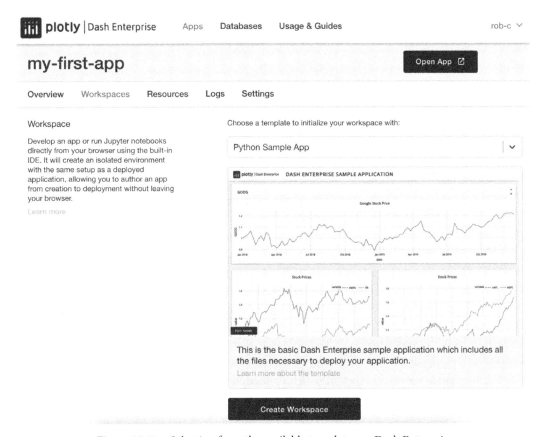

Figure 12.11 – Selecting from the available templates on Dash Enterprise

The Workspaces tool also contains a VS Code-like **integrated development environment (IDE)**, and the ability to run Jupyter Notebooks online, as you can see in *Figure 12.11*:

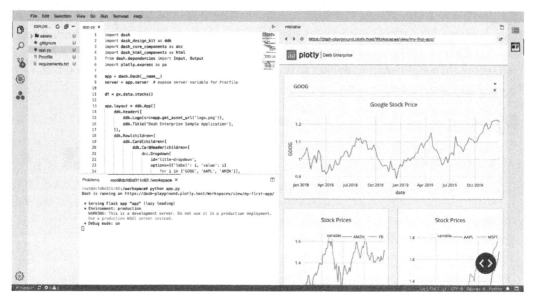

Figure 12.12 – VS Code IDE online on Dash Enterprise

Preparing your project folder

This folder has a very similar structure to the app that we worked with, so it should be familiar. This folder should have three main files:

- The app.py (or index.py) file, containing the app code. The app should also contain the server variable, which is also created by assigning server = app.server.

- The requirements.txt file: This is needed in order to install all dependencies with the correct versions, exactly as we have done previously.

- There is also a Procfile: This is a very simple file containing the commands that are required to run your app. In our server deployment, we ran gunicorn app:server from the command line for example. In this example, this would be included in the Procfile as web: gunicorn app:server. It can include other commands as well, based on your app, and the commands that would go into running it.

Additionally, you may have other optional files in your app's folder:

- The runtime.txt file: This is where you determine the specific Python version that you need.

- An `apt-packages` file: In case your app requires additional system-level packages like database drivers for example.

- An `app.json` file: If you want to call scripts when deploying changes.

- A `CHECKS` file: If you want to customize any pre-release health checks.

- We have now initialized our app, built it, and made sure its folder contains the minimally required files. We now see how to deploy it.

Deploying your application on Dash Enterprise

- The deployment is based on Git, and many parts will be familiar. From the home folder of the app, we need to go through the following steps:

1. Initialize the Git repository to start tracking changes to your app's folder:

   ```
   git init
   ```

2. Set a remote server for your app, which is to be done only once, so Git knows where to send and receive changes:

   ```
   git remote add plotly https://<your-dash-enterprise-
   domain>/GIT/<app-name>
   ```

3. Add the files or folders that you want to commit:

   ```
   git add file1 file2 …
   #OR to add all changes in your working folder:
   git add .
   ```

4. Commit the changes that will be pushed, with a descriptive message, summarizing the changes in this commit:

   ```
   git commit -m "Initial commit"
   ```

5. Push the changes:

   ```
   git push plotly master
   ```

The push to deployment takes about five minutes, after which the app can be accessible on the URL you specified on your domain.

As mentioned, Dash Enterprise is typically used for large scale deployments where changes need to be properly documented, tested, and should meet certain quality checks. So, it also ships with support with various tools that streamline the process.

Every time you make a change, you need to have a set of tests pass before you go live. **Continuous integration** and **continuous deployment (CI/CD)** tools are also part of Dash Enterprise. Also, many of these tools are based on a **graphical user interface (GUI)**, making things easier as well. Another important aspect covered by Dash Enterprise, is its support for the most important authentication systems (LDAP, SAML, simple email authentication and more), making it easy to integrate with IT infrastructure.

We made a big leap in this chapter, and we quickly explored very powerful tools and techniques, so let's recap what we covered in this chapter.

Summary

We started by establishing a simple workflow to manage the cycle of development, deployment, and updates. We defined three main components for this workflow and how they relate to one another. We discussed the relationship between local workstations, a central Git repository, and a web server, and set some guidelines on how work should flow between them.

We then created a hosting account, set up a virtual server, and got ready to do work on the server locally. Then, we explored how we can access the server locally through SSH, and ran some basic security and administration tasks. We cloned our repository and saw that it can run on the server exactly as we do locally.

We then discussed the two other required components for our app to be available publicly. We ran our app slightly differently by using a WSGI server. The last step was to install and configure a web server, using the simplest setup possible. Our app was then accessible on a public IP.

Finally, we explored which ongoing maintenance tasks might be interesting. Most importantly, we ran through the process of upgrading our Python packages, changing a file, committing it to Git, pushing it to the online repository, and merging the changes to our server. This is definitely something that you will be doing continuously.

After having completed our Linux deployment, we went through a similar process with the higher-level and supported product, Dash Enterprise, explored how deployment works, and discussed a few of the tools it provides.

Our final chapter of the book will be about other directions that you might be interested in exploring and other areas that we haven't covered. You now know your way around Dash and can very easily navigate and find out whatever you need to know, yet there are many other things to explore. We will take a quick tour of those options in the last chapter.

13
Next Steps

Welcome to the end of the book, and the beginning of your Dash journey! Even though we covered many topics, use cases, chart types, and interactivity features, the sky is the limit in terms of what you can build with Dash.

By now, you should be as comfortable building dashboards as you would be in creating presentations. You should be comfortable manipulating and expressing data using a variety of data visualization techniques and chart types.

But this book just sets you on the path, and there are many things to explore next, so we will cover some ideas and pointers on how to explore the topics we covered in more depth. We will also look at some aspects that weren't covered in the book that you might be interested in exploring.

The following areas will be covered in this chapter:

- Expanding your data manipulation and preparation skills
- Exploring more data visualization techniques
- Exploring other Dash components
- Creating your own Dash components
- Operationalizing and visualizing machine learning models
- Enhancing performance and using big data tools
- Going large scale with Dash Enterprise

Technical requirements

We will not be doing any coding or deployment, so there won't be any technical requirements for this chapter.

You can learn new things and explore them generally from two directions: the top-down approach, where you want to do something, or are required to do something, and the bottom-up approach, where you start with the tools, and you want to explore the possibilities and what you can do with them:

- **Top-down**: Because of a certain requirement or constraint, often you will be required to do something – make something faster, better, or easier, for example. In order to solve these problems, or satisfy some requirement, you are required to learn something new. The value of this approach is mainly its practicality. You know what is useful and what is required, and this helps focus your mind and energy on the solution that you want, which is focused on solving a practical problem. At the same time, if you only focus on practical problems, you might be missing out on new techniques and approaches that you might learn that can make your practical life much easier.

- **Bottom-up**: This is the approach from the other direction. You start by learning something new just for the sake of exploration or curiosity. It could be something big, such as machine learning, or as small as learning about a new parameter in a function that you use every day. This suddenly opens up possibilities in your mind. It also expands your concept of what is possible. This is something that you can do proactively, regardless of the work requirements that you have. The famous quote, "The more I practice, the luckier I get," seems to fit this situation. The benefit of this approach is that you learn things properly and establish a solid theoretical understanding that allows you to be more in control of the techniques at hand. The drawback is that you might get too theoretical and lose touch with reality and forget what is really useful and what's not.

I find myself alternating between phases where sometimes I spend most of my time focused on solving a particular problem (top-down) and get very practical and produce practical solutions. I then go through a period of stagnation where my imagination doesn't work as much and I'm not that creative. I then slip into a more theoretical mode. Learning new things is very interesting and engaging in this phase. After learning enough new things and having established a good understanding of a certain topic, I find myself getting new ideas and get back to the practical mode, and so on.

You can see what works for you. Let's now explore some specific topics that you might be interested in on your Dash journey.

Expanding your data manipulation and preparation skills

If you have read any introductory text on data science, you will have probably been told that data scientists spend the majority of their time cleaning data, reformatting it, and reshaping it.

As you have read this book, you will have probably seen this in action!

We saw several times how much code and mental effort, and importantly, domain knowledge, goes into just getting our data into a certain format. Once we have our data in a standardized format, for example, a long form (tidy) DataFrame, then our lives become easier.

You might want to learn more pandas and NumPy for a more complete set of techniques on reshaping your data however you want. As mentioned at the beginning of the chapter, learning new pandas techniques without a practical purpose in mind can help a lot in expanding your imagination. Learning regular expressions can help a lot in text analysis, because text is typically unstructured, and finding and extracting certain patterns can help a lot in your data cleaning process. Statistical and numeric techniques can definitely make a big difference. At the end of the day, we are basically crunching numbers here.

Improving data manipulation skills naturally leads us to easier and better visualization.

Exploring more data visualization techniques

We saw how easy it is to work with Plotly Express and how powerful it can be. We also saw the extensive options available for us. At the same time, we are constrained by the requirement to have our data in a certain format, which Plotly Express cannot help with. This is where we have to step in as data scientists.

We covered four main chart types, and this is a very small subset of what's available. As mentioned at the beginning of the chapter, visualization works in a couple of ways. You might be required to produce a certain chart, so you end up having to learn about it. Or, you might learn about a new chart, and it then inspires you to better summarize certain types of data for certain use cases.

You might learn about new types of charts based on the geometric shapes/attributes they use, such as pie charts or dot plots. You can also explore them based on their usage; for example, there are statistical and financial charts. Many chart types boil down to basic shapes, such as dots, circles, rectangles, lines, and so on. The way they are displayed and combined makes them distinctive.

Another interesting visualization technique is using sub-plots. While we extensively used faceting in the book, facets are basically the same visualization for multiple subsets of the data we are analyzing. Sub-plots, on the other hand, allow you to create arrays of plots that could be independent of one another. This can help you produce rich reports in a single chart, where each sub-plot conveys a different aspect of your data.

Having explored and mastered new visualization techniques and charts, you will probably want to put them in an app and make them interactive.

Exploring other Dash components

We covered the basic Dash components and there are many others available. Keep in mind that there are three possible approaches here:

- **Go deeper into components you know**: Although we covered many components, there is always more to explore – more options to learn, use, and gain experience in. You probably want to go deeper into dash_table, which can offer quite complex functionality and spreadsheet-style options.

- **Explore other Dash components**: There are several other components that we didn't cover that could enhance your apps. Two of those are DatePickerSingle and DatePickerRange, which are self-explanatory. The Interval component allows you to execute code whenever a certain period of time elapses. The Store component allows you to store data in the user's browser, in case you want to save some data to enhance the usability/functionality of your apps. There is also an Upload component for uploading files. These are all available under Dash Core Components. There are several other packages that are interesting for other use cases. For example, Dash Cytoscape is great for interactive graph (network) visualizations. We saw it several times when we used the visual debugger and saw how much it simplifies our understanding of our app. This has many applications for various industries. To enable users to draw on your charts, you can check out the image annotation options that Dash provides, as well as the Dash Canvas package. Together, they provide a wide array of options to let users literally draw on the charts with their mouse, using set shapes such as rectangles, or by simply dragging the mouse.

- **Explore some of the community components**: Since Dash is an open source project and has a mechanism for creating and incorporating new components, many people have created their own Dash components independently. One of those is Dash Bootstrap Components, which we have relied on in our work. There are many more and many new ones coming out all the time.

This takes us to another topic, which is creating your own Dash component.

Creating your own Dash component

It's interesting to know that the official strategy for Dash is to be "React for Python, R, and Julia." As you might know, React is a very big JavaScript framework for building user interfaces. There is a massive library of open source React components, and Dash Core Components are basically React components made available in Python. This means that if there is any functionality that is not provided by Dash that you would like to have, you might consider developing it yourself, hiring a developer to build it, or you can also sponsor its development and have the Plotly team build it. Some of the components that we worked with were sponsored by clients who wanted to have certain functionality that wasn't available. This is one way to support Dash as well. It also benefits everyone who uses open source Dash.

There are clear instructions on how to create your own Dash components, and as a Dash developer, it's good to explore this option. It will certainly give you a deeper understanding of how the library works, and maybe you will end up creating a popular component yourself!

With all the data manipulation, visualization, and components, you have a rich vocabulary to do things beyond plotting points on a chart. Exploring what can be done with machine learning can give your models a big boost and can make them usable by others.

Operationalizing and visualizing machine learning models

Machine learning and deep learning are completely separate topics, of course, but with all the previously mentioned skills, you can take your machine learning to a new level. At the end of the day, you will use charts to express certain ideas about your data, and with a good interactive data visualization vocabulary, you can give your users many options to test different models and tune hyperparameters.

Enhancing performance and using big data tools

This is a very important topic, and we always need to make sure that our apps perform at an acceptable level. We didn't tackle this in the book because the focus was mainly to learn how to create a Dash app with all the other details that make it work. We also worked with a very small dataset of a few megabytes. Still, even with a small dataset, it can be crucial to optimize it. Big data can be about handling a massive file, or it can be about a small file that needs to be handled a massive number of times.

These are some things that can be done to optimize performance, but big data is a separate topic altogether, so here are some hints and some areas to explore.

Once we know how our app will behave and what features we will be using, we can clean up some unnecessary code and data that might be hindering our app's performance. Here are some ideas that can be done immediately to our app:

- **Load the necessary data only**: We loaded the whole file, and for each callback, we queried the DataFrame separately. That can be wasteful. If we have a callback for population data only, for example, we can create a separate file (and then a separate subset) DataFrame that only contains relevant columns and query them only, instead of using the whole DataFrame.

- **Optimize data types**: Sometimes you need to load data that contains the same values repeated many times. For example, the poverty dataset contains many repetitions of country names. We can use the pandas categorical data type to optimize those values:

1. Load the sys module and see the difference in size in bytes for a string (a country name) and an integer:

```
import sys
sys.getsizeof('Central African Republic')
73
```

2. Get the size of an integer value:

```
sys.getsizeof(150)
28
```

3. We can see the big difference in size with the string taking almost three times the memory that an integer does. This is what the categorical data type basically does. It creates a dictionary mapping each unique value to an integer. It then uses integers to encode and represent those values, and you can imagine how much space this can save.

4. Load the poverty dataset:

```
import pandas as pd
poverty = pd.DataFrame('data/poverty.csv')
```

5. Get a subset containing the country names column and check its memory usage:

```
poverty[['Country Name']].info()
<class 'pandas.core.frame.DataFrame'>
RangeIndex: 8287 entries, 0 to 8286
Data columns (total 1 columns):
 #   Column        Non-Null Count  Dtype
---  ------        --------------  -----
 0   Country Name  8287 non-null   object
dtypes: object(1)
memory usage: 64.9+ KB
```

6. Convert the column to the categorical data type and check the memory usage:

```
poverty['Country Name'].astype('category').to_frame().
info()
<class 'pandas.core.frame.DataFrame'>
RangeIndex: 8287 entries, 0 to 8286
Data columns (total 1 columns):
 #   Column        Non-Null Count  Dtype
---  ------        --------------  -----
 0   Country Name  8287 non-null   category
dtypes: category(1)
memory usage: 21.8 KB
```

7. With a simple command that encoded our countries as integers, we reduced the memory usage from 64.9 KB to 21.8 KB, making it about a third of the original size.

8. Another thing you might want to consider is to learn more about the available big data technologies and techniques. One of the most important projects right now is the Apache Arrow project. It is a collaboration between leaders from the database community, as well as from the data science community. One of the most important objectives of the project is to unify the effort across disciplines, and crucially, across programming languages.

9. When you want to read a CSV file, for example, you want it represented in memory as a DataFrame. Whether you are using R or Python, or any other language, you will be running very similar operations, such as sorting, selecting, filtering, and so on. There is a lot of effort duplicated, where each language implements its own DataFrame spec. From a performance perspective, it has been observed that a large percentage of computing power is wasted on converting objects from one language to another and reading and writing. This can also happen while saving an object to disk and then opening it in another language. This can cause a waste of resources, and in many cases forces many teams to have to choose a single language for easier communication and to reduce the wasted time and effort.

10. One of the goals of the Apache Arrow project is to create a single in-memory representation for data objects such as the DataFrame. This way, objects can be passed around across programming languages without having to make any conversions. You can imagine how much easier things can become. Also, there are big wins due to the collaborations across the programming languages and disciplines where a single specification is being used and maintained.

11. Each programming language can then implement its own libraries that are based on a single spec. For Python, the package is `pyarrow`, which is very interesting to explore. In many instances, it can be used on its own, and in others, it can integrate with pandas.

12. A very interesting file format that is also part of the project is the `parquet` format. Just like CSV and JSON, `parquet` is language-agnostic. It is a file and can be opened with any language that has a `parquet` reader. And the good news is that pandas already supports it.

13. One of the important features of `parquet` is massive compression that can reduce the size of your files drastically. So, it is ideal for long-term storage and efficiently utilizing space. Not only that, but it is very efficient to open and read those files because of the format. The file contains metadata about the file, as well as the schema. Files are also arranged into separate structures for efficient reading.

14. Some techniques that `parquet` uses are as follows:

- **Column orientation**: In contrast to CSV, for example, which is a row-oriented format, `parquet` mainly stores data in columns. Row-oriented formats are suitable for transactional processing. For example, when a user logs in to a website, we need to retrieve data about the user (a row), and potentially we want to write and update that row based on that user's interactions. But in analytical processing, which is what we are interested in, if we want to analyze the average income per country, for example, we only need to read two columns from our dataset. If the data was arranged in columns, then we can jump from the beginning to the end of the column and extract it much faster than if it was a row. We can read other columns, but only if we want to do further analysis on them.

- **Encoding**: Just like the example we saw with pandas categorical type, `parquet` also performs dictionary encoding. There are several other encoding schemes that it uses. For example, there is delta encoding, which works best when you have large numbers. It saves the value of the first number in the column and only saves the difference between it and consecutive numbers. For example, if you had the following list: [1,000,000, 1,000,001, 1,000,002, 1,000,003], these numbers could be represented as [1,000,000, 1, 1, 1]. We saved the full value of the first element and only the difference between each element and the previous one. This can mean a lot of memory is saved. This can be really useful when using timestamps, for example, which can be represented as large integers with small differences between them, especially in time series data. When you want to read the list, the program can do the calculations and give you the original numbers. Several other encoding strategies are used, but this was just another example.

- **Partitioning**: Another interesting technique is that `parquet` can split a file into multiple files and read and merge them from a folder that contains those files. Imagine a file with data about people, and this file has 10 million rows. One of the columns could be for gender, with "male" and "female" values. Now, if we split the file in two, with one for each value, we don't even need to store the whole column anymore. We can simply include "female" in the filename, and if the column is requested, the program knows how to populate all the values for that column because they are all the same.

- **Summary statistics**: Another technique that `parquet` uses for the groups of data in columns is that it contains the minimum and maximum and some other statistics for each group. Imagine having a file with 10 million rows, and you want to read only the values that are between 10 and 20. Assume that those rows are split into groups of one million each. Now, each group would have its minimum and maximum values in the header of that group. While scanning, if you come across a group where the maximum is six, then you know that your requested values won't be in that group. You just skipped a million values by making a single comparison.

Now, if you have mastered all those techniques and can produce insightful visualizations, nice interactivity, and provide really helpful dashboards, you still might not have the experience (or desire) to handle Dash in large-scale deployments. This is where you might consider Dash Enterprise.

Going large scale with Dash Enterprise

When you have a deployment in a large organization with many users that has an existing infrastructure, several things might come up that you might not have considered or anticipated. Imagine your app is going to be used by hundreds of people in a company. How do you deal with access to the app? How do you manage passwords, and what exactly happens when someone resigns, or joins? Are you experienced enough in security that you are confident that you can handle such a large deployment?

In these cases, data engineering takes on a much bigger role than previously. Storing the data efficiently and securely becomes more important. Scalability and managing it can be tricky if it is not your area of expertise. Your main job is to design and create something that helps in finding insights, rather than maintaining large-scale apps. In some cases, you might have the required skills but don't want to worry about those things and mainly want to focus on the interface, the models, and the visualizations.

This is where Dash Enterprise can help. It's basically Dash, as you know it, but with many options that are specifically designed for large deployments.

Let's explore some of the features available in Dash Enterprise.

Dash Design Kit

This is a set of design and theming tools that are very convenient and easy to use. They allow more granular control of the themes of your app, as well as the components and charts. This becomes more important when you have many changes, and if you work in an environment that requires building many new dashboards all the time. You probably want to spend more time on the models and visualizations, and less time on theming them.

Also, especially in large organizations, you might have branding requirements that have specific color, font, and layout guidelines. These can be made easier with DDK.

App Manager

This is the main tool with which you manage your deployment cycle. The larger and more frequent your releases, the more it makes sense to use such a tool that takes away the headaches of deployment.

The App Manager enables teams to securely deploy, manage, and share apps on a scalable Kubernetes platform.

Snapshot Engine

This is another tool that allows you to more easily manage your app(s) at various stages. As the name suggests, the Snapshot Engine allows you to share a link to a point-in-time Dash app, or snapshot. You can also trigger PDF and/or email reports programmatically. You can also request such snapshots manually, and schedule them to occur periodically.

Another feature is the ability to draw on the screen with your mouse. This allows notes to be shared and can be especially useful if your users are not technical, and want to request a certain feature, or ask a certain question visually. It can also simply be used to annotate certain reports and highlight certain facts.

Better performance with Job Queue

Once you have a large number of jobs that need to be running and/or callbacks that are CPU-intensive, it makes sense to separately manage those jobs in order to improve your app's performance. Job Queue is a set of tools that help with that, most importantly by enabling better scheduling of the incoming web requests, and reducing the likelihood of performance issues that occur when requests become backlogged.

Corporate security

Installing Dash Enterprise is flexible. It can be installed in a virtual private cloud (VPC) environment, as well as in an air gapped bare metal environment. Also, as discussed in the previous chapter, Dash Enterprise integrates with the most important authentication protocols, making accessing Dash apps seamless in a corporate environment.

Consulting services

Finally, you have access to the team that built Dash and has worked with many other similar organizations. Naturally, they can help with highly customized solutions, and have seen many similar situations to the one you are facing.

As you can see, Dash Enterprise would make sense if you have a large enough deployment, that would benefit from those additional features and services discussed here. In some cases, you can build them yourself, and you would have to evaluate whether or not that makes sense, based on the trade-offs involved.

These were some ideas, but most importantly your creativity, domain knowledge, and hard work are what matters at the end, so let's summarize what we covered in this chapter and the book.

Summary

We started by focusing on the importance of basic skills in handling data. We emphasized the importance of mastering data manipulation and cleaning skills, which will allow you to format your data into the shape that you want and make it easy to analyze and visualize. We also mentioned various data visualization techniques and types of charts that can be explored to increase your fluency in expressing ideas visually.

We also discussed the other Dash components that we didn't cover in the book, as well as the community components that are constantly being developed. Eventually, you might decide to develop your own set of components and contribute additional functionality to the Dash ecosystem, and I look forward to `pip install dash-your-components`!

We then discussed exploring machine learning and how we can make our models visual and interactive. Establishing data manipulation, visualization, and interactivity skills will help you a lot in making your models interpretable and usable, especially for a non-technical audience.

We explored some big data options and discussed one of the important projects, although there are many more to consider and explore.

Finally, we talked about the paid enterprise solution that Dash offers, which is Dash Enterprise; this solution might make sense when your project is part of a large organization or deployment.

Thank you very much for reading, and I hope you enjoyed the book. I look forward to seeing your app deployed online, with your own design, models, options, and customizations.

Other Books You May Enjoy

If you enjoyed this book, you may be interested in these other books by Packt:

Hands-On Data Visualization with Bokeh

Kevin Jolly

ISBN: 978-1-78913-540-4

- Installing Bokeh and understanding its key concepts
- Creating plots using glyphs, the fundamental building blocks of Bokeh
- Creating plots using different data structures like NumPy and Pandas
- Using layouts and widgets to visually enhance your plots and add a layer of interactivity
- Building and hosting applications on the Bokeh server
- Creating advanced plots using spatial data

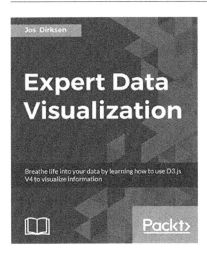

Expert Data Visualization

Jos Dirksen

ISBN: 978-1-78646-349-4

- Learn how D3.js works to declaratively define visualizations
- Create charts from scratch by using SVG and the D3.js APIs
- See how to prepare data for easy visualization using D3.js.
- Visualize hierarchical data using chart types provided by D3.js
- Explore the different options provided by D3.js to visualize linked data such as graphs
- Spice up your visualizations by adding interactivity and animations
- Learn how to use D3.js to visualize and interact with Geo- and Gis-related information sources

Packt is searching for authors like you

If you're interested in becoming an author for Packt, please visit authors.packtpub.com and apply today. We have worked with thousands of developers and tech professionals, just like you, to help them share their insight with the global tech community. You can make a general application, apply for a specific hot topic that we are recruiting an author for, or submit your own idea.

Leave a review - let other readers know what you think

Please share your thoughts on this book with others by leaving a review on the site that you bought it from. If you purchased the book from Amazon, please leave us an honest review on this book's Amazon page. This is vital so that other potential readers can see and use your unbiased opinion to make purchasing decisions, we can understand what our customers think about our products, and our authors can see your feedback on the title that they have worked with Packt to create. It will only take a few minutes of your time, but is valuable to other potential customers, our authors, and Packt. Thank you!

Index

E

U

Uniform Resource Locator (URL)
  about 312
  parsing 289
update workflow
  establishing 302-304
URL-based content
  displaying 293, 294

V

values
  customizing, of sliders 171-176
vertical bar charts
  creating, with many values 116, 117
virtual server
  creating 305-307

W

web server
  configuring 314-316
  setting up 314-316
Web Server Gateway Interface (WSGI)
  app, running with 313
  app, setting up with 313

Made in the USA
Monee, IL
08 March 2022